D1474898

*Congress and the Governance
of the Nation's Capital*

Congress and the Governance of the Nation's Capital

The Conflict of Federal and Local Interests

CHARLES WESLEY HARRIS

GEORGETOWN UNIVERSITY PRESS, WASHINGTON, D.C.

Georgetown University Press, Washington, D.C.
©1995 by Georgetown University Press. All rights reserved.
Printed in the United States of America

10 9 8 7 6 5 4 3 2 1   1995

Library of Congress Cataloging-in-Publication Data

Harris, Charles Wesley, 1928-
    Congress and the governance of the Nation's Capital : the conflict of
Federal and local interests / Charles W. Harris.
        p.   cm.
    Includes bibliographical references (p.   ) and index.
    1. Home rule (District of Columbia)   2. Washington (D.C.)-
-Politics and government--1967-   I. Title.
JK2716.H37   1994
320.8'09753--dc20
ISBN 0-87840-563-1 (cloth). -- ISBN 0-87840-564-X (pbk.)   94-11006

To the memory of my mother and father
Leila (Magby) and John Wesley Harris

Contents

List of Tables

Foreword

This book is a welcome addition to the sparse literature on the government of federal capitals, one of very few case studies of the actual governing of a federal capital. We need studies such as this to increase our knowledge of how to solve the unique problems of governing federal capitals.

In the late 1960s, when I began the research for my book, *The Government of Federal Capitals*, I was surprised to find that no American scholar had made a comparative study of other federal capitals though the lack of self-government and voting rights in Washington had been hotly debated over a long period. Yet most of these capitals, including several within a federal district like Washington, had some form of self-government and voting rights in federal elections. Since then not only Washington but also Canberra and most of the capitals in the Latin American federations have been granted a greater degree of self-government. I am glad to see that Professor Harris has now filled this gap in the American literature by including an updated study of the other federal capitals to see what can usefully be learned for application to the Washington case.

We must not forget that the creators of the District of Columbia recognized an important principle of federalism that was widely adopted by other federations. They understood that the capital of a federation should not lie within the territory of one of the states, because it would come under the jurisdiction and domination of that state, and the federal government would lose control over its own seat of government. Yet some federal countries, such as Canada and Switzerland, have no federal district, and because local government is a state matter, the capital is governed under the laws of the state in which it is situated. Lacking direct control over the capital city, both of these countries have found that their federal government has been unable to control the development of the capital in the national interest. On the other hand, capitals within federal districts, such as Washington and Canberra, have long seen their residents deprived of the elementary democratic rights of self-government and voting.

In any federal capital the interests of the local inhabitants inevitably conflict with those of the federal government. The central task of good government has been to strike a balance between local claims and concerns and the national government's interest in developing its seat of government as a symbol of the nation.

I am naturally pleased that Professor Harris has used my formulation of this conflict of interests as a thesis and central theme for his book. Among the main questions he investigates are whether the reform of 1973 granted enough self-government to Washington, and the extent to which continuing Congressional controls and interventions have been expressions of mere parochial interests rather than true federal interests.

It is hard to believe that the citizens of Washington have been deprived of voting representation in Congress for so long and that the 1978 constitutional amendment to grant them this elementary representation failed to get the necessary approval. In view of this failure, it is not surprising that they have turned to statehood as the only other way to gain this representation. But turning Washington into a state would go against the very principle that caused the District of Columbia to be created: it would place the federal capital city (except for the small Federal Enclave) under the laws of the new state and would prevent the federal government from having ultimate control over the whole city.

However, if the constitutional nature of the new state were different from that of the other states of the union, special provisions could be made to recognize the minimum powers necessary to protect the federal government's interest in its own capital city. On the other hand, if the new state should be no different from the others as a matter of principle, the examples of Ottawa and Bern suggest that this outcome might be workable though very unsatisfactory from the federal government's point of view. In these capitals the local governments in the capital region frequently disregard the national interest. Yet in each case the federal government, because of its superior power (especially its spending power) has been able to largely achieve its objective of developing the capital city and region as a symbol of the nation. Similarly the federal government in the United States, even if it had no constitutional power over the capital city (except for the Enclave) could do likewise.

Because Professor Harris was focusing on the problem of the relations between Congress and the government of Washington, he did not deal fully with another problem that has been typical of federal capitals — the post-war explosion of population beyond the boundaries of the central city. In the case of Washington, four-fifths of the urban population live outside the District of Columbia. This means that four-fifths of the capital's population have full self-government and voting rights in the surrounding states of Maryland and Virginia. But it also means that the federal government has very little control over the development of the capital's metropolitan area because local government and urban planning are under the jurisdiction of the states.

In this respect the position of the federal government of the United States is surprisingly similar to that of Canada's federal government, which has no control over Ottawa's metropolitan area, where nearly two-thirds of the urban population live outside of the capital city, many of them on the north side of the Ottawa river in the province of Quebec. The main difference is that Canada's federal government also lacks control over Ottawa (except on land it owns, such as Parliament Hill and federal parks and driveways), because the Canadian capital is not within a federal district and is governed under the laws of Ontario.

Turning the District of Columbia into a state would not solve the problem of controlling the development of Washington's metropolitan area in the national interest, unless the boundaries of the new state were greatly enlarged to include the whole metropolitan area, and also unless special constitutional arrangements were made to secure the federal interest in the area.

In these pages, Professor Harris deals with the problem of the governance of Washington. Within the parameters that he has set, he has provided us with a balanced and fair-minded account of events since 1973. He has also given us the basic information and food for thought that will be needed for an intelligent decision on the next steps necessary to provide fuller self-government for Washington while preserving and developing a federal capital of which the nation can be proud.

Donald C. Rowat

Preface

At high noon on 2 January 1975 I was one of some fifteen hundred citizens who gathered in front of the District Building in the nation's capital to witness the swearing-in ceremony of the first elected officials for the District of Columbia in more than a century. As we listened to the inaugural address of Mayor Walter E. Washington on this crisp wintry day, the mood was one of accomplishment and joy, and there was a shared feeling that "it's our District Building now, not theirs."

In accepting the challenge of leadership, Mayor Washington lauded the city on how far it had come "to find its rightful place in this nation" and he declared that it was destined "to be a sanctuary of democracy for all the nation and the world to see." He urged all the people to join with him in shaping this new government and in meeting the challenge of democracy that lay ahead. It was on this day that I first thought about studying this new government, and although I did not begin right away, the prospect of doing so remained with me. I followed the local government closely, mainly through media coverage and attendance at public meetings, eventually crafted a prospectus, and began my research.

I soon encountered a certain amount of frustration in my efforts to apply urban political theories and concepts to the District of Columbia. Although it had the same major social and economic problems as other large cities, there was much about its political and governmental framework that was different and even more problematic. With home rule in effect, it now had two masters with overlapping jurisdictions. Much of the national jurisdiction was still fragmented among many agencies and bodies with unclear lines of authority.

It was around this time that I began to look more closely at the work of Donald C. Rowat, a professor at Carleton University, Canada, who was studying federal capital cities of the world as a separate genre. His thesis concerning conflict between the national and local governments in federal capital cities interested me, and I set out to explore it in the context of the District of Columbia. This book is a product of that effort.

The fundamental objectives of this study are threefold: (1) to provide a history of the relationship between Congress and the District of Columbia government during the current home rule period—1975 to the present; (2) to analyze the conflicts between the national and District of Columbia governments; and (3) to investigate statehood and other self-determination options that would render justice to the nation and to the federal district.

The nation's capital is a city of which all Americans should be proud. Washington, D.C. should epitomize what the United States stands for and play a basic role in achieving the country's domestic and international goals. The United States is the leader of the free world and the defender of democracy in principle and in practice. But the six hundred thousand residents of the nation's capital, who carry the same responsibilities of citizenship as other Americans, are denied some of the basic democratic rights enjoyed by all other citizens. The national capital has not become a sanctuary of democracy for the nation and the world to see, as Mayor Washington predicted in 1975.

Several options are available for bringing true democracy to the nation's capital. Statehood has been considered by the 103d Congress (1993–94) and would accomplish both national representation and optimal self-determination. Other options for the District, such as retrocession to or voting with Maryland and full voting rights and local autonomy, have also received consideration. Of course, it is not the procedure but the substance of democracy that is at issue here.

Many persons and institutions have contributed in various ways to this research project. I wish to acknowledge my special gratitude to Director Charles Blitzer and the Woodrow Wilson International Center for Scholars at the Smithsonian Institution, and to the Brookings Institution. The main research for this book and the writing were completed while I was a Fellow at the Woodrow Wilson Center, 1992–93. I was a guest scholar at the Brookings Institution when the initial idea for this research project was conceived. Both of these institutions helped tremendously by furnishing an intellectual and materially supportive environment for research and writing. Without the year at the Wilson Center, the book would not have been possible.

R. Kent Weaver and I collaborated on an article dealing with Congress and the District of Columbia government (*The Brookings Review,*

Summer 1989) that provided a foundation for this study. Donald Rowat was not only generous with advice and counsel but also with documents from his personal library on federal capitals. In addition to reading drafts of the chapters as they were produced and offering constructive criticism, the late Norman Beckman found a host of obscure source materials that were invaluable to this project. Rachelle Brown, John Bailey, and Riordan Roett read parts of the manuscript and nicely managed to be both critical and encouraging in their comments.

Rachael Rezek and John Oberdiek were capable undergraduate research assistants. Graduate students Benjamin Arah, Gustavo Leon, Alberto Föhrig, and Jaime Perales assisted with both research and translations of selected documents from Spanish or Portuguese to English. Finally, this project never would have been completed without the assistance of colleagues in academe, the cooperation of government and political practitioners, and the continual encouragement of family and friends.

1

Introduction

CONCEPTUAL FRAMEWORK

Political scientist Donald C. Rowat argues that all countries with federal systems of government face a difficult problem in governing their national capitals: "There is always a conflict of interests between the national government and the people who live in the capital city." The federal government "wishes to control and develop the capital in the interests of the nation as a whole, while the people of the capital naturally wish to govern themselves to the greatest extent possible." In addition, the governing of a federal capital presents a special problem which is inherent in the very nature of federalism: if the national capital of a federal union comes under the government of any one state of the union, that state is in a position to dominate the federation's capital, denying the national government adequate control over its own seat of government.[1]

That there is a conflict between national governments and the governments of capital cities seems obvious. As students of federalism know, conflict is almost inevitable between any two governments that share jurisdiction over a particular piece of territory. But full control by the national government violates basic democratic principles and the rights of the capital's inhabitants.

If the Rowat thesis is almost a truism, moreover, it also leaves three important sets of questions unanswered. First, is conflict likely to be limited to a few issues or felt across a broad range of areas? And on what issues is conflict likely to be greatest? Second, is the conflict really between the federal interest and city residents' desire for self-government, or are there other forces at work? Federal interventions in local affairs need not be assertions of legitimate national interests; they may also involve parochial forces in the guise of the national interest. "Local interests," too, may be a mask behind which politicians' personal interests or electoral interests of particular constituencies hide.

Finally, when there is conflict between a national government and the government of a capital city, which side is likely to prevail and why?

These questions are not merely of academic interest. They have important policy implications for how capital cities should be governed. If assertions of power by the national government are for the most part disguised parochial rather than real federal interests, then the case for increased autonomy for the capital city is strengthened. If, on the other hand, the federal government is unable to prevail in disputes where legitimate federal interests are involved, it suggests that the governing structure should be altered to increase federal leverage.

For many years (1874–1974), Washington represented a capital governed under the exclusive jurisdiction principle, with Congress serving as the direct legislative body for the federal district. Since 1975, however, limited home rule has been in effect in the District, resulting in shared governmental powers between the national and local governments. Serious problems remain in the home rule relationship. The general conflict between local interests and desires for more autonomy on the one hand, and federal goals on the other, has not disappeared. The fact that the District is largely black and Democratic has influenced both the city government's agenda and the degree of willingness of the federal level to agree to certain governmental changes—notably congressional representation. But, conversely, Congress has failed to develop a consistent notion of the federal interest. In twenty years of home rule in the District, the federal interest has been defined largely on a case-by-case basis, in ways generally tailored to the preferences of specific legislators and/or state or regional concerns. Many of the decisions imposed on the District by Congress in the name of the federal interest have really been driven by disguised parochial or ideological objectives.

The conflicts that have occurred during the current home rule era between the national and District of Columbia governments represent the linking element that runs through this study. I am not suggesting, however, that there has been more conflict than cooperation. The sheer power and dominance of the national government would defy any such relationship. A substantial level of compliance and cooperation at the local level is assured under the present home rule arrangement.

As a means of introducing this study, it is appropriate to provide some background on the nature and scope of the self-government that was provided to District residents. With only a nonvoting delegate in Congress when home rule was approved, the District was not an active player in designing the self-government package. However, it did work through its supporters in Congress to help make the case.

THE LIMITS OF HOME RULE

Of the national capitals in federal districts that began as planned new cities, including Washington and the twentieth-century capitals of Canberra (Australia), Brasilia (Brazil), and New Delhi (India), only in the federal district of the United States did the residents have some form of local government from the beginning. Of course, some of the other cities were established in barren territory, with few residents at the outset. Consequently, it was reasonable to put off for a while the matter of establishing a local government. But the situation in the United States led to early experience with limited home rule.

People living on the land donated by Maryland (1788) and Virginia (1789) formed the federal district, and the respective cession agreements mandated the retention of jurisdiction over the land by the state governments until Congress physically relocated itself within the ceded territories and provided by law for a district federal government. Therefore, the people of the federal district voted either in Maryland or Virginia until December 1800. They actually cast their last votes for a full-fledged member of Congress on 11 November 1800. In legislation passed in early 1801, Congress assumed jurisdiction over the federal district, comprising two counties (Washington and Alexandria) and including the cities of Georgetown (1751) and Alexandria (1749). Congress created a circuit court, called for presidential appointment of judicial and law enforcement officers, and rescinded state jurisdiction over the portions of the federal district in Maryland and Virginia.

The federal district was carved from the two states with the heaviest concentration of blacks in the United States. It is therefore not surprising that there was a significant number of black inhabitants—23.5 percent of the total population of 14,093—when it became the official seat of the national government in 1800. While most of the black residents were slaves, 5.6 percent of the total population was comprised of free blacks.[2]

The first government for the new city of Washington was established in the central portion of the federal district after its incorporation by Congress in 1802. Georgetown and Alexandria continued to operate as autonomous jurisdictions under their own charters. Washington was to be governed by a mayor appointed annually by the president and a twelve-member council elected by the voters. Several changes followed this initial arrangement. In 1812, the city council was permitted to elect the mayor, a practice that continued until 1820, when the people were allowed to elect the mayor. This form remained in effect until 1871.

By the 1840s, the residents of the Virginia portion of the federal district had become dissatisfied with their economic and political status and in 1846 they successfully sought retrocession to the state of Virginia, thus reducing the district to its present size of 68.26 square miles.[3] Apparently, their decision to rejoin their home state was influenced by a number of reasons: disenfranchisement, lack of economic prosperity, the slavery issue and others. Alexandria city was a slave port and slave trading was soon to be abolished in the District of Columbia (1850). When the question of retrocession was put to a vote, the rural people of Alexandria County voted to stay in the District, but Alexandria city outvoted them.[4]

Throughout the Civil War period, the relationship between the District of Columbia and Congress was complicated by the slavery question and the city's predominantly southern attitudes. When slavery in the District was finally abolished in 1862, the pace of black migration escalated, and by 1866 some thirty thousand ex-slaves had made their way to the city. The governance of the city got caught up in the racial and political issues of the Reconstruction era as the District became a testing ground in the drive of radical Republicans to establish black suffrage.

The current home rule era is not the first experience with self-government for the District of Columbia. In 1870 a movement began in favor of establishing a centralized government for the entire federal district. It seemed to many residents that the separate municipal and county governments of Georgetown, Washington city, and Washington County could not handle the social and physical problems facing the District. In their view, Congress had not lived up to its obligation to financially support the city.

The black community viewed this consolidation plan as a setback and their leader Frederick Douglass recognized in these arguments an effort to reduce the influence of the black vote, which had been extended to black males after the Civil War.[5]

In 1871 Congress abolished the existing municipal and county governments and replaced them with a territorial government for the District of Columbia. Congress provided for a local government consisting of a governor, an eleven-member council, and a Board of Public

Works, all appointed by the president. A twenty two-member House of Delegates and a nonvoting delegate to the United States House of Representatives were elected by the people. But this form lasted only three years. In 1874 the corrupt and debt-ridden territorial government was abolished by Congress, including the office of nonvoting delegate, and replaced by a temporary commission of three members, appointed by the president. In 1878 this commission form of government was made permanent and lasted for nearly a century, until 1967, when President Lyndon B. Johnson's Reorganization Plan Number 3 was approved by Congress.

Numerous presidents since 1878 had urged Congress to restore to the District of Columbia the right to elect its city officials, and various bills to effect this recommendation were introduced, but none received final approval of both houses of Congress. The last four presidents who preceded home rule—Dwight D. Eisenhower, John F. Kennedy, Lyndon B. Johnson, and Richard M. Nixon—had all specifically recommended and urged the restoration of suffrage and self-government to the people of the nation's capital.

Supporters and opponents of home rule had wrangled for years over the problems of transferring to the local government routine legislative duties of Congress while protecting the federal interest in the nation's capital. Frustrated by congressional failure to pass home rule legislation, President Johnson in 1967 used his reorganization authority to revamp the city government. The reorganization plan called for the abolition of the three-man board of commissioners and created in its place a single commissioner and a nine-member council to be appointed by the president. The commissioner was given the executive and administrative responsibilities previously exercised by the three-member board of commissioners. Prior to Reorganization Plan Number 3, the executive and legislative functions and powers of the District government were not separate. Although these new officials were not elected, the additional council members allowed the local government to be more representative of the city. President Johnson appointed Walter E. Washington, an attorney/administrator, to serve as commissioner of the new government. The commissioner and five of the nine appointees to the council were members of the black community. In addition to the objective of making the local government more efficient and effective, the reorganization was widely viewed as a preparatory step toward self-government. The main opposition to the reorganization plan came from Republicans and southern Democrats.[6]

The turning point in this struggle to bring self-government to the nation's capital came in 1972 with the defeat of Representative John L. McMillan (D-S.C.), Chairman of the House Committee on the District of Columbia, in his bid for reelection to Congress. From 1949 to 1973, the House District Committee was dominated by eight southern members, including the chairman, who consistently used the power of his post to block home rule legislation.[7]

McMillan was born on a farm near Mullins (Marion County), South Carolina. He was first elected to Congress in 1938 and advanced to the chairmanship of the House District Committee in the 79th Congress (1945–46). During his twenty-four years as chairman, McMillan ruled the city as a kind of local czar.[8] He was viewed as the holder of ultimate authority over almost every aspect of life in the city, from parking space assignments to public employee payrolls. McMillan won praise from city business interests and conservative congressmen who were usually his allies in opposing home rule for the District. A staunch conservative and segregationist, McMillan displayed no sympathy for the political will and desires of the District's black population. Flanked by other rural southern lawmakers who shared his lack of compassion for black people and his inability to appreciate the needs of a large urban area, McMillan used every trick at his command to ensure the continued subjugation of the citizens of the local community. In addition to accusing McMillan of racism, leaders in the black community contended that he ignored the social needs of the city: its housing, employment, welfare, and education problems.[9]

The main difference between the House and Senate with regard to the governance of the federal district was that the Senate District Committee was not chaired or dominated by southern members during the McMillan years.[10] Six times between 1949 and 1965 the Senate passed home rule measures; the first five died in the House District Committee. The sixth bill, approved by the Senate in 1965, was passed by the House in amended form after being discharged from the District Committee. The House version of the bill was so weakened that no compromise could be reached between the two chambers. Strong arguments were advanced in floor debate for and against home rule. With the black population at 60 percent, the fear of black domination of the city government, while unexpressed, was one of the major reasons for opposition to home rule.[11]

Representative Charles C. Diggs, Jr. (D-Mich.), assumed the chairmanship of the House District Committee at the beginning of the

93d Congress (1973–74). The first black member of Congress to chair the committee, Diggs reorganized it, adding a Subcommittee on Government Operations that was chaired by Representative Brock Adams (D-Wash.). The latter panel reported a draft home rule bill to the full committee by late June of 1973, despite a boycott of the subcommittee's work sessions by its three Republican members.[12]

Due mainly to differences over what constituted adequate protection of the federal interest, the District Home Rule Charter was born out of conflict between federal and local interests. Of course, the District had no real clout in this controversy, except through its influence on the national lawmakers. Despite the fact that the home rule movement was endorsed in the platforms of both the Republican and Democratic Parties and was characterized as a bipartisan effort, it was led by the Democrats, who were in control of the Congress.

With Chairman McMillan gone, it was literally a new day in the House, and home rule sponsors and supporters made good on it. For more than two years, home rule advocates had been carefully building a campaign that would lead to congressional approval of a strong home rule bill. Many groups, including Common Cause, participated in the national Coalition for Self-Determination for the District of Columbia. This body activated thousands of concerned citizens who helped convince their congressional representatives that the time for District of Columbia home rule had come.[13]

The 1973 home rule bill passed by the Senate represented the eighth time since 1949 that this body had approved a bill providing some measure of self-government for the residents of the nation's capital. The Senate bill was much stronger than the House version, with the differences finally being resolved in conference.[14] Based on the original House and Senate bills, it seemed that the District was on the verge of gaining the desired control over its own affairs. For many reasons, however, this cherished goal eluded the District. Though rarely spoken of, underlying the arguments on home rule and its different facets were the issues of race and politics. The fact that the population of the District was predominantly black and heavily Democratic left many Republican and southern members of Congress either lukewarm or opposed to a popularly elected local government.

In the District's current form of home rule, the charter provides for a mayor and a thirteen-member council, elected by popular vote. Each of the eight wards of the city elects one member; five members, including the chairman of the council, are elected at large. No political party can nominate more than three candidates to run at large, a requirement to ensure some minority party representation. The mayor and council members are chosen in partisan elections and serve a term of four years. The Senate was steadfast on having partisan elections and prevailed on this provision during the conference. The charter exempted federal employees who were candidates for local office from compliance with the Hatch Act, which prohibits government employees from participating in partisan politics.

The council has broad legislative powers over local affairs, subject to several specific limitations and to a veto by the mayor. The council and mayor have legislative and taxing authority over all local matters except the following: nonresident income tax, property of the United States, height limitations on buildings, the National Capital Planning Commission, jurisdiction of the District of Columbia courts, United States courts, United States attorney and United States marshal.[15] Except for emergency and budget acts and charter amendments, all legislation adopted by the council and approved by the mayor is transmitted to the Speaker of the House and the President of the Senate for a layover period of thirty days (sixty days for criminal laws) before becoming law. The legislation can be vetoed during this period by both houses adopting a joint resolution of disapproval and by the president signing it. Congress reserves the right to legislate for the District at any time.

Practically every possible arrangement was considered for organizing the local judicial system before deciding to essentially leave it as it was prior to home rule. These possibilities included allowing the mayor to appoint the judges of the District of Columbia courts with the approval of the council and allowing the mayor to appoint the judges with the advice and consent of the Senate. The House and Senate took different positions on this question, with the latter body approving a bill that would have allowed the mayor to appoint the judges with the advice and consent of the Senate. The charter authorized the president to continue to appoint the judges of the District courts, but provided that he must choose from among three names submitted to him by a nominating commission that contains local representation. The judicial appointment powers of the mayor are nil when compared with those of the chief executive in the states, where the governor exercises judicial appointment powers.[16]

At one point in the process of drafting versions of home rule bills and forging political alliances, it appeared that the city would control its own expenditures. The earlier bills of both the House and Senate authorized local control of the budget, with Congress appropriating the federal payment. This matter became an issue in the House before the bill reached the floor, and major concessions were made in the original version of the House District Committee bill in order to consolidate support for the measure. Control of the city's spending was a part of the so-called Diggs Compromise. This compromise made six significant concessions to home rule opponents:

- retention of line-item congressional control over the city's budget,
- election of the council and mayor by nonpartisan rather than by partisan elections,
- specific authority to the president to take control of the local police force in an emergency,
- confirmation of judges appointed by the mayor to the District of Columbia Court of Appeals and Superior Court by the Senate rather than the city council,
- a prohibition on the city council from making any changes in the criminal code, and
- a provision that no council action would take effect until thirty days after enactment, so that Congress would have an opportunity to review and veto it. [The original version provided for a congressional veto but did not specify a layover period.][17]

The budget provision was the linchpin in the concessions because it delivered the support of Representative William Natcher (D-Ky.), the powerful chairman of the District of Columbia Appropriations Subcommittee and an influential southern Democrat. The Senate persisted in giving budget control to the city, but the House prevailed during conference. The Diggs Compromise forged some of the major limits of home rule, and many city officials were very critical of Diggs' leadership in this regard. The congressman stood his ground, however, contending that he had successfully shepherded through Congress the first home rule bill in approximately one hundred years.

The White House maintained a low profile in this controversy. President Richard M. Nixon did not take a public position on any of the proposed bills, but reiterated his pledge to "work receptively and cooperatively . . . to achieve true and effective self-government for the District."[18] White House officials met several times with the House sponsors, and the compromise provision giving the president emergency authority over the local police was requested by the administration. The Senate version granted no such authority, but the House provision prevailed during conference.

It appears that, in this crucial political struggle, the residents of the federal district came very close to getting some key powers that, with hindsight, would have made a major difference in District affairs. Control of the budget and authority to appoint judges and prosecute local crimes are cases in point. Another point of contention between the House and Senate centered on the control of comprehensive planning, which was resolved in favor of the local government and in accordance with the position of the House. There were many other thorny issues that generated intense struggles within Congress. One such conflict, over the addition of the federal enclave amendment, is the substance of the next chapter and provides additional background and analysis of the home rule legislation.

OVERVIEW OF CHAPTERS

Soon after home rule took effect in 1975, the new government sought to undo a key provision in the District Home Rule Charter that provided for the National Capital Service Area (federal enclave). The District's elected officials participated in sponsoring and justifying the city's request to Congress to repeal this legislation. The initial conflict between the Congress and the District government is analyzed in chapter 2. The issue resulted in a reargument by elected city officials of many aspects of the recently passed self-government package. Although the city's request was rejected in 1975, the federal enclave provision remains on the statute books, unimplemented. But in a curious turn of events, this provision is now welcomed by city officials who view it as an important stepping-stone in their press for statehood.

The congressional oversight machinery is described in chapter 3. The nature, intensity, and outcome of many of the conflicts, often waged on a partisan basis between the national government and the District, are determined by the makeup of the standing committees and the way in which oversight is handled. In addition to these partisan political influences, the institutional differences between the House and Senate, as well as the racial dimension of the District's politics, are analyzed.

The official challenges and vetoes of District legislation by Congress are discussed in chapters 4 and 5, respectively. While conflicts over land use policy constitute the exclusive subject matter of chapter 7, land use is also involved in two of the vetoes executed by Congress— the location of chanceries and the height limitation. The third veto involved a moral issue: the District's enactment of a reform in the basic criminal code, dealing with the sexual assault laws.

With only three formal vetoes of District legislation in twenty years of home rule, Congress would seem to have an impressive record of self-restraint, from the standpoint of local self-government. Congress's performance regarding self-government, however, is tarnished by the official introduction of some thirty-eight challenges of District legislation. The challenges have an impact on the self-governing prerogative by conveying a warning message to the District government.

But the full impact of congressional intervention in local affairs comes home to roost in the appropriations process. Over one hundred riders and general management provisions pertaining to the District have found their way into the District of Columbia appropriations measures since home rule has been in effect. The analysis in chapter 6, on District appropriations, completes the picture of congressional interventions that is begun in chapter 4, on challenges.

The land use policy conflicts of chapter 7 involved the building of the World Technology Trade Center (Techworld) and the Metropolitan Square complex. The original Pierre L'Enfant plan was the main issue in the Techworld controversy, and the two governments went to court to settle this dispute. The building of Metropolitan Square posed a threat to White House security, and this disagreement focused on the city's use of its planning and development powers under the District Home Rule Charter. Overall, land use policy has been at the cutting edge of the relationships between the two jurisdictions.

Chapters 8 and 9, the final substantive chapters of this study, deal with the challenge of dual democracy in domestic and foreign contexts, respectively. These chapters focus on the objective of trying to strike a balance between federal and local interests. In the domestic context, this issue might be phrased as follows:

The District of Columbia as a national capital
and
The District of Columbia as a place to live.

The analysis in chapter 8 focuses on national representation and self-determination, as represented through statehood, retrocession, and other options for the District. At this time, statehood is the goal of District officials and residents. It is endorsed in the Democratic party platform and by President Bill Clinton, and statehood supporters expect this issue to move forward during his administration (1993–96). However, statehood does not represent a conflict in the same sense as the other issues analyzed in this study, such as land use policy, public safety, and building height limitation, where the battles have already been waged and the respective victor declared. The statehood question is a proposed solution, however, to the problems of increased self-government and national representation for the District. Any study of the current governance of the nation's capital would be expected to assess the statehood question.

With regard to foreign nations, the United States is among approximately eighteen countries with federal systems, the distinguishing characteristic of which is the relative independence of the two levels of government from each other—national versus state. Of course, this is a matter of degree. Whether certain countries are genuine federations is a matter of opinion upon which there can easily be disagreement. I have tried to avoid this problem by including only the countries that claim to have federal constitutions. Two of the countries that traditionally have been placed in the group—the USSR and Yugoslavia—have fallen apart. This reduces the working number to approximately sixteen.[19]

Among the existing federations of the world, there are three types of constitutional arrangements for the government of their national capitals: (1) it may be a city within one of the states or provinces of the federation; (2) it may be a city-state in its own right; or (3) it may be established in a federal district or territory. The various constitutional arrangements, along with the governmental systems in specific federal capital cities, comprise the main content of chapter 9.

The United States is not alone in trying to balance federal and local interests and meet the challenge of dual democracy. This problem is shared with all of the countries whose capital cities are in federal districts. I survey the responses of several foreign countries to this challenge to see what we can learn from their experiences. Apparently, countries such as Australia, India, and Brazil have now moved ahead of the United States in meeting this challenge.

The conclusions of this study, along with some recommendations for repairing the government of the nation's capital, are presented in chapter 10. Many recommendations are made throughout the study in connection with the problems being discussed. Most of these recommendations are restated in the final chapter.

N O T E S

1. Donald C. Rowat, ed., *The Government of Federal Capitals* (Toronto: University of Toronto Press, 1973), xi-xii.

In that most countries are unitary states, they do not face the same kind of problems in governing their national capitals as those faced by federal countries. In a unitary system of government, such as in France and the United Kingdom, the central government is supreme; the regional governments are mere agents of the national government, which can regulate them, overrule them, and abolish them. In a federal system, power is shared between the national and state governments (or subdivisions). The distinguishing characteristic of federalism is the independence of the two levels of government from each other.

2. Over one-half of the 753,430 blacks in the United States in 1790 lived in Maryland and Virginia. By 1840, the year of the last census for the original District of Columbia, blacks comprised 30 percent of its population. Letitia W. Brown, *Free Negroes in the District of Columbia, 1790–1846* (New York: Oxford University Press, 1972), 10, 17.

3. Actually, there had been petitions for retrocession by residents of both Virginia and Maryland portions of the District (Alexandria and Georgetown), but Congress ignored the latter. *Washington Post,* 11 March 1990, B-2. See also Constance McLaughlin Green, *Washington—Village and Capital, 1800–1878* (Princeton University Press, 1962), 178–79.

The records in the Office of the Surveyor of the District of Columbia show the physical size of the District as 68.26: 7.01 square miles in navigable waters (10.26 percent) and 61.25 square miles in land. Information secured via telephone from the Office of the Surveyor, Department of Public Works, District of Columbia Government, Washington, D.C., 31 May 1994.

4. *Washington Post,* 11 March 1990, B-2.

5. William V. Thomas, "Washington, D.C. Voting Representation," *Editorial Research Reports,* published by Congressional Quarterly, Inc. (5 January 1979): 12.

6. The Reorganization Act of 1949 gave the president broad authority to reorganize agencies of the Executive Branch or District of Columbia government. These reorganization plans became effective automatically 60 days after submission to Congress, unless either chamber disapproved by majority vote. Reorganization Plan Number 3 was considered and approved by the House Government Operations Committee. House District Committee Chairman John L. McMillan (D-S.C.) introduced a resolution disapproving the plan as did Representative Joel T. Broyhill (R-Va.), also a member of the committee. The House rejected the disapproval resolution by a 160 to 244 vote, thus allowing the plan to take effect. *Congressional Quarterly Almanac* 23 (1967): 752, 1025.

7. *Congressional Quarterly Almanac* 29 (1973): 735.

8. Due to Republican control of the House during the 80th (1947–49) and 83d (1953–55) Congresses, McMillan's twenty-four years were not consecutive: he served as a chairman of the committee during the 79th (1945–46), 81st-82d (1949–52), and 84th-92d (1955–72) Congresses. House Committee on the District of Columbia, *Legislative Calendar* (Final), 93d Cong., 2d Sess., 31 December 1974, 4.

9. *Washington Post*, 18 September 1972, A-18; Larry White, "Southern Congressional Politics: Change and Continuity Since the 1965 Voting Rights Act" (Ph.D. diss., Yale University, 1978): 1.

10. During the longest period of Representative McMillan's chairmanship of the House District Committee (the 84th through the 92d Congresses (1955–73)), the Senate District Committee was chaired by the following senators: Francis Case (R-S.D.), Matthew M. Neely (D-W.Va.), Alan Bible (D-Nev.), Joseph Tydings (D-Md.), and Thomas Eagleton (D-Mo.). Any senators who leaned against home rule for the District of Columbia could rest assured that the House would take care of the matter.

11. *Congressional Quarterly Almanac,* 21 (1965): 613.

12. Ibid., 735.

13. "Home Rule for District of Columbia is Approved by House." *In Common* 2, no. 11 (19 October 1973): 1.

14. The original version of the House bill was on a par with the bill passed in the Senate, but District Committee Chairman Diggs agreed to a number of compromises in the measure in order to win support on the House floor. *Congressional Quarterly Almanac* 29 (1973): 734.

15. Initially, the mayor and council had no authority over the criminal laws of the District, but that limitation was removed in 1979. Office of District of Columbia Delegate to Congress, Walter E. Fauntroy, *If You Favor Freedom* (Washington, D.C., 1986), 12.

16. The District of Columbia Judicial Nomination Commission is comprised of seven members, only three of which are appointed by the District government: two members are appointed by the mayor and one by the council. *D.C. Self-Government and Governmental Reorganization Act of 1973, As Amended.* Public Law 93-198, sec. 434; 87 *Statutes at Large* 774 (1973)

17. Because of the differences between the respective versions of the House and Senate home rule bills, some of the above provisions were either altered or eliminated from the measure that was finally approved by the two houses. *Congressional Quarterly Almanac* 29 (1973): 737–741. *Washington Post*, 6 October 1973, D-1; 12 November 1973, C-1.

18. *Congressional Quarterly Almanac* 29 (1973): 738.

19. There is considerable variation in the design of federal systems. Some are so politically centralized that the state and lower levels of government have little or no independence. The complete list of federal countries appears in chapter 9, p. 260 n.1.

2

National Capital Service Area

It has been twenty years since the current District of Columbia Home Rule Charter took effect. Yet one of its major sections, calling for the establishment of the National Capital Service Area (NCSA), known as the federal enclave, has not been implemented. With the statehood movement afoot in the 1990s, talk of implementing the NCSA section of the charter has taken on new life, geared to the statehood objective. In the years since the struggle for home rule took place in Congress in 1973, the NCSA issue has come full cycle in terms of the avowed purpose behind its creation and in its supporters and opponents.[1]

BACKGROUND

The NCSA amendment to the home rule bill in the House of Representatives originated under rather unique circumstances. As soon as the 1972 national elections were over, resulting in the defeat of Representative John L. McMillan (D-S.C.), who for twenty-four years had served as chairman of the House District Committee, speculation began about the possibility of accomplishing home rule for the District.[2]

During the previous twenty-five years a total of eight home rule bills had been passed by the Senate, but only one amended version in the House, mainly because the bills could not get through the House District Committee. The last home rule bill to be debated on the House floor was in 1965.[3]

With the opening of the 93d Congress (1973) a new chairman, Representative Charles C. Diggs, Jr.(D-Mich.), was in charge of the District Committee and eleven new members took their seats on this twenty-five-member body. The committee was younger and stronger with respect to pro-home rule Democrats, and both Representatives Diggs and Brock Adams (D-Wash.), Chairman of the Subcommittee on Government Operations of the District Committee, emphasized their commitment to working for home rule for the District.[4] Initial hopes centered on passage of some version of home rule for the District before the end of the 93d Congress, but as time passed and optimism increased, hopes began to focus on the first session. Work by the home rule supporters intensified, but no one was sure what would happen should the home rule bill reach the full House. Who would line up on which side?

The conservative members, led by Washington metro-area Representative Joel Broyhill (R-Va.), were opposed to home rule, but some left the door open for a possible compromise, depending upon the substance of the bill. One year earlier, in 1972, when the House District Committee was about to vote on a home rule bill, Broyhill had deprived the panel of a quorum by standing outside the room for thirty minutes. Inside, Representative Earl F. Landgrebe (R-Ind.) argued that home rule was a "scary" notion and complained: "This community, with the makeup of its population, I don't know who these people would elect, Jane Fonda? Or what's his name—Stokely Carmichael?"[5]

Since all members concurred in the primary objective of protecting the federal interest in the nation's capital, the differences centered around how best to achieve acceptable self-government without violating this objective. Most members agreed that strictly local policies should be decided by local citizens, but where was the line to be drawn between federal and local interests?

Once the House District Committee bill was drafted, members began to take sides and a variety of positions began to surface. Although some of the pro votes were not firm, the home rule bill was voted out of the District Committee by the overwhelming majority of twenty to four.[6] This bill provided for the nonpartisan election of a mayor and a thirteen-member council to which was transferred considerable authority.[7] The initial committee bill was subjected to a number of changes both prior to and during floor debate. Most of the former changes were conceded by supporters in order to give the measure a better chance for success on the House floor. The most important concession was to give up budgetary authority for the local government and allow Congress to remain in control of the city's finances. Judicial appointments, initially given to the mayor and council, were allowed to remain in the hands of the president. In spite of these concessions, a flurry of substitute bills and amendments were proposed by members dissatisfied with the Committee bill.

While there were some members who were generally opposed to any kind of home rule for the District, the main battle would be waged over what type of self-government the District should have. Once the

House District Committee presented its bill, the struggle was largely between those who supported it and those who did not. Some conservative members preferred a legislative body of elected and appointed members, with a mayor elected from within its own ranks. There was considerable support among Republicans for a compromise measure, sponsored by the ranking Republican on the House District Committee, Representative Ancher Nelsen of Minnesota, and by Democratic Representative Edith S. Green of Oregon. Their bill proposed an elected council, with the president continuing to appoint the mayor. This measure had the support of such prominent House Republicans as Minority Leader Gerald Ford of Michigan, who vowed to work against the committee bill.[8] Some of the amendments that were subsequently offered to the committee bill on the House floor represented key provisions in the failed substitute bills. Such was the case with the amendment calling for the creation of the National Capital Service Area.[9]

From the very outset, the home rule movement was characterized as a bipartisan struggle and so was the opposition to it. Home rule lobbyists viewed Representative Ancher Nelsen (R-Minn.) as their most "important opponent." Nelsen was the ranking Republican on the House District Committee and had recently served as chairman of the Commission on the Organization of the Government of the District of Columbia (Nelsen Commission—1970–72). This twelve-member congressionally authorized body was appointed by President Richard M. Nixon to study and make recommendations concerning the reorganization of the District government. Although he opposed the committee bill, Nelsen never took a hard line against home rule and finally cast a vote in favor of reporting the bill out of committee in order that it might be debated on the House floor.[10]

Representative Edith S. Green (D-Ore.) was the first Democratic member of the House to indicate that she would actively work against the committee bill, which was supported by the Democratic leadership in Congress. A member of the prestigious Appropriations Committee, Green was considered one of the most powerful Democrats in the House. For years, she had been a member of the Education and Labor Committee, where she chaired one of its special subcommittees on education and was the second ranking Democrat behind the chairman. She became a member of the Appropriations Committee at the beginning of the 93d Congress (1973–74).[11]

Representative Green emerged as the leader of the Democratic opposition to the committee bill. Under her leadership, and with the strong assistance of Representative Nelsen, the home rule bill was successfully amended to create the National Capital Service Area. This core area of the federal district, running from Capitol Hill to Theodore Roosevelt Island, contained the Capitol and related buildings, monuments, federal offices, and historical sites.[12] It was to be administered by a director appointed by the president.

As will be shown in detail below, the leaders and supporters of the home rule movement were strongly opposed to the Green amendment, which carved up the District in an unprecedented way by removing its core area from local control. Those members who took a moderate position on the home rule question viewed the amendment as unnecessary to protect the federal interest and felt it would create another layer of bureaucracy.[13]

When the District Home Rule Charter took effect on 2 January 1975 nothing was done toward implementing section 739, which contained the NCSA provision. But local leaders and some members of Congress were worried over the possibility that at any time the White House might take steps to implement this section of the charter. Consequently, as soon as home rule took effect, this provision of the charter became an issue and steps were taken to repeal it in the first session of the 94th Congress (1975). In the sections below, I explain why this bipartisan effort, including support from the Ford administration, was doomed to failure.[14]

Because the NCSA provision was added during the final stages of debate and was not included in the hearings and markup sessions, it received a more comprehensive examination during the repeal effort than at the time of passage. Therefore, much of the analysis given below is from the repeal stage.

THE NCSA AND THE FEDERAL INTEREST

The basic idea of the Founding Fathers to create a federal district might be considered an ingenious one, and to stake out a part of this district, where there is heavy federal concentration, for special administration would not appear to be that unusual. But the timing of this step in relation to the granting of home rule to the District, and the failure two years later to implement the provision or repeal it, presents an anomalous political situation. For example, the District of Columbia Task Force, appointed by President Jimmy Carter in 1977 and headed by Vice President Walter Mondale, hardly raised the issue of the NCSA in carrying out its assignment to study the District of Columbia government, for fear that it might result in demands from Congress that this provision of the Home Rule Charter be implemented.[15]

In many respects, the NCSA issue represents a microcosm of the theoretical and practical problems involved in governing the federal district. A main theoretical consideration centers on the need to identify and accommodate both federal and local interests, while the practical problems focus on the operational machinery necessary for a smooth delivery of basic services in an area of concentrated federal establishments. Under the thesis advanced by Donald C. Rowat, the question centers on the extent to which both federal and local interests can be accommodated within the framework of the federal district.

The establishment and current status of the NCSA are to some extent intertwined with the larger issues of full home rule, voting representation in Congress, and statehood. Any permanent resolution of these issues is likely to influence the final decision to retain and implement the NCSA provision of the charter or eventually repeal it. During the initial stage of home rule, it appeared that the future handling of this matter by Congress would serve as an index of the chances for increased local autonomy. Yet little has changed in the two decades since home rule was enacted; the NCSA legislation remains unimplemented and unrepealed.

The purpose given for establishing the NCSA was to protect the federal interest and "preserve the monumental proportion of the District of Columbia for all American citizens." Utilizing the District's governmental services "to the extent practicable," the main function of the NCSA was to assure the provision of basic operating services in "an area of heavy federal concentration."

The director of the NCSA was to be appointed by the president at Level IV of the Executive Schedule. Acting through the director, the president was to see that adequate fire protection and sanitation services were provided to the NCSA and, with certain areas excepted, give the same assurance for police protection and the maintenance of streets and highways.[16]

The introduction and eventual success of the Green amendment (section 739) caught many members by surprise, particularly some of the main sponsors of the home rule bill.[17] When the measure went to conference, comments on the NCSA amendment were solicited from various federal agencies and Representative Green gave testimony, but no regular public hearings were held nor any in-depth analysis made of this section of the bill.

Although section 739 of the Home Rule Charter has been claimed as a base of support by those local leaders and organizations who advocate statehood for the District of Columbia, the section actually was sponsored and supported mainly by members who were opposed to any kind of self-government or statehood for the District; they probably would have preferred retrocession to Maryland.[18]

LOCATION

Although there are bits and pieces of the federal establishment located throughout the country and in other parts of the District of Columbia, the physical presence of the federal government is mainly concentrated in the NCSA. Approximately twenty million visitors come to the nation's capital each year, and each one of these American and foreign visitors is likely to spend time in the federal enclave.[19] Few if any of them know that the jurisdiction over this area, at least for certain services, is officially separate from the remainder of the District of Columbia.

A line drawn around the NCSA would include the federal buildings along the Mall area, the Capitol, the Senate and House Office Buildings, the Supreme Court, Union Square, the White House, the Kennedy Center, and all of the federal buildings up and down Independence Avenue.[20] It would also include Fort McNair, the Washington Navy Yard, Bolling Air Force Base, the Naval Research Observatory, and some smaller establishments.[21]

Some federal land and buildings in the District of Columbia are outside of the NCSA as delineated in the Home Rule Act. These include the main buildings which house the Department of Housing and Urban Development, the Department of Transportation, the Environmental Protection Agency, and several additional agencies or segments of agencies located in offices in the northwest section of the District. There are approximately eighty-seven federally owned and General Services Administration (GSA) operated buildings in the NCSA, exclusive of the leased space for which GSA is responsible. Altogether, the NCSA contains twenty-two million square feet of space.[22]

DELIVERY OF SERVICES

The sponsors of section 739 of the Home Rule Act said its purpose was to assure the delivery of basic operating services to the federal establishment within the federal enclave. These services included fire and police protection, sanitation, and road service. With few exceptions, these responsibilities were being carried by the District government at the time the Home Rule Charter was passed, and because the NCSA has not been activated, there has been no change in the scope of services provided in the enclave by the District of Columbia government.

Fire.

With the exception of Bolling Air Force Base, Washington Navy Yard, and the Naval Research Laboratory, the District is totally responsible for providing fire protection throughout the federal enclave. This holds true in spite of the fact that enforcement of the District fire code is not required in the federal buildings of the enclave. The GSA fire inspectors, the architect of the capitol, and the National Capital Park Service usually coordinate their fire protection programs with that of the District Fire Department. The fire inspectors for these agencies provide the District Fire Department with precise information on building layouts, including the location of alarms, extinguishers, and exits.[23]

Police.

In the area of police protection, the main coordination is between GSA and the Metropolitan Police Department (MPD). Although there is some mutual cooperation on an ad hoc basis, there is no official relationship between GSA's Federal Protective Service (FPS) and the police of the National Capital Park Service. If it happens that both the FPS and the park police arrive at a GSA building, they will then agree on who has jurisdiction. If GSA apprehends someone in one of their buildings, they will call the District police, who will come and get the person, book him/her, and incarcerate the individual if necessary. Prosecution is through the District of Columbia Superior Court system rather than the federal court system.

GSA has a small investigative police force of usually not more than ten persons who handle thefts and misdemeanors in federal buildings and who call the MPD for serious offenses. The MPD can go into GSA buildings without getting consent from the FPS; its jurisdiction is concurrent with that of GSA, a relationship which is different from that in any other state or city. The FPS has authority to write traffic tickets within certain areas, mostly around federal buildings, but not on major streets and highways within the District.

Street Maintenance.

The streets throughout the District are maintained by its government except where they are totally within federal property. Although GSA takes care of the sidewalks around its buildings, this service is usually provided on a contract basis through the District government. The Park Service provides a complete road maintenance program for thirty-nine miles of road and thirty-six miles of sidewalk as well as complete maintenance for twelve bridges.[24]

The Park Service provides sanitation services for 1,203 out of the 1,448 acres defined as the NCSA. The District provides service for the remainder of this area. In other jurisdictions across the country where federal government or GSA buildings are located, water and sewer services are provided to the federal government at cost; the District also provides these services in all government buildings and is reimbursed at cost.

CREATING THE NCSA

Although the sponsors of the amendment establishing the NCSA gave a number of reasons in support of their actions, some of the motivations behind the successful effort to add section 739 to the home rule bill have to be inferred from statements, floor debates, and votes of members of Congress. The debates on the rule of procedure, the main bill, substitute bills, and amendments all tend to shed light on some of the underlying motivations.

In presenting the case for the establishment of the federal enclave, its sponsors placed heavy emphasis on the fact that the capital belonged to "all of the people of the United States," and that the people who happen to live very close to it (inhabitants of the District) should not have any greater control over it than those people who live far away. Representative Green stated:

> I see absolutely no reason why anybody who wants this home rule vote for the residents of the District—and I favor home rule, and I favor full citizenship for all residents of our country—I see no reason why they should ask that they should have control over this Federal area any more than the people of Virginia or the people of Alexandria County who were one time a part of the District of Columbia, should insist that they have jurisdiction over this Federal City. . . .

Why is it that the people who live 3 or 5 miles away, on one side of the Potomac River only, should have a greater voice than anybody else? Why is this, for them, a requirement for home rule?[26]

Representative Green argued further that it was intended that the representatives of all the people of the country should control "this one city, and to prevent its being controlled by the parochial spirit that would . . . govern men who did not look beyond the city to the grandeur of the nation. . . ." Representative Joel Broyhill of Virginia argued in much the same vein, stating that he would not vote for any bill that would deny his constituents "and all other American citizens, their right of control and voice in the management of our Nation's Capital."[27]

The sponsors of the amendment to establish the NCSA also argued that George Washington and the framers of the United States Constitution intended to retain the District of Columbia as a federal city, operated by the federal government. According to Green, government under the home rule bill could only be viewed as a temporary stage for the District. At some point in the future, a new solution would be necessary, which she saw as either retrocession to Maryland or statehood. She believed that the passage of the enclave provision would facilitate either of these ends.[28]

In order to get at some of the subtle factors behind the amendment to establish the NCSA, it is necessary to examine the comments and fears articulated during floor debate on the home rule bill and the context in which they were made. At the time of this debate, the black population of the District was above 70 percent, the highest percentage of any large city in the United States.[29] The city was being labeled the "crime capital" of the nation and crime was extensively reported and played up in the media, particularly in the two major papers of the city—the *Washington Post* and *Washington Star.* An atmosphere of fright and panic was not an unusual situation in the city at that time, especially among its white residents, over crimes which were either committed or assumed to be committed by blacks. During the 1960s and 1970s, presidential candidates made campaign promises across the country to clean up Washington, D.C., based upon crime statistics and impressions about the public safety and security in the nation's capital. Senatorial and congressional candidates in the states adjacent to the District had waged similar kinds of political campaigns, promising to assist in controlling crime in the District of Columbia.

The majority of the members of the 93d Congress were residents of Washington and its metropolitan area during the 1968 riots by the black population following the assassination of Dr. Martin Luther King, Jr.[30] Members still harbored degrees of fear about what was viewed as the lawless and destructive potential of certain elements in the population of the District of Columbia.

The public use of racial terms and labels can arouse sharp reactions, sometimes resulting in a preference for the use of code terms, such as "law and order," when referring to the black community. Although it was not stated directly, the thought of turning full authority over to the local government was either unacceptable or discomforting to members. Representative Delbert L. Latta (R-Ohio), a member of the Rules Committee, alluded to this fear when he cautioned his fellow members to protect federal property. Citing the possibility of a riot as an example, the representative stated:

> . . . in case of a riot, I would fear for the city as the President would not have the authority to mobilize the police force of the city as he may see fit.[31]

On this particular point, Representative Green voiced her concern as follows:

> The question I want to ask you is, as a Member of this House representing your constituency, do you want the time to come when the Metropolitan Police Force, responsible to a locally elected mayor and council, shall be the ones who have control over the Federal buildings in this city?[32]

Representative Steven D. Symms (R-Idaho), a member of the House District Committee was more explicit in his comment:

> We live in an age of demonstrations and we can expect more, not fewer, demonstrations in this city in the years ahead. This, of course, is perfectly proper since any citizen has a constitutional right to petition this Congress for the redress of their grievances. At the same time, however, other citizens have an equal right to have their Government continue to function. . . .
>
> What would happen, Mr. Chairman, if there were a large demonstration in this city which effectively blocked the operations of

the National Government? . . . Suppose that the City Council of Washington had control over the Metropolitan Police and suppose further that the local government was in sympathy with a particular demonstration. Let us suppose that the majority of people elsewhere in the United States, however, disagreed with the aims of these demonstrators and that their Congressmen also disagreed. Could we have a situation where the representatives of the majority could be blackmailed into enacting a law opposed by that majority? This would make a travesty of representative government.[33]

These statements from supporters of the NCSA emphasized a line of separation between local and national interests that apparently was driven by the racial composition of the District population. The latter dimension overshadowed the traditional conflict between national and local interests.

DIVERGENT VIEWS OF THE FEDERAL INTEREST

Taking a position against the Green amendment, Representative Ronald Dellums (D-Calif.) raised points that were to become prominent two years later during the effort to repeal section 739 (the Green amendment) of the Home Rule Charter. He focused attention on the need to draw the line between local and federal interests and on the question of satisfying the constitutional requirement to establish and protect the "Seat of Government." Dellums argued that the home rule bill and the NCSA amendment were totally incompatible—that the main bill was designed to protect the federal interest in the District of Columbia. If the NCSA amendment were passed, Dellums saw no need for Congress to play any further role in the lives of the residents of the District of Columbia on matters of a local nature:

> . . . if we in fact adopt this Federal enclave to this piece of legislation then we will have for all time separated out and protected the Federal interest, . . . there would be no reason whatsoever for the Congress to play any further role . . . in the lives of the residents of the District of Columbia that is of a clearly local nature.[34]

If Dellums's view represented one extreme, the opposite extreme was voiced by Representative Earl F. Landgrebe (R-Ind.), who opposed the creation of the NCSA but for reasons different from those of most of its opponents. After voicing his feelings that the city belonged to his constituents and all of the people of the United States, Landgrebe stated:

> . . . this city was established by congressional action and is the Capital City. Yes, there is a lot of talk about the Federal interest and the local interest, but I beg to tell you that the Federal interest must be the only legitimate concern in our Capital City. I cannot for the life of me see any reason why we should at this time under the pressures of the proponents of the so-called home rule bills, . . . consider shrinking the National City and why we should shrink it down to an enclave or turn the control of the city over to the local people. . . .[35]

In spite of the arguments made by the chairman and members of the House District Committee and other supporters of the main bill, the amendment to establish the NCSA was added to the home rule bill by the close vote of 209 to 202, with 24 abstentions (see table 2.1). Some members justified their votes in favor of what were termed by key supporters as "crippling amendments" (e.g., the NCSA) on the grounds that they would save the main bill. The amended measure was approved in the House on 10 October 1973 by a lopsided vote of 343 to 74 (see table 2.2) and was sent to conference, where the differences between the House and Senate versions were resolved.[36] The bill was signed by President Nixon on 24 December 1973, received referendum

TABLE 2.1   House Vote: NCSA Amendment to Home Rule Bill, H.R. 9682 (1973)

	Yes	%	No	%	Not Voting	%
Democrats	81	34%	151	63%	11	4%
N Dems 30–120						
S Dems 51–31						
Republicans	128	67%	51	26%	13	7%
Total	209		202		24	

Congressional Quarterly Placement of nonvoters: Democrats 1–3; Republicans 7–3; Unidentified 10. %—percentage of total party membership.
Source: *Congressional Quarterly Almanac* (1973).

TABLE 2.2   Home Rule Bills: House/Senate Votes (94th Congress—1973)

	House Vote—H.R. 9692					
	Yes	*%*	*No*	*%*	*Not Voting*	*%*
Democrats	205	85%	27	11%	4	2%
N Dems 150–02						
S Dems 55–25						
Republicans	138	72%	47	24%	2	1%
Total	343		74		6	

	Senate Vote—S. 1435					
	Yes	*%*	*No*	*%*	*Not Voting*	*%*
Democrats	41	73%	7	13%	9	16%
N Dems 35–0						
S Dems 6–7						
Republicans	28	67%	10	24%	4	10%
Total	69		17		13	

%—Percentage of party membership in respective body.
Source: *Congressional Quarterly Almanac* (1973).

approval from the citizens of the District on 7 May 1974, and became effective on 2 January 1975.

EFFORT TO REPEAL THE NCSA

When the Home Rule Charter became effective in 1975, President Gerald Ford took no steps to implement section 739. There is no indication that the matter of implementation was raised by either the Congress or the District government. During 1975, however, a strong bipartisan effort was made in Congress (House District Committee), the executive branch, and the District government to repeal that portion of the Home Rule Charter which called for the establishment of the NCSA.

The effort to repeal section 739 was led by Republican Representative Gilbert Gude of Maryland, ranking minority member of the House District Committee, with strong support from Delegate Walter E. Fauntroy (D-D.C.), Representative Charles W. Whalen, Jr. (R-Ohio), and other members of the District Committee and Congress. In March 1975, Gude introduced a bill to amend the Home Rule Act of 1973 by deleting the National Capital Service Area and the office of its director. Later in the month, an identical bill was again introduced by Gude, along with eight cosponsors, all members of the House District Committee.[37] In June 1975, the Subcommittee on Government Operations of the House District Committee, chaired by Fauntroy, began hearings on the repeal measures. It was significant that the move to repeal section 739 was being led by a minority party member of the District Committee. Although there had been changes in the membership of the committee since the home rule bill was passed in 1973, seven of the eleven Republicans on the committee at that time had supported the addition of the amendment establishing the federal enclave.[38]

The effort to repeal section 739 provided an opportunity not only for an in-depth analysis of its contents (which had not taken place due to its addition to the main bill during floor debate), but also for an examination of the coordination of the delivery of basic operating services in the District of Columbia as handled by the federal executive agencies and the District government.

A wide range of organizations and agencies presented testimony during public hearings on the repeal measures. Included were representatives of the District of Columbia Statehood Party, Georgetown University Law Center, Coalition for Self-Determination for the District of Columbia (Coalition for Self-Determination), General Services Administration (GSA), National Capital Park Service, and the District of Columbia government; testimony was also given by the architect of the capitol. Statements on the repeal measures were entered into the record from the Office of Management and Budget (OMB), District of Columbia Mayor Walter E. Washington, District Council Chairman Sterling Tucker, and former members of Congress Edith Green, Ancher Nelsen, and others.

All of the agency heads involved in the delivery of basic operating services within the NCSA testified that smooth administrative links between the federal and District governments already existed. They pointed out that implementation of the NCSA provision would add an unnecessary layer of bureaucracy. None of the officials who testified or submitted statements for the record thought that the NCSA arrangement would really provide more efficient or economical services to the federal government. Moreover, many of them felt that implementation of section 739 would confuse and further complicate a delicate and complex administrative system in the nation's capital.

Under the existing arrangement, the District is not reimbursed for the delivery of most basic operating services to the federal government. If the NCSA were put into operation and administered in accordance with the Home Rule Charter, reimbursement to the District would be necessary. Both the District government and GSA (the main federal agency involved) felt that this would be a monumental and costly administrative task.

OMB agreed with this position and also specified some of the serious potential administrative problems. The Home Rule Charter called for the director of the NCSA to be appointed by the president as part of the executive office. Taking issue with this arrangement on theoretical grounds, OMB argued that the responsibility of the NCSA director did not fit in with the mission of the executive office, which was created to deal with broad national matters that required the involvement of the president. OMB did not consider the purely local responsibilities to be handled by the director to require or merit the attention of the president. OMB also objected to the decision to place the position of the director at Level IV of the Executive Schedule. The director's duties and responsibilities were not considered to be commensurate with those of other Level IV positions, which are usually held by senior policy officials, "administrators of large and complex programs, and members of regulatory commissions. The duties of the Service Area Director do not warrant such designation."[40]

In spite of wide-ranging support, including that of President Ford, for the bills to delete the NCSA provision from the Home Rule Charter, this effort was defeated in the House by a final vote of 201 to 150.[41] The defeat came in the form of a substitute amendment that in effect killed the bill to repeal section 739. This loss was a major setback for the bipartisan effort of the House District Committee, which had given its unanimous approval to the bill. Republican Representative William Ketchum of California caught the repeal advocates off guard with an amendment that had the effect of reversing the intent of the original amendment sponsored by Representative Gude and others. The substitute amendment retained the federal enclave but authorized the president to designate an existing federal officer as overseer, thus avoiding another layer of bureaucracy, which had been the main thrust behind the repeal movement. The net result of this amendment was that Congress refused once again to give the local government official authority over the entire District of Columbia.

Whether the racial makeup of the District population was a major factor, a complicating factor, or no factor in the failure of the repeal effort, Ketchum probably came closest to giving the main reason for what happened, which he termed as maintaining the "comfort level" in the matter of the federal interest. He argued that when constituents come to the nation's capital, it is important for them to be in a federal area where services are provided by federal officials "who are directly responsible to the federal government and not some local agency."[42] Apparently, there is "comfort" in this statute remaining on the books, even if it is not implemented.

CONSTITUTIONAL AND LEGAL ASPECTS

Although it came after the fact, much of the debate and testimony on the repeal of section 739 of the Home Rule Charter centered on two important questions connected with the establishment of the NCSA. How would the creation of the NCSA affect the constitutional definition of the seat of government of the United States? How would the creation of the NCSA affect the legal jurisdiction of the District government?

As the holder of national legislative authority, Congress may delegate to local legislative bodies broad jurisdiction over territories, ceded areas, or a federal district, provided it retains ample power to revise, alter, or revoke the local legislation.[43] Section 739 partitioned off a part of the District as an area of particular federal interest. Statehood supporters and many others argue that by doing so, Congress has officially defined that part of the seat of the government that needs to be under direct congressional control.

The NCSA was made independent of outside sources of police, fire protection, sanitation, and street services. If this is the part of the District which is necessary for the smooth functioning of the federal government, then the remainder of the District, it may be argued, should be removed from the exclusive jurisdiction of the Congress. Because section 739 authorized the NCSA director to assure that certain basic utility-type services be provided within the federal enclave, "utilizing District of Columbia governmental services to the extent practicable," it was not clear how much official separation or independence the NCSA was to have from the District. This specific point concerned

Mayor Walter E. Washington in his testimony on the bills (H.R. 4394 and H.R. 5642) to repeal section 739:

> Of more importance in our view is the critical question of whether the National Capital Service Area is to be administered as a separate and distinct geographic entity or merely for the purpose of ensuring proper liaison and coordination in an area of the District of Columbia in which there is a concentration of Federal activity.[44]

The mayor was inclined toward the latter interpretation, under which the existing jurisdiction or responsibilities of the District government would hardly be diminished at all. In the mayor's view, the NCSA director's authority to assure the provision of basic services was not inconsistent with continued provision of these services by the District government. The absence of language specifically limiting the District's jurisdiction and responsibility in those portions of the federal enclave outside the Capitol grounds was viewed as a strong indication that no such limitation was intended.[45]

THE STATEHOOD PARTY

An extreme position against elimination of the NCSA was taken by the District of Columbia Statehood Party. Its representatives argued that the official establishment of the federal enclave made it easier, procedurally, to gain statehood for the District. They called the efforts to delete section 739 a backward step and the first piece of "post-reconstruction" legislation for the District during the home rule era. The Statehood Party representatives felt that section 739 had helped to clarify the situation regarding the "District that is required as the Seat of Government." They also emphasized that the 730,000 people in the District were not a part of the seat of government and were not necessary to the "function of the Federal government which could carry on its business without depriving us of our rights as American citizens."

> The enclave renders unto Caesar that which belongs to Caesar and lays the groundwork for giving the rest of the City to the people.[46]

Spokespersons for the Statehood Party went so far as to accuse executive branch officials of not wanting the NCSA to become a reality because it would limit their power and control to a designated area. With the NCSA clearly defined as the seat of government, as required by the Constitution, the party saw the possibility that the remainder of the city might move into a territorial status. The city could then follow the same constitutional procedure as that followed by most states, which were able to move from territorial status to statehood through a constitutional convention and petition to the House and Senate to grant statehood pending the execution of a successful referendum. (Further discussion of the Statehood Party is presented in chapter 8, National Representation and Statehood.)

SUPERIOR POSITION OF FEDERAL GOVERNMENT

A major point made both at the time the NCSA amendment was passed and during the effort to repeal it was that the federal government already had sufficient authority to protect the federal interest without any additional statutory power. The Home Rule Charter (section 601) states in very clear language that Congress has the right to pass any law that it deems appropriate for the District. In addition, it places restraints (section 602) on the legislative authority of the District, prohibiting it from taking any action concerning the functions or property of the United States that would repeal any act of the Congress.[47]

During floor debate on the amendment establishing the NCSA, Representative Green made much of the fact that the Metropolitan Police Force would be under the mayor of the District. Consequently, the NCSA director was given the power to call out the militia to suppress riots. Few, however, would question the fact that the president had adequate powers both before and after home rule to control any emergency situation in the District of Columbia.[48]

In addition to these specific charter provisions, certain general powers of control are held by the federal government because of its superior position. In local communities where federal establishments are located, the respective jurisdiction (city or state) is always called upon to provide basic operating services to the federal government (on a reimbursable basis) such as those being provided by the District of Columbia—fire, police, sanitation, and street maintenance. Under existing statutes, it has been construed that these jurisdictions do not have the authority to tell the federal government that they will not provide these services.[49]

OTHER ARGUMENTS FOR REPEAL

Probably no thoughts or influences on policy decisions go unspoken more often than those of race and racism. Consequently, no overt racial issues were injected into the debates on creating or repealing the NCSA provision. Yet the rioting in the nation's capital following the assassination of civil rights leader Martin Luther King, Jr. in 1968 was a reality that must have been vivid in the minds of both white and black members of Congress. The liberal members were probably inclined to think of the underlying and precipitating causes behind civil disobedience, to consider remedial social steps that should be taken, and to view any recurrence of riotous behavior as extremely remote, without serious provocation. The conservatives and/or racist members probably viewed civil disobedience as a strict public safety issue to be dealt with by an increase in security forces and expansion in prison and detention facilities. Although phrased as humanistic and moral concerns, the talk around the racial issue continued with the testimony of the spokesman for the Coalition for Self-Determination.[50]

The debate on the repeal of section 739 was centered to only a small degree on moral and humanistic concerns. The representative of the Coalition for Self-Determination stated at the very outset that he found no moral or legal justification for the establishment of the federal enclave, nor could he find that it would serve any practical purpose. Consequently, he could only draw the conclusion "that there are other more obscure reasons for the establishment of the NCSA."

The coalition argued that the establishment and operation of the NCSA would have a polarizing effect in the District. Essentially, it would move the national government, symbolized by the national policymakers, further away from the people who were actually providing services indispensable to its day-to-day operation:

> We exist today in an age of increased polarization between the affluent and the poor, the blacks and the whites, the young and the old, the city dweller and the suburbanites. Shall we perpetuate an act which works to further polarize one part of the city and the other?[51]

Approximately twelve organizational groups and/or agencies from federal and local governments or the private sector testified or entered statements in the record concerning the NCSA. Only one, the District of Columbia Statehood Party, was opposed to the deletion of the NCSA provision.

In spite of the decision by Congress, implementation of the federal enclave provision of the charter is seen by the executive branch as either unworkable or so costly and difficult to administer as to nullify any real benefits that might result from its implementation. The decision by President Ford not to execute the federal enclave provision when home rule became effective was policy making of a type. You might say it was a de facto item veto of the respective section of the charter. The record now shows that this matter has been allowed to remain dormant at the chief executive level through the administrations of Presidents Jimmy Carter, Ronald Reagan, George Bush; and, as of 1994 there is no indication of interest in the matter by the administration of President Bill Clinton.

THE NCSA AND STATEHOOD

Although the sponsors of the NCSA amendment to the home rule bill mentioned statehood in 1973 as a future possibility that would require the carving out of a core federal unit, the idea of statehood was too remote at that time to be given serious consideration. As predicted by Representative Green during the home rule debate, the District has come back to demand statehood, and the NCSA has become a vital element in this quest.

Most of the local leaders and supporters of full citizenship rights for District residents who, initially, opposed the creation of the NCSA and, subsequently, sought to repeal it, now view its de jure existence as a major asset in the struggle to gain voting representation in the national legislature via the statehood route. The original sponsors of the NCSA and/or their "descendants" are largely in the camp of those who oppose statehood.[52] Our main concern at this point is with the relationship of the NCSA to statehood. A general discussion of the latter topic is presented in chapter 8.

The transfer in purpose of the NCSA from a service unit, as originally intended, to the official seat of the national government is not without complications. Some of the most serious problems fall into the following three categories:

- difficulties connected with clarifying the physical area of the NCSA as described in the Home Rule Act,
- the complexity of surveying and establishing metes and bounds for the NCSA, and
- complexities of trying to establish a clear geographical separation between the NCSA and the state of New Columbia.

The particular physical boundaries of the NCSA are not adequately described in section 739 of the Home Rule Act. A proper description is necessary before the series of surveys can be conducted, leading to the establishment of metes and bounds, which is a standard but highly technical procedure.[53]

The purposes of the NCSA within the Home Rule Act and the New Columbia Admission Act, respectively, are different. The NCSA within the Home Rule Act, through its director, assures the provision of four types of services to the federal establishment: fire, police, sanitation, and street maintenance. The purpose of the NCSA within the New Columbia Admission Act is to redefine the District of Columbia as the seat of the national government.[54] The National Capital Planning Commission has identified a number of federal interests relevant to its statutory authority that would necessarily influence the configuration of the boundaries of the NCSA as the seat of the national government. These interests include federally leased property, scattered federal property, foreign missions, federally owned streets within the new state, the security of the White House, the Capitol, the Supreme Court, and the vice president's residence, and the future expansion needs of the federal government.[55]

THE NCSA AND THE ROWAT THESIS

The NCSA amendment to the home rule bill reflected the disposition of Congress toward the idea of self-government for the District and what it saw as its responsibility to protect the seat of the government and the federal interest within the nation's capital. Many who voted in favor of the amendment defended their action on the grounds that it was necessary to win approval of the House District Committee's bill. The failure of the repeal effort stands on its own as an unimpaired conflict between the national and District governments. While the controversy generally fits under the Rowat thesis, further analysis is necessary in order to explain the outcome.

In his study of federal capital cities in 1973, Rowat identified a unique reason that does not exist in other federal capital cities to explain the lack of self-government. Attributing the absence of home rule in the District of Columbia to the politics of race, he stated:

> There are special reasons why self-government has not been granted to Washington. Most of the white population have moved into the surrounding metropolitan area in Maryland and Virginia, where they have local government and full voting rights, leaving a large Negro majority in the city.[56]

Few people would take issue with Rowat's conclusion and they would include the NCSA provision under the same rubric. Although racism may have been the main factor behind the approval of and the failure to repeal the NCSA section of the charter, without further analysis there is a danger of oversimplification. It appears that a portion of Rowat's theory on state-controlled capitals might be useful here. Some of the capitals under state law, such as Ottawa and Bern, have dominant cultural influences that either render them, or create the perception that they are, less representative of the nation as a whole. The French-speaking populations in both Canada and Switzerland represent cases in point.

With a minority population in control of the District of Columbia government, is it not possible that we have a situation that parallels that in the above countries, based not so much on language or a subculture but mainly on race? Certainly, as in Bern and Ottawa, the District of Columbia is not a microcosm of the country as a whole. Because of the dominant minority population in the District, the capital city gets caught up in the existing or perceived racial polarization in the country as a whole—a point that was made by the Coalition for Self-Determination when it urged that the interests of the sovereign people of the United States not be separated from that of the District of Columbia. The parallels between the United States and the above two countries, with regard to language/subculture and race, cease abruptly at a point because there is no place in the United States creed or its governmental system for arrangements based on race. The development of the national capital city should not become a civil rights issue, a challenge that is much deeper than nomenclature. The country as a whole should resist this through both deeds and behavior.

As will be shown in the discussion of foreign capitals in chapter 9, the basic problems faced in federal district capitals are not that different—be it Washington, Brasilia, Caracas, or other capitals. The racial dimension in the United States may intensify some of the controversies in its federal district or cause degrees of difference in handling them, but not really change the nature of problems that it shares with many other federal countries. For example, it is by no means alone in having to wrestle with the question of how to conciliate the autonomy of the government of the capital city with the assurance that public safety can be guaranteed.[57]

Finally, there were partisan political factors that influenced the outcome of the NCSA conflict. Although it was billed as a bipartisan effort, the Republican commitment to self-government for the District has not been as consistent as that of the Democrats. It was a Republican congressman who caught the sponsors of the repeal effort off guard with a substitute amendment that nullified their efforts.

The residents of the District take great pride in their city as the seat of the national government. It may be that the District's strategy with regard to the NCSA should have included a greater effort to get this point across to Congress. The repeal of the section of the Home Rule Charter dealing with the NCSA turned out to be a volatile issue. Its ultimate defeat by a margin of over fifty votes indicated that the sponsors underestimated the intensity of the resistance.

NOTES

1. The original supporters and opponents of the NCSA have virtually changed sides on this issue, with the current plan for the NCSA to comprise the reduced federal district. Most of the opponents of the NCSA in 1973 now applaud its creation, while its original sponsors are generally opposed to the statehood movement.

2. McMillan was first elected to Congress in 1938 and advanced to the chairmanship of the House District Committee during the 79th Congress (1945–46). By this date and for many years thereafter, his district base in South Carolina was so well consolidated that he faced no opposition at all. *Washington Post*, 4 September 1979, D-3.

3. With support from President Lyndon B. Johnson, a Senate-passed home rule bill was discharged from the House District Committee in 1965 and debated on the House floor, where an amended version of the bill was passed.

The respective versions were so different that the two chambers could not reach a compromise. *Congressional Quarterly Almanac* 21 (1965): 613; *Washington Star,* 9 October 1965, A-1.

4. As chairman of the subcommittee that would sponsor hearings and otherwise guide the measure, Adams was an enthusiastic leader in the home rule struggle. *Washington Post,* 3 April 1973, C-1.

5. The position of many members on the home rule question varied to some extent with the different stages in the struggle and with the substance of the particular bills under consideration. Ibid., 29 April 1973, B-1; 25 October 1981, A-17.

6. The four "no" votes were cast by Republicans and one Republican voted "present." Some of the members who voted "yes" at the committee stage indicated that they might change their votes when the full House voted on the measure. Ibid., 13 September 1973, C-1.

7. The council could, for instance, change sales or income tax laws, including tax rates, and pass other general legislation previously handled by Congress. There were a number of specific prohibitions on its authority: it could not enact laws to tax federal property in the District, to change the city's building height limitations, or to affect the local courts, the United States attorney, or the United States marshal. For two years the council would be prohibited from changing the city's criminal code. Ibid., 7 October 1973, B-1; 20 December 1973, A-21.

8. Ibid., 4 October 1973, C-1.

9. Representative Broyhill proposed an alternative bill that, among other provisions, would have reduced the size of the federal district to a small enclave containing the Capitol and related federal buildings, monuments, federal offices, and historical sites. The remainder of the District would have been a self-governing jurisdiction, not entitled to a federal payment. Ibid., 10 September 1973, C-1.

10. Ibid., 16 September 1973, B-1; 31 July 1973, C-1.

11. Representative Green was first elected to Congress in 1954 from Oregon's Third District (east Portland). During her years on the Education and Labor Committee, she was a leader in the movement to change the antipoverty program, giving state and local governments tighter control over community action programs (1967).

She was also known for her strong stand against school busing to desegregate public schools. Ibid., 3 October 1973, D-1; *Congressional Quarterly Almanac,* 23 (1967): 107–76; 27 (1971): 610.

12. Roosevelt Island is located in the middle of the Potomac River, adjacent to the Roosevelt Bridge and near the Kennedy Center on the District side. Provisional map prepared by the District of Columbia Office of Planning and Management in cooperation with the National Capital Planning Commission, Washington, D.C. (April 1974).

13. House Subcommittee on Government Operations of the Committee on the District of Columbia, *National Capital Service Area: Hearings on H.R. 4394 and H.R. 5642,* 94th Cong., 1st sess., 10 and 13 June 1975, 193–94 ff.

14. At the time the NCSA amendment to the home rule bill was debated on the floor of the House, Representative Gerald R. Ford (R-Mich.) was minority leader and spoke strongly in favor of it but was among twenty-four members not voting on the amendment. By the time home rule took effect, he had become president of the United States and was responsible for implementing the measure. He took no steps in this regard and, subsequently, supported the effort to repeal the NCSA process.

15. Pursuant to certain statements and promises made by President Carter during the 1976 presidential campaign concerning his support for changes in the government of the District of Columbia, the basic mission of the task force was to come up with proposals for the president on expanded home rule and representation in Congress for the District. *Washington Post,* 4 May 1977, B-1; 22 September 1977, A-23.

16. *Congressional Record,* 93d Cong., 1st sess., 9 October 1973, 119 pt. 26: 33358 ff.

17. Introduced in the House on 30 July 1973, the home rule bill (H.R. 9682) was a product of the House District Committee. Led by Committee Chairman Charles C. Diggs, Jr. (D-Mich.), the bill was sponsored by sixteen of the twenty-five members of that committee: Brock Adams (D-Wash.), Donald M. Fraser (D-Minn.), Ronald V. Dellums (D-Calif.), Thomas M. Rees (D-Calif.), Walter E. Fauntroy (D-D.C.), James J. Howard (D-N.J.), James R. Mann (D-S.C.), Ramano L. Mazzoli (D-Ky.), Fortney H. (Pete) Stark, Jr. (D-Calif.), Gilbert Gude (R-Md.), Les Aspin (D-Wis.), Charles B. Rangel (D-N.Y.), John Breckinridge (D-Ky.), Henry P. Smith III (R-N.Y.), and Stewart B. McKinney (R-Conn.). House Committee on the District of Columbia, *District of Columbia Self-Government and Government Reorganization Act,* 93d Cong., 1st sess., 1973, H. Rept. 482.

18. This point was emphasized in the statement of Representative Gilbert Gude in the hearings on the National Capital Service Area. House, Subcommittee, *National Capital Service Area,* 140–41.

19. An average of 54,795 people visit Washington, D.C. each day. Washington Convention and Visitors Association, Office of Public Relations, telephone conversation with the author, 12 July 1993.

20. It was determined that the District Building and an adjacent parking lot were transferred from the federal government to the District in 1903. Therefore, the District Building is excluded from the NCSA. *Washington Evening Star,* 28 November 1973, D-1.

21. For a particular description of the boundaries of the NCSA by streets, avenues, and major landmarks, see House, *Amending Section 739 of Public Law 93-198 National Capital Service Area,* 94th Cong., 1st sess., 3 November 1975, H. Rept. 616, 19–25.

22. House Subcommittee, *National Capital Service Area,* 46.

23. House, *Amending Section 739 of Public Law 93-198—National Capital Service Area,* 3.

24. House Subcommittee, *National Capital Service Area,* 56–57.

25. Fairly extensive debate took place on the substance of the home rule bill during consideration of the rule—H. Res. 581—to govern debate on the main bill as proposed by the House Rules Committee. The fight by Representative Green to create the NCSA began with the debate on the rule for taking up the home rule bill. *Congressional Record,* 93d Cong., 1st Sess., 9 October 1973, 119 pt. 26, 33352–53, 33358 ff.

26. Ibid., 33359; 10 October 1973, 33611.

27. Ibid., 9 October 1973, 33356.

28. House Subcommittee, *National Capital Service Area,* 200.

29. In 1973 blacks comprised 71.1 percent of the District of Columbia population. Bureau of the Census, *Statistical Abstracts of the United States, 1970 Census of Population* (Washington, D.C., 1973).

30. At the time of the home rule debate, major sections of the city, for example, 14th Street Northwest, H Street Northeast, and other areas, had not been rebuilt and were daily reminders of the riot devastation. *Washington Post,* 2 June 1982, A-1; 7 July 1982, C-1.

31. *Congressional Record,* 93d Cong., 1st sess., 9 October 1973, 33355.

32. Ibid., 10 October 1973, 33645.

33. Ibid., 33648–49.

34. Dellums was a supporter of statehood for the District and had introduced a statehood bill (H.R. 9599) during the first session of the 92d Congress (1971) which provided for the carving out of the federal enclave. Coalition for Self-Determination for District of Columbia, "A Look at Congressional Proposals in the Last 25 Years," unpublished document, in Home Rule Papers (1965), Washingtoniana Collection, Martin Luther King Memorial Library, Washington, D.C. See also House Subcommittee, *National Capital Service Area,* 204.

35. House Subcommittee, *National Capital Service Area,* 186–87. The House voted final approval of the home rule conference report on 17 December 1973. Landgrebe introduced a resolution on the following day, calling for the appointment of a commission to consider relocating the nation's capital. H. Res. 751, 93d Cong., 1st sess. (1973).

36. Although the Senate agreed to most of the major provisions of the House bill that were not contained in the Senate version, four Republican House conferees refused to sign the conference report: Ancher Nelson (Minn.), Earl F. Landgrebe (Ind.), William H. Harsha (Ohio), and Joel Broyhill (Va.). *Congressional Quarterly Almanac,* 29 (1973): 740. See also *District of Columbia Self-Government and Government Reorganization Act—Conference Report,* 93d Cong., 1st sess. 6 December 1973, H. Rept. 703.

37. The initial bill, H.R. 4394, was followed by H.R. 5642. The eight cosponsors were Delegate Walter E. Fauntroy and Representatives Thomas Rees (D-Calif.), Stewart McKinney (R-Conn.), Helen Meyner (D-N.J.), Tom Railsback (R-Ill.), Edward Biester (R-Pa.), Charles Whalen (R-Ohio), and Donald Fraser (D-Minn.).

38. For a listing of these members, see the *Congressional Quarterly Almanac* 29 (1973): 119H.

39. The present reimbursement to the District for basic operating services provided to the federal government is generally considered to be covered by the annual federal payment by the United States government to the District of Columbia. A specific cost or reimbursable charge is attached to some services that are easily identified. Some examples include water and sewer services and repairs and solid waste disposal. District of Columbia, *The Federal Payment—FY 1981* (Washington, D.C., 1979): 16. See also House Subcommittee, *National Capital Service Area*, 45–49 ff.

40. Letter from James Frey, Assistant Director, OMB, to Walter E. Fauntroy, dated 4 June 1975, in House Subcommittee, *National Capital Service Area*, 13–14.

41. There were eighty-two members not voting on the substitute amendment, including several members of the Congressional Black Caucus. The absent Caucus members, however, were paired against the substitute amendment which killed the repeal measure. *Congressional Record*, 94th Cong., 1st sess., 10 November 1975, 10864.

42. Ibid., 35594.

43. House, *District of Columbia Self-Government and Governmental Reorganization Act*, 58.

44. Letter from Mayor Walter E. Washington to Representative Charles C. Diggs, Jr., dated 10 June 1975, in House Subcommittee, *National Capital Service Area*, 56–57.

45. Ibid.

46. Ibid., 131.

47. Ibid., 43–44.

48. Section 740 of the charter, dealing with emergency control of the Metropolitan Police Force (MPF), states: "Notwithstanding any other provision of law," the president shall determine when emergency conditions exist that require the use of the MPF. He may then "direct the Mayor to provide him, and the Mayor shall provide, such services of the Metropolitan Police Force as the President may deem necessary and appropriate." House Committee on the District of Columbia, *The District of Columbia Self Government and Governmental Reorganization Act of 1973, As Amended*, 94th Cong., 1st sess., 3 January 1974, Committee Print, 60–61.

49. House Subcommittee, *National Capital Service Area*, 54.

50. The coalition was a citizens' group that played a major role in the struggle for home rule and for increased local autonomy after home rule was achieved. At the time of its testimony in 1975, it was composed of approximately twenty-five individuals and about twenty-five local and ten national groups. House Subcommittee, *National Capital Service Area*, 175–78. See also Charles W. Harris and Neeka Harris, "Conflicting Vistas in the Nation's Capital," *Catholic University Law Review* 38, no. 3 (Spring 1989): 604.

51. House Subcommittee, *National Capital Service Area*, 176.

52. The significant constant factor here is the political party affiliation of the supporters and opponents of the NCSA. Generally, the Republicans supported the creation of the NCSA in the home rule bill but are opposed to statehood, which is expected to require NCSA implementation; again, in general terms, the reverse is true of the Democrats. While the 1992 Democratic platform contains a strong endorsement of District of Columbia statehood, the Republican platform makes an equally strong statement against it.

53. House Subcommittee on Fiscal Affairs and Health of the Committee on the District of Columbia, D.C. Statehood: *Hearings and Markups* on H.R. 51, 100th Cong., 1st sess., 110–11.

54. Ibid., 112.

55. Ibid.

56. Donald C. Rowat, "Ways of Governing Federal Capitals," (paper presented at Colloquium on Capital Cities, Canada's Capital Tri-University Study Group, Ottawa, Canada, 6–8 December 1990), 4–5. Canada's Capital Tri-University Study Group is comprised of political scientists and other scholars from Carleton University, the University of Ottawa, and the University of Quebec in Hull.

57. Due to the occurrence of agitated demonstrations in the capital city, this was a very hot issue in Brazil when the constitution of 1988 was being drafted. Diogo Lordello de Mello, "Overview of the Different Political and Legislative Structures of Capitals and the Issues and Problems Relating to Them," paper presented at the Capitals of the World Conference, Ottawa, Canada, October 1987.

3

Oversight Mechanisms

Before the District Home Rule Charter came into effect in 1975, the real legislative branch of the city was Congress, where the burden of local lawmaking fell to the House and Senate District Committees. For better or worse, these committees were constantly considering, enacting, and killing strictly municipal measures of varied significance.

With home rule in effect, oversight or the review of legislative action by the District Council is the most consistent activity of the House District Committee; it has little legislative function. Oversight mainly involves efforts by Congress to supervise the executive establishment that administers the laws it has enacted. Implemented through its committees, oversight activities fall into three areas: authorization, appropriation, and investigation. The objectives of oversight often vary from committee to committee and the process suffers from a lack of consensus on goals and procedures. The fiscal oversight of the District is part and parcel of the national budget arrangement and a regular oversight agenda is maintained in accordance with the appropriations process; but the District is not a federal agency, and there is some question as to whether there is an adequate agenda for a full authorizing committee.

During the 93d Congress (1973–74), which ended just prior to the effective date for home rule, the District Committee sent twenty-seven bills to the House floor for action. With home rule in effect during the 94th Congress (1975–76), only fifteen bills were sent to the floor. As shown in table 3.1, this reduced number of bills reported by the committee to the House floor has remained consistent in subsequent congresses. Considering their typical substance, it is not surprising that there was an even greater reduction in the number of resolutions reported to the floor by the committee after home rule became effective. For example, in the two congresses before home rule (92d and 93d), the District Committee had averaged over 200 resolutions per congress. With home rule in effect, the main resolutions considered by the com-

TABLE 3.1   House Committee on the District of Columbia
Bills Reported to the House and Senate

Congress	House Bills	Senate Bills	Total
92d (1971–72)	57	8	65
93d (1973–74)	27	3	30
94th (1975–76)	15	0	15
95th (1977–78)	12	5	17
96th (1979–80)	14	2	16
99th (1985–86)	10	0	10
102d (1991–92)	14	0	14

Source: House Committee on the District of Columbia, Legislative Calendars (Final),
92d through 102d Congresses.

mittee dealt with challenges to District legislation, most of which were
not reported to the floor.[1]

ADJUSTMENTS IN MECHANISMS: SENATE AND HOUSE

With the advent of home rule, the question of what to do with the District Committees in the House and Senate was frequently raised. It was
expected that these two committees would have less and less to do
with a jurisdiction beginning to practice a limited form of home rule.

Initially, the chairman of the House District Committee, Charles
C. Diggs, Jr. (D-Mich.), had hopes of making the committee into a sort
of "urban workshop," through which various problems of urban areas
would be explored. The ranking Republican on the committee, Gilbert
Gude (R-Md.), thought that the idea had merit, but he would take it
one step further. In 1976 Gude introduced a resolution to replace the
House District Committee with a committee on urban and District of
Columbia affairs.[2] Gude's proposal received only a lukewarm recep-
tion from Chairman Diggs, who, by this time, preferred expanding the
committee's jurisdiction to include responsibility for the territories of

the United States.[3] While neither of these proposals was implemented, there were still other recommendations to abolish the House District Committee during the early years of home rule.

Senator Charles McC. Mathias (R-Md.), while supporting the proposal by Representative Gude, recommended that the Senate District Committee expand its focus to include the entire national capital region. Mathias argued that since almost one-half of the federal employees in the Washington area were working at suburban locations, the federal interest in the nation's capital was not limited to the District of Columbia.

Effective with the 95th Congress in 1977, and without significant opposition either on Capitol Hill or from city leaders, the Senate District Committee was downgraded to a subcommittee of the Governmental Affairs Committee.[4] Thus the Senate District Committee, which for generations had been an influential leader in the colonial cabinet that ran the District's local affairs from Capitol Hill, died of natural causes at the age of 160 years.[5] In the heyday of congressional control over the District's legislative affairs, the Senate District Committee won a reputation as the more compassionate of the city's two foster parents. For example, decades before the House District Committee agreed even to let the city have its own elected school board, the Senate District Committee was voicing its approval of full self-government for the District.[6]

As the intermittent talk of abolishing the House District Committee continued, Representative Stewart B. McKinney (R-Conn.), ranking minority member of the District Committee and a strong supporter of full local authority, recommended in 1985 that this committee be abolished. McKinney asserted that the District government was now able to conduct its own affairs and did not need a congressional overseer. Home rule was by no means total, McKinney admitted, but the elected mayor and council did in fact formulate and execute policy for the District with what he termed as minimal congressional interference. The essence of the proposal was that the panel's responsibilities, including review of District legislation and administrative actions, would be downgraded and shifted to a subcommittee. The proposal drew an angry response from Representative Ronald Dellums (D-Calif.), chairman of the committee. Dellums said he was not concerned about a loss of position or power but felt that he and other committee members should have been consulted before McKinney went public with the proposal.[7] Mayor Marion Barry and Delegate Walter E. Fauntroy were

divided over the proposal, with the mayor favoring the swift disman-
tling of the District Committee and the delegate arguing that the committee should be retained until the District achieved statehood or
resolved other thorny self-government issues.[8]

When the Home Rule Charter was approved in 1973, no one
could have anticipated the frequency of congressional challenges to
District of Columbia legislation. As long as Congress retains its present
power to review District legislation, responsible execution of this
power requires adequate support staff to stage hearings, conduct research, and prepare reports. These procedures are essential to responsible review by Congress. With only an authorizing subcommittee to
deal with District affairs, the Senate has neither the time nor the staff
for a full-fledged review of challenged legislation. This means deferring to the House or making a decision without adequate preparatory
work. The home rule experience seems to strengthen the case for a full
committee or adequate support staff in at least one of the chambers.

Because Congress retained final control over the District budget
and issues thought to involve a federal interest, appropriate oversight
mechanisms were necessary. How the congressional mechanisms are
used depends not just on their availability but on the willingness of
those in control to use them. Moreover, these mechanisms are not set in
stone; Congress can revise the home rule controls in directions that
give the District more or less autonomy.

ADJUSTMENTS IN PROCEDURES: THE CHADHA DECISION

The legal procedures for congressional oversight were unexpectedly
called into question in 1983 after the Supreme Court, by a seven to
two vote, struck down the legislative veto in the case of *Immigration
and Naturalization Service v. Chadha.*[9] The District Home Rule Charter
and the provision in it that allowed Congress to veto District legislation became an issue after this decision was rendered, which nullified
the legislative-veto provisions contained in more than 200 laws.[10]
Legislative-veto provisions allowed all or part of Congress to block
executive action, with or without the president's approval. In ruling
them unconstitutional, the Court not only altered the balance of
power between Congress and the president, but also threw into
doubt the constitutionality of provisions of the District Home Rule
Act. A provision in the Charter allowed Congress to overturn District
criminal laws by a majority vote of either house and civil laws by a

vote of both houses—in each case, without the approval of the president. For a period of time after the Supreme Court ruling was handed down, the city was not able to issue bonds because of the cloud over home rule authority.

Legislative experts were uncertain as to whether or not the ruling applied to the Home Rule Act, since the Constitution gives Congress specific and exclusive legislative authority over the District. Congressional leaders decided, however, that Congress should act to bring the process involving the District in line with the Supreme Court ruling, which required that veto action be executed through a statute enacted in the manner prescribed by the Constitution.

After months of deliberations between city officials and key members of Congress concerning the method of disapproving council acts, identical bills were introduced in the House and Senate that required a joint resolution either passed by a majority of both houses and signed by the president or passed by a two-thirds majority of both houses over the president's veto. But the matter reached an impasse due to the desire of the Reagan administration and a handful of Republican senators to keep tighter controls over the District's criminal laws to ensure, they argued, public safety and security.[11] The White House sought a requirement that every District-passed criminal bill would have to have the active, formal approval of the House, the Senate, and the president. The objections of the Reagan administration kept the Senate from considering the House-passed bill for much of 1984.

On the eve of the conference to resolve the differences between the House and Senate proposals, the administration dropped its objections and decided to support the House-passed legislation. This means that a formal veto of District legislation must be approved by both houses of Congress and signed by the president. A longer congressional review period was agreed upon for criminal laws—sixty days instead of thirty—to preserve a distinction between criminal and non-criminal legislation that was in the original Home Rule Charter. The bill also included provisions that would revalidate all laws that were passed under the Charter that had not been overturned by Congress. This was intended to take care of challenges to criminal convictions made under those laws.

District officials were relieved and reassured by the settlement. A Republican-controlled Senate, a Democratic-majority House, and the Reagan administration had thoroughly reviewed proposals to tighten federal control over certain local lawmaking powers, and had agreed that they were not necessary. On the contrary, the process could be made more uniform and left more to local discretion without any damage to the federal interest.[12]

ANALYSIS OF OVERSIGHT MECHANISMS

There are in fact important differences among the potential controllers. Congressional oversight of the District of Columbia is concentrated in four bodies: in the House, the District of Columbia Committee and the Appropriations Subcommittee on the District of Columbia; and, in the Senate, the Governmental Affairs Subcommittee on General Services, Federalism and the District of Columbia and the Appropriations Subcommittee on the District of Columbia. The composition of these bodies provides some important insights into the objectives that their members are likely to pursue, the likelihood that their respective chambers will defer to the oversight bodies' wishes, and potential sources of federal-District conflict. Table 3.2 presents a breakdown of the membership of the four oversight bodies between the 93d(1973) and 102d(1992) Congresses. It shows that there are in fact several different membership patterns on these bodies, and that there has been substantial change in these patterns since the 1970s on the House side.

The greatest change has occurred in the House District of Columbia Committee. Until 1972, the House District Committee was dominated by Southern conservatives. But in 1973 it acquired a black chairman, Charles C. Diggs, Jr., and since the 96th Congress (1979–80), Democratic membership has been concentrated among black legislators. From 45 percent in the 101st Congress (1989–90), the percentage of blacks on the committee fell to 36 percent during the first session of the 102d Congress (1991), when Representative William Gray (D-Pa.) resigned his seat in Congress to become president of the United Negro College Fund.[13] Moreover, contradicting the reputation of the District Committees as unpopular assignments which members switch out of as soon as possible, Democratic members on the House District Committee now tend to serve for a longer period of time—an average of 7.1 years at the beginning of the 102d Congress (1989–90), compared with only 2.9 years of experience at the beginning of the 95th Congress in 1977 (see table 3.3). Leadership has been even more stable, with only four chairmen since 1955, and the chairman at the end of the 102d Congress (1992), Representative Ronald V. Dellums, had been in the position for fourteen years. The change to a more stable, black-dominated

District Committee resulted in large part from a substantial downsizing of the committee (from twenty-four members in the 93d Congress to eleven in the 100th Congress, as shown in table 3.2) and increasing norms of self-selection for committee membership in the House, as opposed to involuntary assignment. In addition to the District of Columbia delegate and members from suburban Virginia and Maryland, the committee consistently has had a significant number of members from the western states in recent years, including five from California during the 102d Congress (1991–92).

Despite the changing demographic and turnover trends among the committee's Democratic members, one feature remains constant: with the exception of the chairman, the District's delegate, and the ranking minority member, it is a low-priority committee assignment for most members. For other members, the committee is a secondary choice, a stepchild, and members are usually either threatened or promised something to get them to serve on it. In their study of congressional committees, political scientists Steven S. Smith and Christopher J. Deering placed the District Committee along with three others (House Administration, Post Office and Civil Service, and Standards of Official Conduct) in the category of "undesired committees" in the House.[15] The committee is of little interest to most congressmen largely because the District is far removed from their own congressional districts and District residents are not voting constituents. When they direct their attention to the District, it is only for a fleeting moment. With the opening of the 95th Congress (1977–78), there were forty-eight new House Democrats, but none volunteered to serve on the District Committee, which had six vacancies on the twenty-member committee.[16] The Democratic caucus voted to change certain committee membership rules as a sweetener. Members were allowed to serve on the District Committee as well as two other standing committees so as not to block them from their priority assignments.[17]

Because most District Committee members of both parties are not very active, the committee's Democratic leadership has been able to count on (if only by proxy votes) a stable pro-District majority in recent years. In fact, since the advent of home rule more than twenty years ago, the District Committee has provided almost unbroken support for the city's position on issues. During most of the 1980s, the committee had a very pro-District ranking minority member in Representative Stewart B. McKinney of Connecticut.[18] The level of partisan conflict on the committee increased substantially after McKinney's death.

TABLE 3.2 Membership of Congressional Committees with Oversight Responsibility for the District of Columbia. (percent of committee members)

Congress	93d (1973–74)	94th (1975–76)	95th (1977–78)	96th (1979–80)	97th (1981–82)	98th (1983–84)	99th (1985–1986)	100th (1987–88)	101st (1989–90)	102d (1991–92)
House District of Columbia Committee										
Democrats	58	68	70	67	67	67	67	64	67	64
Black	17	14	20	33	42	42	42	45	45	36
White—MD/VA	0	9	10	13	8	8	8	0	0	0
White Northern	25	32	20	13	8	8	8	9	18	45
White Southern	17	14	20	6	8	8	8	9	0	0
Republican	42	32	30	33	33	33	33	36	36	36
Maryland/Virginia	8	9	10	27	25	25	17	18	18	9
Other	33	23	20	7	8	8	17	18	18	27
Number	(24)	(22)	(20)	(15)	(12)	(12)	(12)	(11)	(11)	(11)
Senate Governmental Affairs Subcommittee on General Services, Federalism and the District of Columbia*										
Democrats	57	57	50	50	33	40	33	60	60	60
White—MD/VA	0	0	0	0	0	0	0	0	0	0
White Northern	57	57	25	50	33	20	33	40	40	40
White Southern	0	0	25	0	0	20	0	20	20	20
Republicans	43	43	50	50	66	60	66	40	40	40
Maryland/Virginia	14	14	25	25	33	20	33	0	0	0
Other	28	28	25	25	33	40	33	40	40	40
Number	(7)	(7)	(4)	(4)	(3)	(5)	(3)	(5)	(5)	(5)

House Appropriations Subcommittee on the District of Columbia

Democrats	58	73	75	71	63	67	67	67	67	67
Blacks	8	9	13	29	25	22	22	22	22	22
White—MD/VA	0	0	0	0	11	11	11	11	11	11
White Northern	33	36	38	14	0	11	22	22	22	22
White Southern	17	18	25	29	38	33	11	11	11	11
Republicans	42	27	25	29	38	33	33	33	33	33
Maryland/Virginia	0	0	0	0	0	0	11	0	0	0
Other	42	27	25	29	38	33	22	33	33	33
Number	(12)	(11)	(8)	(7)	(8)	(9)	(9)	(9)	(9)	(9)

Senate Appropriations Subcommittee on the District of Columbia

Democrats	60	60	60	60	40	40	40	60	60	60
White—MD/VA	0	0	0	0	0	0	0	0	0	0
White Northern	40	0	60	40	20	40	60	60	40	40
White Southern	20	60	0	20	20	0	0	20	20	20
Republicans	40	40	40	40	60	60	60	40	40	40
Maryland/Virginia	20	20	20	20	0	0	0	0	0	0
Other	20	20	20	20	60	60	60	40	40	40
Number	(5)	(5)	(5)	(5)	(5)	(5)	(5)	(5)	(5)	(5)

*Senate authorizing bodies: 93d and 94th Congresses—Senate District Committee
95th and subsequent congresses—subcommittee of Governmental Affairs Committee

TABLE 3.3 Experience of Members of Congressional Committees with Oversight Responsibility for District of Columbia. (prior years of service on body at beginning of the term of Congress) (number in parentheses is number of legislators in category)

Congress	95th (1977–78)	96th (1979–80)	97th (1981–82)	98th (1983–84)	99th (1985–86)	100th (1987–88)	101st (1989–90)	102d (1991–92)
House District of Columbia Committee								
Democrats	2.9(14)	4.4(10)	4.5(8)	6.5(8)	7.8(8)	10.3(7)	10.0(7)	7.1(7)
Blacks	6.0(4)	6.0(4)	4.4(5)	6.4(5)	7.2(5)	9.2(5)	11.2(5)	9.0(4)
White—MD/VA	2.0(2)	2.0(2)	2.0(1)	2.0(1)	4.0(1)	—	—	—
White Northern	0.8(5)	2.0(2)	6.0(1)	8.0(1)	10.0(1)	12.0(1)	7.0(2)	4.6(3)
White Southern	2.7(3)	6.0(1)	8.0(1)	10.0(1)	12.0(1)	14.0(1)	—	—
Republicans	1.3(6)	2.8(5)	2.5(4)	4.5(4)	5.5(4)	3.5(4)[a]	5.0(4)	3.5(4)
MD/VA	1.0(2)	4.0(1)	0.0(3)	2.0(3)	4.0(2)	6.0(2)	8.0(2)	8.0(1)
Other	1.5(4)	2.5(4)	10.0(1)	12.0(1)	7.0(2)	1.0(2)	2.0(2)	2.0(3)
All Members	2.0(20)	3.9(15)	4.0(12)	6.0(12)	7.0(12)	7.8(11)	9.4(11)	5.8(11)
Senate Governmental Affairs Subcommittee on General Services, Federalism and the District of Columbia								
Democrats	4.0	5.0(2)	12.0(1)	7.0(2)	16.0(1)	1.3(3)[bc]	1.3(3)[d]	2.0(3)
White—MD/VA	—	—	—	—	—	—	—	—
White Northern	8.0(1)	5.0(1)	12.0(1)	14.0(1)	16.0(1)	1.0(2)[b]	0.0(2)	1.0(2)
White Southern	0.0(1)	—	—	—	—	2.0(1)[c]	4.0(1)[d]	4.0(1)
Republicans	4.0(2)	6.0(2)	6.0(1)	5.3(3)	10.0(1)	0.0(2)	3.0(2)[e]	1.0(2)
MD/VA	8.0(1)	10.0(1)	12.0(1)	14.0(1)	16.0(1)	—	—	—
Other	0.0(1)	2.0(1)	0.0(1)	1.0(1)	4.0(1)	0.0(2)	3.0(2)[e]	1.0(2)
All Members	4.0(4)	5.5(4)	8.0(3)	6.0(5)	12.0(3)	0.8(5)[bc]	2.0(5)[de]	1.6(5)

House Appropriations Subcommittee on the District of Columbia

Democrats	6.3(6)	5.4(5)	7.6(5)	8.0(6)	9.3(6)	9.7(6)	9.6(6)	12.3(6)
Black	0.0(1)	3.0(2)	5.0(2)	7.0(2)	9.0(2)	11.0(2)	10.0(2)[f]	12.0(2)
White—MD/VA	—	—	—	—	0.0(1)	2.0(1)	4.0(1)	6.0(1)
White Northern	6.0(3)	8.0(1)	—	0.0(1)	2.0(1)	2.0(2)	1.0(2)	5.0(2)
White Southern	10.0(2)	12.0(2)	9.3(3)	11.3(3)	18.0(2)	30.0(1)	32.0(1)	34.0(1)
Republicans	2.0(2)	0.0(2)	0.0(3)	1.3(3)	2.7(3)	4.0(3)	2.6(3)	2.0(3)
MD/VA	—	—	—	—	0.0(1)	—	—	—
Other	2.0(2)	5.4(7)	0.0(3)	1.3(3)	4.0(2)	4.0(3)	2.6(3)	2.0(3)
All Members	3.8(11)	5.4(7)	4.8(8)	6.0(9)	7.1(9)	7.8(9)	7.3(9)	8.9(9)

Senate Appropriations Subcommittee on the District of Columbia

Democrats	0.0(3)	0.7(3)	3.0(2)	5.0(2)	0.0(2)	1.3(3)	0.0(3)	2.0(3)
White—MD/VA	—	—	—	—	—	—	—	—
White Northern	0.0(3)	1.0(2)	4.0(1)	6.0(1)	0.0(2)	1.3(3)	0.0(2)	2.0(2)
White Southern	—	0.0(1)	2.0(1)	4.0(1)	2.7(3)	—	0.0(1)	2.0(1)
Republicans	2.0(2)	3.0(2)	0.0(3)	0.7(3)	2.7(3)	0.0(2)	2.0(2)[g]	0.0(2)
MD/VA	4.0(1)	6.0(1)	—	—	—	—	—	—
Other	0.0(1)	0.0(1)	0.0(3)	0.7(3)	2.7(3)	0.0(2)	2.0(2)[g]	0.0(2)
All Members	0.8(5)	1.6(5)	1.2(5)	2.4(5)	1.6(5)	0.8(5)	0.8(5)[g]	1.2(5)

a Figures for the House District Committee for the 100th Congress do not include years of service of Rep. Stewart McKinney, who died early in the first session.

b Includes one term of non-consecutive service by Senator Levin in the 96th Congress.

c Includes one term of non-consecutive service by Senator Sasser in the 95th Congress.

d Includes two terms of non-consecutive service by Senator Sasser in the 95th and 100th Congresses.

e Includes two terms of non-consecutive service by Senator Stevens in the 95th and 96th Congresses.

f Includes full term for Rep. Gray who resigned in the first session of the 102d Congress.

g Includes two terms of non-consecutive service by Senator Domenici in the 98th and 99th Congresses.

The next ranking minority member, Stan E. Parris (R-Va.), was a consistent critic of the District until his defeat in 1990. His congressional district housed the District's major correctional institution, the Lorton Reformatory, and much of his criticism focused on the District's management of this prison. In 1991, Representative Thomas Bliley, also from Virginia, became the ranking Republican member. Although the interests of his district and state may at times clash with those of the District, so far he has not been accused of District-bashing.

The House Appropriations Subcommittee on the District of Columbia, like the authorizing committee, has also had increasing black membership (and leadership) in recent years. Representative Julian C. Dixon of California has chaired the subcommittee since 1980, when he succeeded Representative Charles Wilson of Texas.[19] This membership trend has been weaker and later than on the District Committee because of the small number of black congressmen serving on the Appropriations Committee.[20] By 1983 blacks equaled the number of white Southerners among House Appropriations Subcommittee Democrats but, through the 102d Congress, their percentage of the total membership did not rise above 22 percent.

The rise of Dixon to the chairmanship of the subcommittee provides further evidence of members' views of service on District committees. Dixon had been a member of Congress for only fourteen months when he became chairman. First-term House members generally do not get the chance to chair subcommittees. But the House District appropriations chairmanship, while very important to the city, often went begging on Capitol Hill. Representative Louis Stokes, a black member of the House Appropriations Committee from Ohio, was next in line for the position but did not want it.[21]

Bolstered by the long years of service of Representatives William R. Natcher (D-Ky.) and, to a lesser extent, Louis Stokes (D-Ohio) and Julian Dixon (D-Calif.), the members of the House Appropriations Subcommittee have a creditable experience record. At the beginning of the 102d Congress, the average number of years experience for all nine members of the subcommittee was 8.9. The experience level for the Democratic members was very high, with an average of 12.3 years, while the Republicans were at the other end of the spectrum, with an average of 2.0 years.

In the Senate the pattern among both Democrats and Republicans on both District oversight bodies has been largely one of very high turnover and low interest. The Senate lacks the sizable corps of black members to serve on the District oversight bodies out of a concern for minority issues. Indeed, there have been no blacks in the Senate during most of the current home rule period.[22]

In spite of these problems, there have been some positive moments and pleasant surprises for the District under the Senate oversight bodies. Senator Alfonse M. D'Amato (R-N.Y.) was promptly stuck with the chairmanship of the District Appropriations Subcommittee upon his arrival in the upper chamber in 1981. The local officials feared the worst: a self-described conservative Republican from Long Island who had campaigned on a strong law-and-order, antiabortion platform being given financial control over a large, mostly black, and Democratic city. But the senator and his subcommittee turned out to be more supportive of the city on budget matters, as well as significant issues of home rule, than anyone had expected. Within a week of taking over the subcommittee, the senator had established a good working relationship with District Mayor Marion Barry and evinced a deep interest in District affairs.

While establishing himself as a strong ally of the city on most budgetary and home rule issues, D'Amato's relationship with the District was not without problems. When the city's chief of police announced his plans to retire in early 1981, there was a long list of candidates vying for his position. Senator D'Amato sent a letter to Mayor Barry endorsing one of the names on the list. The letter immediately set off criticism around town because it touched on two sensitive nerves. The Senator endorsed the only white candidate for the job and his letter angered local residents who viewed his advice as an intrusion on their limited home rule powers. Upon leaving the subcommittee after two years, the Senator took pride in the fact that he had been a defender of home rule and had spent a lot of time trying "to get Congress not to nit-pick everything the District does."[23]

The senators from neighboring states do not involve themselves in District issues as much as the representatives from nearby jurisdictions. Since 1969 only one senator from Virginia or Maryland, Republican Charles McC. Mathias of Maryland, has taken sufficient interest in District issues to serve on the Senate's authorizing body. For some eighteen years each party had one resident expert serving on the authorizing body—Mathias for the Republicans and Thomas Eagleton of Missouri for the Democrats. The chairman of the authorizing body in the 103d Congress (1993–94), Senator James R. Sasser of Tennessee, has served in the position since 1987, a total of eight years. No other senators in the past two decades have served for more than six years and most have served less. This lack of senatorial interest, combined with the factor of less staff than the House to work on District issues, has been reflected in Senate deference to the lower chamber on most District legislative matters.

Turnover is even more prevalent on the Senate's District Appropriations Subcommittee. Only two senators in the past two decades have served as long as eight years on the subcommittee. The subcommittee has had ten chairmen since 1967, compared to only three since 1961 for its House counterpart. The average number of years of prior service for all members of the subcommittee at the beginning of the 102d Congress was at a low 1.2.

TENURE ON OTHER COMMITTEES

Some turnover on committees is a normal result of attritional factors such as electoral defeat, retirement, and deaths. To gain some perspective on the turnover rate on other congressional committees, I ran statistics on the experience records of the members of one of the comparatively high demand committees in each house for the 102d Congress. The selection in the Senate was the Finance Committee which, along with the Appropriations Committee, is a traditional high demand body. At the beginning of the 102d Congress, the average number of years experience on the Finance Committee for its 20 members was 10.2. The turnover rate on the committee was higher among Democratic members than Republicans. The average number of years of service for Republicans was 11.8, compared with 8.9 for the Democratic members.

In the House, the Rules Committee was chosen for statistical calculations. Although the Rules Committee may have lost some of its attraction in recent years, it is still viewed as one of the "Big Three" in the House, along with Appropriations and Ways and Means, that enjoy premier status. The average number of years of prior service on the Rules Committee for its twelve members at the beginning of the 102d Congress was 9.0, with the Democratic average at 10.0 and the Republican average at 7.0.[24]

PARTNERSHIP/COOPTATION

The varying membership patterns and powers of the four congressional oversight bodies for the District suggest that they will vary both in the interests they advance and in their ability to gain congressional approval for their views. If there is a partnership between the District government and the national legislature, the crux of this relationship is with the House District Committee. Yet they are partners with different purposes: the main purpose of the local government is to make and execute public policies, while that of the District Committee is to protect the federal interest. From the beginning of home rule through the 102d Congress (1991–92), the committee's record is probably second to none in the art of bottling up bills that the city does not want. As will be shown in Chapter 4, dealing with congressional challenges, the committee has successfully buried most of the veto proposals on District legislation introduced in Congress. The committee will presumably continue as a strong champion of District interests, but, because it is perceived as such, it may have trouble winning approval for its measures on the floor of the House. The abortive effort to repeal the legislation on the National Capital Service Area is a case in point.

In the Senate, contrasting with the situation in the House, members tend to side with the District committee leaders. The rejection of the bond issue and the call for an audit of city finances during the early years of home rule are examples of this trend.[25] The Senate's authorizing body is likely to follow the lead of final House action rather than that of the House District Committee and to play a fairly passive role. The House District Appropriations Subcommittee will give the most consistent and detailed scrutiny to District affairs. Senate District Appropriations Subcommittee actions are likely to be intermittent and to change over time as the subcommittee chairmanship changes, reflecting that body's high turnover and its low priority for most members.

Generally, little of the federal intervention in city affairs is exercised by means of the authorizing committees; they are rarely successful channels for assertion of federal interests, whether they are genuine national interests or disguised parochial interests. Indeed, Democratic majorities on the House District Committee have for the most part been strong proponents of increased District autonomy during the home rule period. When Representative Dellums became chairman of the committee in 1979, he paid a call on new mayor Marion Barry, promising to be "an advocate, not an overseer, for District affairs."[26]

The role played by the House District Committee results in large measure from the identification of the committee's black leadership with the self-government objectives of the District's black majority. But this role has not been without costs for the committee. Like other committees that are seen as "captured" by the interests they oversee, the House District Committee has had difficulties in winning floor approval for its own agenda. Since the enactment of the Home Rule Act in 1973, the committee has been largely unsuccessful in its efforts to gain increased autonomy for the District of Columbia, such as through a statehood initiative or even local control over judicial appointments. The House District Committee has had more success in pursuing a negative agenda—blocking federal initiatives that challenge local autonomy. And even here it has sometimes lost out, as in the 1981 vote on changing the sex offender provisions of the District of Columbia criminal code.[28] There is, of course, a significant irony here: the pre-1973 House District Committee, dominated by Southern conservatives, also pursued a largely negative agenda in the opposite policy direction— prevention of home rule. On the Senate side, the authorizing subcommittee has been relatively inactive for a different reason: District affairs have been a low priority for senators, who serve on more committees than their House counterparts.

The success of the House District Committee in defending District interests has forced critics of the District government to find other channels to override District government decisions. The fact that the process became more difficult in the mid-1980s, after the Supreme Court ruling on legislative vetoes, has also discouraged the use of that mechanism. The appropriations process has taken up the slack as a channel of control. Specific provisions that do not arouse opposition from interest groups or threaten members' interests can be buried in big packages that are unlikely to be challenged on the floor.

Somewhat surprisingly for a policy arena that is supposed to be of low salience for most senators and representatives, neither the authorizing nor the appropriations committees have been able to control the agenda on District affairs. Actions initiated on the chamber floors have therefore been an important mechanism of federal influence, especially in the House of Representatives. Some of these floor challenges have been amendments to committee bills (for example, on abortion, gun control, and retention of the federal enclave), while the 1981 legislative veto barring changes in the criminal code took the form of a discharge petition.[29]

The frequency of floor activity becomes more understandable, however, when we consider that (1) norms of deference to specialists, especially the House District Committee, were weak; and (2) most of the challenges to specialized authority occurred on issues with a high degree of symbolic resonance. Abortion, gay and lesbian rights, gun control, and public safety all provide blame-generating opportunities for conservatives to put their colleagues on the spot and to win at least local victories for their supporters' values. The greater frequency of floor challenges in the House can be attributed to three factors: (a) the more frequent electoral cycles in the House, which make representatives more subject to pressures to avoid controversial issues; (b) the fact that the House usually acts first on legislative matters, which allows controversies to arise and sometimes be resolved in the latter chamber before the Senate acts; (c) and lack of deference to the House District Committee.

LOSING AT THE DISTRICT BUILDING

In the years since home rule has been in effect, the citizens of the District have strongly asserted their right to elect their own local officials. What is less apparent is that many District residents, including some ostensible supporters of home rule, also like the idea that Congress has some say in local affairs. They especially like having a friend in Congress when things are not going their way in the District Building. As one longtime District resident and actor on the political scene explains: "What you've got to understand is that Congress was a back door that suited people who had the key. . . . Now it suits people who don't have full faith in the people in the District Building. The Congress checks on them."[31] An example of this dual approach occurred when the gambling initiative won voter approval in 1980 and a group of local ministers and politicians, who had opposed it, went to Capitol Hill to get Congress to overturn the bill before it became law. They made the point that going to Congress is a part of the home rule process.

It happens that the District is a hybrid jurisdiction with both state and local functions among its limited powers. The above kind of "end run" could not happen at the state level because there is no higher legislative body with formal review and veto power over a state's actions before they become effective law. It is not that unique to the District when wearing its "city hat" because other local jurisdictions are subjected to various types of control by their state legislatures.[32]

A WHIPPING BOY

Instead of implementing oversight based on consideration of the federal interest, many national legislators use the District as a handy target for making a point with the folks back home or some national interest group. Taking the common path of the appropriations process, the fight usually is over whether the citizens of the District should be allowed to spend their own money—not federal money—for their own purposes. No other jurisdiction is in the District's position, subject to the ulterior motives and whims of overseers without the opportunity to participate in their election to office. As District residents gain experience with home rule, increasingly they would rather live with a law that they do not like, but was enacted by their own representatives, than to have the power of self-government snatched away by national lawmakers who have no roots or direct responsibilities in the District.

Other large cities have large delegations in their state legislatures to look out for their political interests. Depending on the size of the city, its delegation may comprise a formidable bloc. Even the representatives of small cities can link up with their compatriots in the state legislature to protect their political interests. The lack of leverage in this regard is a unique fact of political life for the District.

THE THREAT OF ACTION

The impact of congressional oversight is not fully consumed in official vetoes, challenges, or policy directives issued through the appropriations process. The threat of congressional disapproval through a resolution, an appropriations bill, or public criticism is always present for District of Columbia lawmakers. In the District's situation, even a strong media reaction to its decisions and steps may trigger a congressional response. A comment by Senator Thomas F. Eagleton (D-Mo.), during his chairmanship of the authorizing body in the upper chamber, illustrates the extremity of this situation: "I don't want them to have to say every time they want to do something, 'Oh, we'd better call that son-of-a-bitch Tom Eagleton and see what he says.'" He emphasized the fact that this was the kind of thing that would compromise home rule.[33]

It all serves to underscore the District's still precarious form of limited home rule, under which local politicians must constantly look over their shoulders and assess the potential fallout from the congressional system before certain decisions or steps are taken. The political question either spoken or in the minds of local officials is, "Do we want to antagonize them now--on this particular question?"

Although the District's congressional members during the home rule period, Delegates Walter E. Fauntroy and Eleanor Holmes Norton, have earned the high respect of their colleagues for their struggles to represent and defend the District, the real congressional power over the city resides, as before home rule, in persons representing states far removed from the federal district. Whether it is the desire to work on minority issues, the racial dimension, or other factors, there are key home rule advocates on the authorizing and, to a lesser extent, the appropriations bodies who play a unique role in the oversight system. In recent Congresses (103d and before), there has been no mention of abolishing the House District Committee. In some respects, the committee functions as a buffer between Congress and the District government, and it seems that District leaders and supporters are comfortable with the existence and role of the committee. As of mid-1994, it does not appear likely that this committee will be phased out before the District achieves either statehood or true self-government.

STANDARDS OF EVALUATION

It remains a problem that the charter did not set forth criteria for Congress to apply in deciding how to exercise its appropriations and veto powers over the District. The House District Committee has attempted to deal with this by establishing criteria based on three grounds: constitutionality, accord with the District Home Rule Charter, and impact on the federal interest.[34] The objective is to focus congressional oversight on those aspects of local policy which are most fitting subjects for congressional concern. Of course, one could define the "federal interest" broadly enough to embrace every detail of District policy. But that is not what even a limited concept of local self-government means or contemplates.

In this chapter we have dealt with some of the unique aspects of congressional oversight of the District of Columbia government. We have described the House District Committee in a very close partnership with the local government, yet raised questions about the need for a full oversight committee after twenty years of home rule. It is demeaning to a self-governing jurisdiction to be monitored like an executive branch department. If congressional review of District legislation were reduced or eliminated, the oversight function in the House could be downgraded to a subcommittee. If a full committee was needed at the outset to protect the federal interest, this is no longer the case, considering the other checks that are in place. Although it is not an issue of conflict between the two governments, the oversight mechanisms provide necessary background for the study of congressional challenges and vetoes, the subject matter of the next two chapters.

NOTES

1. The highest number or challenges in a single Congress is twelve (94th Congress). See chapter 4 for a full discussion of congressional challenges to District legislation. House Committee on the District of Columbia, *Legislative Calendars*, (Final), 92d through 96th Congresses, 1971–80.

2. *Washington Post,* 10 August 1976, A-16.

3. The U.S. territories included Puerto Rico, the Virgin Islands, Guam, American Samoa, the Panama Canal Zone, and numerous islands in the South Seas. Emphasizing his interest in the territories and his former service on the Interior and Insular Affairs Committee, Diggs argued that this concept made sense in light of the District's territorial status. Ibid., 29 September 1976, C-1.

4. This plan permitted the chairman of the Senate District Committee, Thomas F. Eagleton (D-Mo.), and its ranking minority member, Charles McC. Mathias, Jr. (R-Md.), to transfer to the new subcommittee of the Governmental Affairs Committee—expanded from 14 to 20 members. Ibid., 25 January 1975, C-2.

5. Created on 18 December 1816, the Senate Committee on District of Columbia was the twelfth oldest standing committee in the upper house. Senate, Committee on the District of Columbia, *The Senate Committee System*, 94th Cong., 2d sess., July 1976, Committee Print, 11.

6. *The Washington Post,* 10 February 1977, A-14.

7. McKinney presented his proposal to the House Administration Committee without consulting with the chairman or members of the House District Committee. Ibid., 1 March 1985, C-3.

8. In 1985 the District Committee had a staff of approximately thirty nine persons and a budget in the range of $1.7 million. *Congressional Directory,* 99th Cong., (1985–86):315; *Washington Post,* 1 March 1985, C-3; 4 March 1985, A-10.

9. *Immigration and Naturalization Service v. Chadha,* 462 U.S. 919 (1983).

10. *Congressional Quarterly Almanac,* 39 (1983): 565; 29 (1973): 734.

11. *Washington Post,* 17 September 1984, A-1.

12. Ibid., 18 October 1984, A-20.

13. Gray announced his departure plans on 20 June 1991, with the effective date of his resignation being 11 September 1991. As majority whip of the House, Gray was the highest-ranking black member in the Congress.

14. Representative John McMillan became chairman of the House District Committee in 1945. He was relegated to ranking minority member in the

80th (1947–49) and 83d (1953–55) Congresses, then served continuously as chairman from 1955 to 1973 when Representative Charles C. Diggs, Jr. (D-Mich.) became chairman. Representative Ronald V. Dellums (D-Calif.) replaced Diggs as chairman in 1979 after the latter, in November 1978, requested to be relieved of the post following his conviction and sentence to a federal prison for illegal diversion of staff pay. At the beginning of the 103d Congress (1993), Representative Fortney (Pete) Stark (D-Calif.) became chairman, replacing Dellums, who left the position to chair the Committee on Armed Services. *Washington Post,* 22 November 1978, C-8; 27 January 1979, B-4.

15. Steven S. Smith and Christopher J. Deering, *Committees in Congress* (Washington, D.C.: Congressional Quarterly Press, 1984), 90, 118–19.

16. The District Committee's membership was reduced from its previous authorized total of 25 to 19 at the beginning of the 95th Congress (1977). It was not the only committee, however, that had a recruiting problem with the opening of the 95th Congress. The House leadership also had to use some "friendly persuasion" to fill vacancies on the Judiciary, International Affairs, and Agriculture Committees. *Washington Post,* 27 January 1977, B-2.

17. Ibid., 27 January 1977, B-2.

18. McKinney was regarded as so favorable to District interests that the District's nonvoting delegate to Congress, Walter Fauntroy, referred to him as "my vote on the floor." *Washington Star,* 30 May 1978, B-1.

19. Representative Dixon became chairman of the subcommittee in March 1980 when Representative Charles Wilson (D-Texas) gave up the position for a seat on the more prestigious Defense Appropriations Subcommittee. *Washington Post,* 5 March 1980, A-1.

20. During the 102d Congress, only two of the fifty-nine members of the House Appropriations Committee were black. Both of them served on the District of Columbia Subcommittee.

21. Ibid.

22. After the defeat of Senator Edward Brooke (D-Mass.) in 1978 (95th Congress), there was no black member until Senator Carol Mosely Braun (D-Ill.) took her seat in the 103d Congress (1993).

23. Saying that he was elected to be something other than a "full-time overseer" of the District, the Senator commented on the large amount of time devoted to District affairs. *Washington Post,* 26 December 1982, D-6.

24. Computation of years of service on respective committee as reported in *Congressional Quarterly Almanac* for relevant years.

25. *Washington Post,* 6 January 1975, B-1.

26. Ibid., 17 January 1979, B-1.

27. Other committees with close ties to their clientele, for example, Agriculture, at least have resources that can be used in building logrolling coalitions. The District Committee has little to offer other members in exchange for support on the floor. R. Kent Weaver and Charles W. Harris, "Who's in Charge Here? Congress and the Nation's Capital," *The Bookings Review* 7, no. 3 (Summer 1989): 33n.

28. See p. 112 ff.

29. Ibid.

30. On 14 December 1992 the offices of the mayor and many other city agencies were moved from the District Building (1350 Pennsylvania Avenue, Northwest) to a new eleven-story office building at One Judiciary Square (441 Fourth Street, Northwest).

The District Council chose to remain in the District Building. *Washington Post,* 17 December 1992, J-2.

31. *Washington Post,* 4 September 1980, A-17.

32. In addition to great influence on the financing of local governments, the states have preeminent leverage on how local governments are organized—the rules and laws which apply to local governments—and how land is to be used. For a detailed discussion of this subject, see Patricia S. Florestano and Vincent L. Marando, *The States and the Metropolis* (New York: Marcel Dekker, 1981), 12–13.

33. *Washington Post,* 6 January 1975, B-1.

34. On at least one occasion Senator Mathias suggested that Congress ought to evaluate city legislation by applying these criteria. Ironically, these standards led the senator to urge a veto of the franchise tax extension (District of Columbia Revenue Act of 1975), on the grounds that it was really a tax on nonresident income and as such was a violation of the charter. Ibid., 8 October 1975, A-10.

4

Congressional Challenges

Home rule had been in effect for several years before the first District legislation was vetoed by Congress, but congressional challenges of District legislation began in 1975, the first year of home rule, and have been a continuing activity in the relationship between Congress and the District government. This chapter briefly summarizes the more serious challenges, determined largely on the basis of the consideration given by Congress to the respective challenge as indicated through the staging of hearings. All of the subjects challenged receive some comment.

Probably in every act of the Council of the District of Columbia on which there is sufficient difference and controversy between the council and Congress to generate a disapproval resolution by the latter body, there may be some arguable degree of federal interest. Most of the failed challenges, however, involved primarily local policy matters rather than true federal interests. As will be shown later in this chapter, more often than not the prime motivating factor behind the effort to veto the District legislation originated from the parochial interests of neighboring states, moral issues that could be exploited by single-issue interest groups on a national level, and local lobbying groups and leaders who were unsuccessful at the council level. In some of the latter cases, Congress has allowed itself to be used as an appeal body by dissident groups unwilling to accept the policy decision at the local level. If we place a conservative label on the sponsors of most of the disapproval resolutions, it should not be surprising that most of them were Republicans (see tables 4.1 and 4.2).

The Democratic-controlled 94th Congress (1975–76) convened in January 1975, as did the new home rule government for the District of Columbia. The 94th Congress produced more challenges to District of Columbia Council action than any Congress since home rule has been in effect. A total of twelve disapproval resolutions were introduced in Congress on five different subjects. For example, the District of Columbia gun control law generated seven disapproval resolutions, all in the

TABLE 4.1 Congressional Challenges to District of Columbia Home Rule Legislation 1975–93

Policy Area	Legislation	Year	Main Sponsor(s)	Resolution Number	Motivation	Ultimate Winner
Revenue	Revenue Act of 1975	1975	Harsha (R-Ohio) *Mathias (R-Md.)*	2	Parochial (Va./Md.)	Compromise
	Bonds	1975	*Eagleton (D-Mo.)*	1	Federal Interest	Compromise
	Lottery	1981	Holt (R-Md.) *Hatfield (R-Ore.)*	3	Parochial/Moral	Compromise
	Omnibus Budget Act	1992	Moran (D-Va.)	1	Parochial (Va.)	Federal
Land Use	Rental Accommodations	1975	Stuckey (D-Ga.)	1	Parochial (D.C.)	District
	Foreign Chanceries	1979	Stark (D-Calif.) *Pell (R-R.I.)*	2	Federal Interest	Federal
	Condominiums	1980	Wilson (D-Texas)	1	Parochial (D.C.)	District
	Building Height	1990	Combest (R-Texas) Rohrabacher (R-Calif.) *Levin (D-Mich.)*	3	Federal Interest	Federal
Public Safety	Gun Control	1976	Paul (R-Texas)* Ashbrook (R-Ohio)	7	Moral Conflict	District
	Prison Release	1987	Parris (R-Va.)	1	Parochia (Va.)	District
	Gun Liability	1991	Bliley (R-Va.) *Stevens (R-Alaska)*	2	Federal Interest	District

Policy Area	Legislation	Year	Resolution Main Sponsor(s)	Number	Motivation	Ultimate Winner
Health/Human Services	Natural Death Act	1982	Siljander (R-Mich.)	2	Moral Conflict	District
	AIDS Insurance	1986	Dannemeyer (R-Calif.)	3	Parochial/Moral Conflict	Federal
	Health Care Benefits	1992	Holloway (R-La.) *Lott* (R-Miss.)	2	Moral Conflict	Federal
General Government	Statehood Convention	1981	Daniel (R-Va.)	1	Federal Interest/Parochial	District
	Statehood Constitution	1987	Parris (R-Va.)	1	Federal Interest/Parochial	Compromise
Civil Liberties/Rights	Affirmative Action	1976	Collins (R-Texas)	1	Federal Interest	District
	Criminal Code	1981	Crane (R-Ill.) *Denton* (R-Ala.)	2	Moral Conflict	Federal
	South Africa Disinvestment	1983	Crane (R-Ill.)	1	Parochial (Business)	District
Public Works/Transportation	Service Stations	1977	Archer (R-Texas)	1	Parochial (Business)	District

Note: Names of senators in italic.
* Resolutions and concurrent resolutions with different cosponsors.

67

TABLE 4.2   Breakdown of Congressional Challenges to Home Rule
Legislation 1975–1993

| | *Resolutions* | | | | |
| | *House* | | *Senate* | | |
Congress	*Dem*	*Repub*	*Dem*	*Repub*	
94th (1975–76)	1	9	1	1	Firearms, Revenue, Housing
95th (1977–78)	0	1	0	0	Service Stations
96th (1979–80)	2	0	1	0	Chanceries, Housing
97th (1981–82)	0	6	0	2	Lottery, Statehood Natural Death, Criminal Code
98th (1983–84)	0	1	0	0	South Africa
99th (1985–86)	0	1	0	1	Insurance
100th (1987–88)	0	3	0	0	Insurance, Statehood, Prison
101st (1989–90)	0	0	0	0	
102d (1991–92)	1	4	1	2	Gun Liability, Building Height, Budget
103d (1993–94) (1st Session)					
	4	25	3	6	

Totals:	Disapproval Resolutions Introduced	38
	Average Number per Congress	4.2
	Subjects	20
	Average Number per Congress	2.2
	Disapproval Resolutions Passed	3

Source: Congress, House, Committee on the District of Columbia, official records.

House of Representatives. Overall, during this initial two-year period, both the District of Columbia government and Congress were adjusting to a new relationship. Although there had been an appointed local council for the city since 1967, most members of Congress were still accustomed to taking action on any policy matter for the District, local or federal, that they saw fit.

With regard to the minimum number of challenges to District home rule legislation, there was only one challenge during the 95th Congress (1977–78) and none in the 101st (1989–90), the only Congress to date with this distinction.[1] Table 4.1 shows all of the District of Columbia Council acts challenged during the period from 1975 to 1993. Including both vetoed and challenged legislation, a total of thirty-eight disapproval resolutions of District of Columbia Council actions on twenty different subjects were introduced during the nineteen years of home rule, an average of two resolutions on slightly more than one subject (1.05) per year, as noted in table 4.2.

The most serious challenges resulted in vetoes—a total of three—which are discussed in the next chapter. There were a total of thirty-one challenges on seventeen different subjects that did not result in vetoes. The largest number of the twenty subjects challenged—a total of four—were concerned with revenue and land use, respectively, followed by public safety, civil liberties, and health and human services, with three subjects each. For the purpose of summary and analysis, the challenges are grouped into the following seven policy areas and are discussed in the order listed: revenue measures, land use, public safety, health and human services, general government, civil liberties and rights, and public works and transportation.

The most serious challenges of District of Columbia legislation, of its laws not overturned through the formal disapproval route, were the Prison Overcrowding Act of 1987 (Lorton Prison) and the AIDS Insurance Act of 1986. The action of the District government to deal with prison overcrowding survived the most serious challenge of any act that was not overturned through a formal veto. The challenge of the Prison Overcrowding Act of 1987, led by Representative Stan E. Parris (R-Va.), failed by only ten votes and involved power dynamics on a par with the vetoed legislation. The critical congressional vote in the House came on a substitute motion to table (a discharge motion) which carried by only ten votes. In spite of the bitter struggle that took place in Congress, driven mainly by parochial interests, there was little or no federal interest involved and the case offers no support for the Rowat conflict of interest thesis. Although the AIDS Insurance Act was not officially vetoed by Congress, the continuing pressure on the District government and threats in the Senate, led by Senator Jesse Helms (R-N.C.), to repeal the measure forced the city to yield to congressional power.

REVENUE MEASURES

The parochial factor played a dominant role in congressional resolutions to disapprove District home rule legislation dealing with raising revenue. With the exception of the local legislation on general obligation bonds, parochial interests were involved in three of the four resolutions to disapprove home rule legislation concerned with revenue. Included are the District of Columbia Revenue Act of 1975, the lottery (1981), and the Omnibus Budget Act of 1992.

District of Columbia Revenue Act of 1975

The first congressional challenge of District of Columbia legislation during the current home rule era came approximately eight and one-half months after home rule went into effect. It was mounted against the Revenue Act of 1975, a $1 billion tax package that contained a controversial professional tax. Although this act comprised eight titles that included new or revised taxes on a wide range of services and some goods, including motor vehicle registration, water and sewer charges, and dry cleaning and laundry services, it was Title VI, which levied the tax on professionals, that generated sharp congressional opposition. The tax on doctors, dentists, lawyers, accountants, engineers, and other professionals was to be levied at the 12 percent rate after deductions for salaries and other expenses and would raise an estimated $8 million annually.

Although the disapproval resolution was introduced by Representative William H. Harsha (R-Ohio), the strongest opposition to the measure came from congressmen representing the neighboring states of Maryland and Virginia. They charged that the tax was too high and that it discriminated against Virginia and Maryland residents who, unlike District of Columbia residents, would also have to pay state taxes on the same income. The veto resolution was considered initially by the Fiscal Affairs Subcommittee of the District Committee, which approved it by a six to five vote. However, District Committee Chairman Charles C. Diggs, Jr. (D-Mich.) worked hard to block the veto move, and there was some reluctance on the part of the full committee to veto the first major bill that the District Council had sent to Congress under the Home Rule Charter.

The critics of the bill were amenable to a compromise on the measure, involving a reduction in the tax on professionals, and the council acted quickly to forestall the veto by drafting revised legislation that modified the controversial provision. When this step was taken, the veto effort lost many of its supporters. Some members who were not firmly identified with either side of the tax fight indicated that they did not feel a sufficient "federal interest" was at stake in the controversy. Essentially, it was the intensity of parochial interests in the House, led by Representatives Gilbert Gude (R-Md.) and Herbert E. Harris (D-Va.), that constituted the driving force in the veto effort. The main arguments were that the tax was illegal under the Home Rule Act, which prohibited a commuter tax, and that it discriminated against Maryland and Virginia residents, who could not claim the same income tax credit as District of Columbia residents.

Shortly after the House Committee action, this issue resurfaced in the Senate as Senators Charles McC. Mathias and J. Glenn Beall, both Maryland Republicans, introduced their own veto resolution. With the House on record against the veto measure, the Senate move did not gain momentum. In the final analysis, however, the congressional veto effort failed because the District of Columbia Revenue Act was essentially a local policy matter that did not involve the federal interest.

General Obligation Bonds

In 1975 the city was making plans for a $50 million bond sale which required congressional approval, after which the sale would be floated at the most advantageous time. The bond issue would be used to refinance existing debt to the United States Treasury which, by law, had been the District's only source of loans prior to home rule. The Treasury generally charged a higher rate of interest than the commercial bond market and the city wanted to refinance about 5 percent of its existing $1 billion debt to the Treasury. Mayor Walter Washington was confident of getting an interest rate sufficiently low to yield some $400,000 in annual savings, or $12 million over the thirty-year life of the bonds.

The bond proposal ran into immediate trouble in the Senate, where Senator Thomas F. Eagleton (D-Mo.) contended that the city was on the verge of such deep financial trouble that its books should be independently audited before it ventured into the bond market. Eagleton proceeded to introduce a resolution to veto the bond authorization bill, which won the unanimous backing of the Senate District of Columbia Committee (which Eagleton chaired) and later sailed through the full Senate by a vote of eighty to three.[2]

Chairman Charles C. Diggs, Jr. (D-Mich.), a strong home rule advocate, and House District Committee members were troubled by the Senate action. The House Committee had bottled up earlier veto resolutions but was concerned that it might run the risk of a retaliatory move by the upper chamber to loosen its grip on veto resolutions if it refused to let the House vote on a Senate-passed resolution. A summit meeting between the two committee chairmen, in Diggs's office, was rather fruitful. It was hard to contest the wisdom of the city's proposal to refinance $50 million in District debt but, apparently, Eagleton's concerns were broader than the bond authorization. He wanted to call attention to other fiscal shortcomings of the District that he considered very serious. In addition to the pressing need for an audit of the city's books and a reform of its accounting system, there were the problems of unfunded pension commitments, a $46 million budget deficit from the previous year, and other concerns. While admitting some of the problems, Diggs was inclined toward a different approach in resolving them.

The House District Committee held three days of hearings on the Senate resolution, and most of the committee members made it clear that they saw bonding authority as a clear-cut prerogative of home rule government. By a vote of nineteen to one they refused to send the Senate-passed resolution to the House floor.[3]

Diggs became the chief negotiator with city and Senate officials. Embracing the proposals for reform in the city's financial management system as well as an independent audit, Diggs was able to firm up the offer from Mayor Walter Washington to consult with him and Eagleton before selling the bonds. The offer was made explicit in private conversations and on paper. If the mayor refused their advice, Congress could simply ban the bond sale by law.[4]

In addition to avoiding a congressional veto of a local policy matter, there were other positive results of the approach taken by the House District Committee. These included the proposed audit of District books and reform in the District's accounting system, the reaffirmation of a good working relationship between the House and Senate District Committees, and the demonstration to city officials of the need for adequate consultation with the District's supporters in Congress before sending up problematic legislation.

On balance, the bond issue was a local policy matter. Yet the municipal bonding proposal came on the heels of the New York City fiscal crisis, causing municipal bonds to be scrutinized as never before.[5] Finding itself on the verge of defaulting on its financial obligations, New York City, in May 1975, had petitioned the federal government for assistance. From the perspective of the members of the Senate District Committee, avoiding a similar crisis in the nation's capital was a federal interest matter, but with home rule in effect, the House Committee prevailed in placing Congress on a different track.

The Lottery

Initiative #6, Legalized Lotteries, was approved by the voters of the District of Columbia on 4 November 1980 by a margin of nearly two to one, but under the terms of the Home Rule Charter, review and approval by Congress were still required before the initiative became law. Essentially, this initiative, as conveyed to Congress by the District Council, authorized a city-run lottery and numbers game in addition to bingo and raffles for charity.

After this citizens' initiative was approved and sent to Capitol Hill, an effort to overturn it began to gain momentum. The conservative Christian lobby Moral Majority, two members of the District Council, and business leaders from the neighboring state of Maryland who feared that their own lottery receipts might suffer, all announced plans to push for congressional rejection of the gambling legislation.[6]

The Moral Majority said that it would mount a full-fledged lobbying campaign to try to get the measure vetoed by Congress and would welcome a recorded vote on the issue. Council members Jerry A. Moore (R-At Large), a Baptist minister, and William R. Spaulding (D-Ward 5) were opposed to legalized gambling and announced that they had sent letters to all members of the Senate, asking them to disapprove the initiative. The two veteran council members said they believed that the gambling initiative was potentially so harmful to the city that it warranted drastic steps. Business leaders and entrepreneurs from Maryland, mainly Princes George's County, asked their state legislators to lobby Maryland's congressional delegation to vote against the initiative.

With the opposition forces growing, a resolution proposing a veto of the gambling initiative was introduced in the House by Representative Marjorie Holt (R-Md.). Many of her constituents earned a part of their livelihood selling Maryland lottery tickets to District residents. The leading gambling opponent in the upper chamber was Senator Mark O. Hatfield (R-Ore.), who introduced a veto resolution to kill the gambling bill and lobbied other senators for support. He was unable to generate much interest in his measure, and after the veto resolutions languished for a time, the congressional opposition to the gambling initiative swiftly disintegrated.

After staging full committee hearings and markup sessions, the House District Committee voted unanimously to reject the disapproval resolution to overturn the initiative. Later the same day, Senator Hatfield dropped his plans to push for a veto in the Senate.

Omnibus Budget Support Act of 1992

Facing a projected budget deficit of approximately $90 million in early 1992, the District was desperately seeking additional sources of revenue. The purpose of the Omnibus Budget Support Act of 1992 was to support the revised fiscal year 1992 budget and the fiscal year 1993 budget. It included measures to generate revenues as well as structural reorganizations needed in government to reduce costs. Through certain provisions of the act, the District proposed a new fee in lieu of taxes on the users of the Blue Plains Waste Water Treatment Facility.[7] The fee would be collected for the District's general fund rather than for Blue Plains operation. The suburban users contended that this new payment would not only violate the 1985 Intermunicipal Agreement, drawn up between the city and suburban jurisdictions, but would be a commuter tax in disguise, which is prohibited by the Home Rule Charter.

A disapproval resolution introduced against the Omnibus Budget Support Act by Representative James P. Moran (D-Va.) and cosponsored by Representatives Constance Morella (R-Md.) and Frank Wolf (R-Va.) was withdrawn when the problem was resolved through the appropriations process. The House appropriations bill for the District included language to block the fee increases.[8]

LAND USE

Two of the major federal interest issues among the challenges deal with land use—foreign chanceries and building height limitation. Both resulted in vetoes and are discussed in the next chapter. The remaining two challenges are concerned with rental accommodations and condominium conversion, both of which were motivated largely by parochial rather than federal interests.

Rental Accommodations

Rent control was the second challenge of District of Columbia legislation during the current home rule era and came a few days after the first (Revenue Act of 1975). Led by the Apartment and Office Building Association of Metropolitan Washington (AOBA), the landlords in the city were up in arms over the new rent control bill, the District of Columbia Rental Accommodations Act of 1975, enacted by the council and transmitted to Congress for the thirty-day review period. From consideration of a flat, citywide percentage increase in the rent ceilings, the council turned to a formula that would permit a 4 percent increase in the rents for the current year plus 50 percent of increases in the cost of utilities. In another draft bill, a landlord rate-of-return factor was injected into the mathematics of allowable rent increases.

Things got rather confusing, leading to a veto by Mayor Walter Washington of the first bill passed by the council, after which the mayor and members of the council got together to hammer out a new version that would be acceptable to both parties. This new version allowed a rate-of-return formula of 8 percent on the assessed valuation of an apartment building in determining landlord profits and a 5 percent allowable increase in rents over the next two years, with no provision for permitting landlords to pass on to tenants increased utility costs.

Rent control had become a key populist issue in the city and with many ex-social activists on the council, there was high motivation to collar the landlords and deliver an effective pro-tenant bill that protected the interests of the poor. As an issue, there had not been anything like rent control in the short history of self-government in Washington. It had set landlord against tenant and both against the District Council. It had clogged the courts, all but collapsed the bureaucratic machinery established to administer it, and created a new legal specialty, rent control law, practiced on the one hand by highly paid specialists at some of the city's premier law firms and, on the other hand, by poverty lawyers whose fees were collected by tenant representatives on nighttime rounds. In the fog of statistics, one stood out with clarity: more than 70 percent of the voters were tenants. It was the city's chief political issue, and not a single vote in the thirteen-member council was cast against the concept of rent control in the 1975 deliberations.[9]

The AOBA argued that the 8 percent/5 percent formula was "confiscatory" of the owners' property and was therefore unconstitutional.[10] Among other assertions, they argued that the measure would result in a halt to all new construction of apartment buildings in the city. When the second bill was finally passed by the council and signed by the mayor, the AOBA and the landlords took their case to Capitol Hill.

A disapproval resolution was introduced by Representative Williamson S. (Bill) Stuckey, Jr. (D-Ga.), who sat on the District Committee and chaired its Subcommittee on Commerce, Housing and Transportation. The subcommittee held hearings on the bill, but the full committee by voice vote discharged the subcommittee from further consideration of the resolution and approved a motion to table same. District of Columbia Delegate Walter Fauntroy, also a member of the District Committee, put forth a valiant negotiating effort on behalf of home rule on this local policy matter. Under an agreement worked out by Fauntroy and Stuckey, the information gathered by the latter s subcommittee, including an Urban Land Institute study, would be turned over to the District Council without any directive for reconsideration. Before the conflict was over, even Representative Stuckey, the sponsor of the veto resolution, questioned whether the law encroached on the federal interest.[11]

Condominium Conversion

District officials concluded that the rapid pace of conversion of apartments to condominiums was creating a serious housing problem in the District. The main purpose of the Rental Housing Conversion and Sale Act of 1980 was to restrict condominium conversion and to develop appropriate policies under which conversions would take place. The council approved the measure by a twelve to one vote, stating that all of the provisions of the act and others were necessary to prevent the accelerating trend to conversions that was "threatening to squeeze out of the city low- and moderate-income people who cannot afford to buy apartments they now rent."[12]

The rental housing act required a majority vote of the current rental tenants before any rental apartment building could be converted into a condominium. It gave tenants the first option to purchase the building and granted continued rental rights at legally controlled rents to elderly persons (over sixty-two years of age) with under $30,000 annual family income as long as the law remained in effect. Although protection of tenants was one of the main purposes of the bill, both tenant organizations and developers objected to the provision that only owners could apply for the right to convert buildings. This provision was especially onerous because tenants would have to buy their buildings, often requiring large sums of money, before they could apply for permission to convert.[13]

Representative Charles Wilson (D-Texas), chairman of the House District of Columbia Appropriations Subcommittee, said that he was concerned about the condominium bill. He argued that this bill and the city's rent control law were destroying the local tax base and predicted that the city would encounter real trouble in persuading Congress to raise its federal payment with the above policies in effect. Wilson's recommendation was that government action should take the form of a rent subsidy program to help the poor rather than restrict condominium conversions that end up subsidizing the non-poor who live in fashionable high-rise apartments west of Rock Creek Park.

Wilson backed up his views by introducing a resolution to veto the District's condominium law. The District Committee held one day of hearings on the resolution and despite strongly voiced misgivings over the economic impact of the District law, the committee unanimously rejected the veto resolution. In accordance with its established criteria, the committee concluded that the local legislation neither involved the federal interest nor did it violate the Home Rule Charter. Consequently, the members of the committee preferred not to interfere with city affairs in this instance.

Remembering that Representative Wilson had played an active role in opposing rent control while he was chairman of the House Appropriations Subcommittee as well as a landlord in the city, the *Washington Post* carried an editorial that made a scathing attack on the congressman, asking him to get off the city's back and to use his energy to oppose the condominium law not in Congress but before the District Council, where it thought the merits of his case would have some support. The *Post* conceded, however, that it thought that Wilson was right in condemning both rent control and the limitations that had been placed on condominium conversion. But these issues should be dealt with as local rather than federal interests.[14]

PUBLIC SAFETY

Public safety in the nation's capital is a legitimate federal concern. The fact that the local government has broad powers in this area, including control of the police department, has not been reassuring to national lawmakers. In its efforts to cope with an extended drug and homicide crisis, the city has taken many steps over the years to improve security and deal with the growing problem of inadequate prison facilities. Members of Congress have often disagreed with the remedies adopted by the city, especially its efforts to relieve prison overcrowding and control the use of handguns. After a brief discussion of the challenges to firearms control and gun liability, major attention in this section is devoted to the confrontation between Congress and the District over the prison early release program, which originated from both federal and parochial interests.

Firearms Control and Gun Liability

The District Council action on firearms control was driven by the council's perception of the need to significantly improve the local government's capacity to monitor the traffic of firearms within the District of Columbia. The Firearms Control Act of 1975 evolved from a series of gun control bills that had been introduced and considered by the council, and were aimed at reforming the current firearm registration and licensing regulations.[15] The goals of this legislation were twofold: (1) to reduce the potential for the occurrence of gun-related crimes and deaths; and (2) to strengthen the capacity of the District government to monitor the traffic in firearms and ammunition within its jurisdiction.

The council measure banned the possession of handguns by anyone except police officers and guards unless the weapons were registered with the city at the time that the new regulations took effect. After the effective date of the act, no other handguns could be registered. All firearms must be kept unloaded and dismantled or trigger-locked except in business establishments or when in use for lawful recreational purposes, namely, on the firing range. The ownership of rifles and shotguns was not prohibited, but sawed-off shotguns, machine guns, and short-barreled rifles would continue to be illegal.

There was a strong expression of community support for gun control but if the city had expected some reaction from gun-lobbied members of Congress, it was not to be disappointed. A disapproval resolution, introduced by freshman Representative Ron Paul (R-Texas), was referred to the House District Committee. Hearings were held on the resolution but, repeatedly, the committee failed to muster a quorum whenever the gun control resolution was on its agenda. There were many known opponents of the tough new gun control act in Congress and Paul tried unsuccessfully to force a floor vote on his resolution, but he was ruled out of order by Speaker Carl Albert (D-Okla.). Failing in his efforts to get the issue to the floor, Paul predicted that the validity of the District of Columbia law would have to be challenged in the courts to block its implementation. The powerful National Rifle Association (NRA), arguing that the District Council did not have authority to pass the gun control bill, was solidly opposed to the legislation and promised to make good on the prediction by Paul that the measure would be challenged in court. The city's gun control law took effect in 1976 and was subsequently upheld by the courts in spite of legal action by the NRA that continued until 1978.[17]

Although handguns had been banned in the District by the strict 1976 gun control law, in recent years most of the guns recovered in shootings were traced to distributors in Maryland and Virginia.[18] The rate of violent crime in the District continued to increase. By 1989 the District Council was making a serious effort to go after the manufacturers and distributors of deadly assault weapons by holding them liable for damages and injuries suffered by victims in the District. It was another effort by the council to do something about the record pace of homicides in the city.[19]

By a vote of eight to three in December 1990, the District Council approved the Handgun and Machine Gun Manufacturing Strict Liability Act of 1989, better known as the Gun Liability Act. Considered one of the strictest gun control bills in the country, the measure held gun manufacturers, dealers, and importers of assault weapons liable when their product was used to cause injury or death in the city. Instead of making all handgun manufacturers liable for shooting injuries or deaths, a decision it initially considered, the council opted to limit the bill to cover only some semiautomatic assault weapons.[20] The act allowed shooting victims or their families to seek damages against gun manufacturers and dealers.

About a month after the gun liability law was approved, the council temporarily repealed it upon the request of new Mayor Sharon Pratt Dixon, who felt that congressional opposition to the law would interfere with the District's chances of getting a $100 million budget supplement. After the city received the funding, the council permanently repealed the law.[21]

After the council dropped the gun control law, scores of ministers and gun-control groups organized a campaign to revive it. The Committee for Strict Liability was created, which gathered 27,000 citizen signatures and demanded a referendum on the issue. In a special election with no one running for office, District voters gave overwhelming approval to a reenactment of the gun liability measure, which effectively aborted the permanent repeal legislation. The measure won in each of the city's eight political wards by at least a two to one ratio and passed with 77 percent of the vote.[22]

With support from the NRA, disapproval resolutions were introduced in the House by Representatives Dana Rohrabacher (R-Calif.), a member of the District Committee, and Larry Combest (R-Texas). Their main argument was that the law was unconstitutional and would illegally give the District authority to regulate interstate commerce.[23] Another staunch opponent of the law, Representative Thomas Bliley (R-Va.), said that it was not a local matter and that Congress intended to prohibit the District from enacting "such overreaching laws."[24]

The District's gun liability law was sustained by the District Committee on a straight party-line vote, with the Democrats supporting and the Republicans in opposition. Several members of the upper chamber, including Senators Ted Stevens (R-Alaska) and Steve Symms (R-Idaho), considered taking the District of Columbia act to the full Senate floor by attaching it to another piece of District legislation. In early 1992, Senator Bob Smith (R-N.H.) introduced legislation, ultimately successful in the Senate, that would repeal the gun liability law.[25]

Stepping up efforts to overturn the District's assault-weapon liability law, Representative Bliley, joined by the three other Republican members of the House District Committee, sued top city officials in an effort to invalidate this statute. They contended that Congress's power over the District was being undercut in that the final version of the law had never been submitted to Congress for formal review, and that the city violated the law by failing to do so. District leaders contended that Congress reviewed the original act and made no attempt to overturn it; consequently, there was no need for the statute to be retransmitted.[26]

The suit brought by Bliley and others to overturn the Strict Liability Act was dismissed by the United States District Court on the grounds that it was inappropriate for the court to intervene in the issue. As pointed out by the judge, Congress can directly invalidate the statute by legislation to this effect. There was no indication of such action by the 103d Congress (1993–94).

Prison Overcrowding

The action of the District government to deal with prison overcrowding survived the most serious challenge of any act that was not overturned. The struggle between political forces was intense and the final vote in the House was extremely close. Consequently, it provides a viable test, on a par with vetoed legislation, of the Rowat thesis on conflict of federal and local interests. In spite of the bitter struggle that took place in Congress, driven mainly by parochial interests, there was little federal interest involved and the case provides limited support for the Rowat thesis.

Controlling crime and incarcerating convicted or charged offenders are problems throughout the United States. In 1987 the District of Columbia along with forty-five of the fifty states, Puerto Rico, and the Virgin Islands were under some form of court order or were parties in pending litigation involving prison overcrowding.[28] The District of Columbia, as well as twenty-six states, had at least one major prison operating under a court order or a consent degree. Eight of these states were operating their entire prison systems, under court orders or consent decrees concerning crowding or other conditions.[29] The severe crowding crises resulted in court-ordered limits at most of the District's correctional facilities.

The District of Columbia prison system consists of nine facilities at the Lorton Reformatory, the District of Columbia Detention Facility (District of Columbia Jail), and eight halfway houses. With more than 6,500 persons behind bars, the District has the highest incarceration rate in the United States.[30] Dating back several years, the District of Columbia prison system had been under a series of court orders and decrees mandating population limits and reductions at the District of Columbia Jail and most of the nine prison facilities at the Lorton Reformatory.[31]

Emergency Action.

In June 1987 Mayor Marion Barry requested the council to declare an emergency regarding the overcrowding in the District prison system and to enact emergency legislation granting him authority in certain defined circumstances to release prisoners.[32] The council approved the emergency legislation for a period of ninety days, beginning on 22 June, the date of the mayor's signature, and ending on 30 September, 1987.[33] The mayor was authorized to declare a prison overcrowding state of emergency whenever the population of the District of Columbia prison system exceeded its rated designed capacity for thirty consecutive days. Essentially, this act authorized the mayor to follow two different procedures to reduce the prison population. First, the mayor was allowed to reduce maximum sentences by ninety days or 10 percent, whichever was less, of inmates convicted of nonviolent crimes, thus accelerating their mandatory release date. Generally, these prisoners were denied parole at some point or chose to serve their full sentences rather than be under parole supervision later. Second, the Mayor was allowed to reduce by ninety days the minimum sentences of some inmates convicted of nonviolent crimes, thereby accelerating parole eligibility by three months of a different group of prisoners.

When the first state of emergency was declared by the mayor on 3 July the prison population was 8.6 percent above design capacity, with most of the crowding at Lorton's three Occoquan facilities where 1,970 prisoners—689 above the design capacity of 1,281—were housed.[34]

The early release program became enmeshed in politics soon after it was enacted. The Lorton Reformatory is located in Southeast Fairfax County, Virginia, which was in the congressional district of Representative Stan E. Parris (R-Va.), a longtime critic of the District's operation of the Lorton facility. Immediately after the emergency legislation was enacted, Parris, warning that the early release program posed a serious danger to public safety in the District and suburban communities, introduced a bill to repeal it. Although District officials emphasized the fact that inmates convicted of violent crimes—homicide, rape, assault with a dangerous weapon, armed robbery—and those serving mandatory sentences on drug convictions would not qualify for the program, Parris insisted that the emergency legislation would permit the early release of "quite dangerous" criminals, especially drug offenders who were not covered under the District of Columbia sentencing statute.[35]

Permanent Legislation.
On 14 July, the District Council approved legislation (Bill 7-177; Act 7-56) that would continue the early release program on a permanent basis. This bill, which was very similar to the emergency act, was signed by the mayor and delivered to Congress on 21 July 1987.[36]

At the time that the mayor declared the first emergency, he estimated that about 350 prisoners would be released during the three-month period. Instead, approximately 815 inmates were freed. Parris charged that in its haste to comply with court-ordered limits on inmate population, the District had jeopardized public safety by releasing potentially dangerous criminals. However, the effect of the early release program was not significant in terms of the net reduction in the overall inmate population. When the emergency was declared, the city's prisons held 7,950 inmates, or about 600 more than the rated design capacity. Despite the early releases, the prisons still held 7,840 inmates, or about 500 more than capacity, when the emergency measure expired on 30 September.

Parris introduced a bill to repeal the ninety-day emergency legislation (the District of Columbia Prison Overcrowding Emergency Powers Emergency Act of 1987) and later, after the District enacted legislation to continue the early release program on a permanent basis (the District of Columbia Overcrowding Emergency Powers Act of 1987), he introduced a joint resolution to disapprove the latter act.[37]

Since emergency legislation becomes effective immediately and without congressional review, Parris took immediate action to repeal it. Both measures were referred to the District Committee, on which Parris was the ranking Republican member. The hearings on these measures began on 10 September, but the emergency legislation had expired prior to further committee consideration on 7 and 8 October, by which time the emergency legislation (Council Act (7-40)) and the bill to repeal it (H.R. 2850) had become moot for legislative purposes.[38] If it was an advantage to the city to have the emergency act run its course without interruption, the flip side of this situation was that the program could be evaluated and the results used as a part of the congressional review of the permanent legislation, which did not augur well for the city. The critics questioned the District's ability to handle the early-release program, charging that the city violated its commitment to release only prisoners convicted of nonviolent crimes.[39]

The minority (Republican) members of the District Committee participated in the initial subcommittee hearing in September but boycotted the subcommittee and full committee markup sessions scheduled for 7 and 8 October.[40] The full committee proceeded with the markup on October 8 and by a unanimous vote of eight to zero rejected House Joint Resolution 341. Similar to the action taken on the Sexual Assault Reform Act of 1979, the minority members were gearing up for an effort on the House floor to discharge the District Committee of its responsibility on the resolution and to seek a vote by the full House on the disapproval resolution.

Less than one week after the committee's rejection of the disapproval resolution, Parris and the Republican members of the committee made good on their promise to take the issue to the floor of the House. Parris's first move was to offer a privileged motion to discharge the District Committee from further consideration of the disapproval resolution.[41] This step was taken in spite of the unanimous committee vote against the resolution.

Although the debate on the discharge motion was limited to one hour, a battle royal took place on the floor over the ultimate fate of the disapproval resolution. For those who supported the disapproval of House Joint Resolution 341, the issue was *public safety* in the nation's capital and its suburban communities. For those who opposed it, the issue was *home rule,* and not closing the last door available to the District for dealing with an overcrowded prison system and the resulting court orders.[42]

At the very outset the Republicans, led by Parris, took issue with the use of the three criteria that had been utilized by the District Committee (of which Parris was a member) to determine action on a veto resolution. Rather, they pointed to the broad power of Congress to legislate on the District of Columbia at any time and on any subject.[43] They argued that the application of the criteria "is tantamount to total abdication of the congressional responsibility for oversight."

Representative Dellums, chairman of the District Committee, countered by pointing to the statement of purpose in the congressionally enacted Home Rule Charter that granted to the inhabitants of the District the powers of local government with the objective of relieving Congress of the burden of legislating upon essentially local District matters. In his counterattack, Dellums also charged that the privileged motion to discharge was being misused by the minority members of the District Committee—that it was not intended to be used as a procedural device to bring a substantive issue before the body.[44] He angrily described Parris's action as an unnecessary intrusion on home rule and an affront to him and the committee, which he argued had dealt openly and fairly with Parris's resolution.[45]

Although the disapproval resolution had become largely a partisan issue, there was no way that the Republicans could win on a straight party-line vote. Consequently, Parris set about the task of enlisting Democratic allies by appealing to their growing concerns about crime and their belief that Congress must retain some control over public safety in the nation's capital.[46] Parris and other critics summarily charged that the District had violated its commitment to release only prisoners convicted of nonviolent crimes, that the program was hastily prepared and sloppily managed, and that any easing of overcrowding was very temporary at best.[47]

At the end of the debate, Dellums offered a motion to table the privileged motion, which set up a showdown vote on the House floor. Parris had claimed to have lined up the unanimous support of the 170 House Republicans and was successful in persuading a surprising number of Democrats to cross over with two carefully crafted "Dear Colleague" letters that emphasized what he called the dangers to public safety posed by the early release program. His goal was to recruit the remaining forty-eight votes required for a majority from conservative Southern Democrats.

In the end the Democrats pulled themselves together to block a vigorous GOP assault. The Democratic-controlled House voted 210 to 200 to block the Republican effort, but not before Democratic leaders twisted arms to avert widespread defection by other Democrats. The vote to table was so close that Democratic Majority Whip Tony Coelho (D-Calif.) scrambled, with no time remaining on the electronic tote board, to persuade over a half dozen Democrats to change their votes in favor of the motion to table.[48] In the end, 34 Democrats broke ranks to vote with 166 Republicans against the motion.[49] Trying to salvage something good from this hard-fought battle, the leaders of the veto effort, Representatives Parris and Bliley, said the closeness of the vote would force the city to tighten regulations for releasing prisoners.[50]

Since arriving in Congress in 1973, Stan Parris had positioned himself as a critic of the District of Columbia government; some called his stance bashing the District. With the District of Columbia prison facilities located in Parris's congressional district, the driving force behind the effort to overturn the District of Columbia program was parochial. Parris was good at galvanizing Republicans and Democrats as he pursued largely his own local interests, often at the expense of the District, which has no voting representation in Congress.[51]

The Rowat thesis is about the conflict between national and local interests. This struggle over the early release of District prisoners was waged by opponents in the name of the national interest but it was propelled by members of the Virginia delegation. Public safety in the District and the national capital area is a legitimate national concern. But the hub of this problem was in Virginia, and less than a majority in the House saw it as a serious enough threat to the public safety of the nation's capital to treat it as a federal interest matter. Although the local position was narrowly sustained, the close vote is a true reflection of a near collision between federal and local interests, driven by parochial forces.

HEALTH AND HUMAN SERVICES

Two of the three challenges under health and human services—natural death and health care benefits (domestic partners)—involved moral conflicts that divide the nation. Although the moral dimension was involved in the challenge of the AIDS insurance legislation, it was dominated by a parochial business interest.

Natural Death Act

Based on a Kansas law that was drafted for use as a model bill, the Natural Death Act of 1981 permitted individuals to declare in advance that they should not be kept alive by extraordinary means should they become terminally ill. The act enabled any adult person eighteen years or older to state explicitly in a will-type document his or her desire to have life-sustaining procedures withheld or withdrawn in the case of a terminal medical condition. Detailed procedures were provided in the legislation for both executing and revoking such directives, with the aim of providing a guide to health professionals in dealing with the terminally ill. The essential purpose of this act was to ensure that the rights of patients may be respected even after they are no longer able to participate actively in decisions about themselves.[52]

Contending that the measure was susceptible to abuse, among other reasons, the Moral Majority, some members of the local clergy, and one member of the council took a strong position against the Natural Death Act, providing the impetus for the challenge of this legislation.[53] Two disapproval resolutions against this act were introduced by Representative Mark Siljander (R-Mich.), which were referred to the House District Committee. Somewhat late in the thirty-legislative-day review period, hearings on these resolutions were scheduled but were not held.

The local groups opposing the Natural Death Act were joined by the District of Columbia Federation of Citizens Associations, which asked Mayor Marion Barry to veto the bill, but Barry refused. It turned out that before the expiration of the congressional review period, the act's chief adversary, Representative Siljander, dropped his effort to persuade Congress to veto the measure.

AIDS Insurance and Health Care Benefits

The District of Columbia passed the following legislation to deal with different aspects in the provision of individual health insurance: the

Prohibition of Discrimination in the Provision of Insurance Act of 1986 (AIDS Insurance Act) and the Health Care Benefits Expansion Act of 1992 (Domestic Partners Act). This legislation dealt with the prevention of discrimination in health insurance and coverage of a domestic partner. Both of these acts became enmeshed in controversy focusing on the gay and lesbian community. Neither act was officially vetoed by Congress but nevertheless both were derailed by other available tactics and means.

The AIDS Insurance Act of 1986 was passed by the council to prevent health and life insurance companies from denying coverage to persons who test positive for exposure to the AIDS virus and from charging higher rates to such persons for at least a five-year period. In addition, the measure banned companies from using factors such as age, sex, marital status, or sexual preference in deciding whether to provide coverage. The AIDS Insurance bill, passed unanimously by voice vote, would not force insurance companies to provide coverage for anyone diagnosed as suffering from AIDS.

Opponents of the AIDS Insurance Act spoke of increased insurance premiums for all people in the District to subsidize protection for persons at high risk. They maintained that such a law would establish the District as a mecca for people who test positive for AIDS exposure elsewhere in the nation.

The insurance industry lobbied heavily to defeat the bill before the District Council but, reaffirming its respect for home rule, steered clear of official involvement in the effort to get Congress to veto the measure. Although no one charged that a federal interest was involved, Senator Jesse Helms (R-N.C.) and Representative William Dannemeyer (R-Calif.) introduced joint resolutions in the Senate and House, respectively, to disapprove the District legislation. The veto effort was backed by the Moral Majority and some family-oriented church groups.[54]

The House District Subcommittee on Fiscal Affairs held a hearing and a markup session where the disapproval resolution was defeated by a vote of five to two. The members of the subcommittee said that the issue before them was not the substance of the legislation but whether there was a basis for Congress to interfere with a local decision. An effort to bring the issue to a vote on the House floor through a procedural motion was blocked.[55] By a vote of fifty-three to forty-one, legislation in the Senate was approved as a rider to a debt ceiling bill that would veto the District's AIDS Insurance Act.[56] Consequently, consideration by a

House-Senate conference was necessary to resolve the major difference between the respective bills, namely, the AIDS provision.

Even after the AIDS Insurance law took effect in August 1986, it still remained the target of an intense lobbying effort by the Moral Majority and other fundamentalist antihomosexual groups, who wished to see the measure repealed.[57] Later in 1986, the Senate voted for the second time to repeal the AIDS Insurance Act.[58] The repeal provision, again offered by Senator Helms, was added to an omnibus appropriations bill by a voice vote, requiring this measure to be sent to conference with the House. As it turned out, the House and Senate conferees agreed to drop the challenge to the District of Columbia law.

But the final chapter in this struggle was not over. Although Congress did not formally overturn the act, it gave the council a deadline (31 December 1988) for amending the AIDS law.[59] The city had no choice but to bow to congressional power, to either repeal the law or face a total freeze on District funds. By October 1988, council member John Ray (D-At Large), the lead sponsor of the statute, had begun drafting legislation that would repeal the city's pioneering AIDS law barring insurance companies from routinely testing applicants for the AIDS virus. The council approved the repeal measure on 13 December 1988 and it became effective law after the congressional review period expired in March 1989.[60]

In early 1992 the council was again considering legislation that focused attention on the gay and lesbian community. For approximately five years, gay rights leaders had been pushing for the official right to become domestic partners, and the initial legislation, proposed by Council Chairman John A. Wilson (D), received the unanimous vote of the council. Although the momentum in the council was slowed by media reports and general reactions, it resisted a furious campaign by local religious leaders and passed the bill, which allowed unmarried adult couples who live together to register with the city government as domestic partners. This act allowed live-in partners of District of Columbia government employees to receive a range of new medical benefits and offered tax breaks to private companies that extended the same privileges. Hospitals were required to grant partners the same visitation rights as spouses. Although attention focused on what the bill would do for the gay and lesbian community, it included any unmarried couple—a mother and her adult son, for example.

When the Health Care Benefits Expansion Act of 1992 reached Capitol Hill for congressional review, it aroused immediate opposition. Opponents of the measure settled on Representative Clyde Holloway (R-La.) to sponsor the veto resolution because he did not have a reputation for "gaybashing." The Senate was also prepared to take up the domestic partnership issue, led by the conservative members of that body.[61]

The District Committee upheld the domestic partnership law on a straight party-line vote, with the Democrats stating that Congress should not interfere in District affairs and the Republicans saying that they believed the law to be in violation of federal statutes.[62] Holloway responded to the committee's action by announcing that he would be looking at other options, including an amendment to the District of Columbia appropriations bill, working with other opponents to challenge the law in court, and hoping that District ministers would seek a referendum to repeal the law.

The gutting of the domestic partners law was accomplished through the appropriations route, a path well-trodden by Congress to block District policies without passing a formal disapproval resolution. As an amendment to the District's appropriations bill, both the House and Senate voted overwhelmingly to prohibit the city from spending money to implement the domestic partners law although, technically, it remained on the books.

Of course, there is some difference between formal disapproval of a District of Columbia law and disallowing the expenditure of funds for a particular program. In an unprecedented act of brinkmanship, Mayor Sharon Pratt Kelly ordered city officials to continue registering "domestic partners" despite the overwhelming congressional vote to intentionally block the program. Conceding that the practical benefits of the program had been eliminated, the mayor said that her decision was part of a broader campaign to protest congressional interference in city matters.[63]

GENERAL GOVERNMENT

Local government action on statehood and the subsequent challenges to it are discussed here as "general government." These two congressional challenges—involving the statehood convention and constitution—are discussed together in the follwong section.

Statehood: Convention and Constitution

Both Initiative #6, Legalized Lotteries, and Initiative #3, Statehood Constitutional Convention, were approved by the voters of the District of Columbia on 4 November 1980. The statehood initiative provided for the selection of delegates to a convention to draft a state constitution for the nation's capital that would later be put before the city's voters and Congress. Representative Robert W. Daniel, Jr. (R-Va.) introduced a resolution to veto the District of Columbia initiative calling for convening a constitutional convention as a step in achieving statehood. Citing the United States Constitution, costs, and bureaucratic proliferation as the basis for his action, Daniel said, "The Constitution provided for a federal capital and that's what it ought to be."[64]

Full District Committee hearings and markups were held on the veto resolution, which was defeated on a committee roll call vote of five to four and not reported to the floor. As both initiatives quietly became law in March 1981, the city had its first voter-initiated legislation since home rule but no readily identifiable funds to put the laws fully into effect. The cash-strapped government had no money allocated in the current or next fiscal year's budget for either initiative. The statehood initiative was estimated to cost about $750,000—including an estimated $400,000 for the convention alone.[65]

By November 1981 the District was ready to implement the citizen-approved statehood act and forty-five delegates were elected to a constitutional convention, authorized to draft a state charter. The delegates were elected from the District's eight wards (five from each ward), with five delegates elected at large. In May 1982 the convention delegates completed and signed the constitutional charter for the "State of New Columbia," the name chosen by the convention.

Statehood for the District has been a continuing issue during the 1980s and into the 1990s and its ultimate fate will be determined by legislation originating in Congress rather than council acts that require congressional review and approval. The constitution of the new state, however, would have to be submitted through a council act, and some critics of statehood were concerned about certain provisions in the proposed constitution such as the guarantee of the right to employment to every resident of the new state. In order to alleviate some of those concerns, the District of Columbia Council and the nonvoting delegate to Congress, Walter E. Fauntroy (D-D.C.), carried out a revision of the constitution to concur more with the Home Rule Charter that eliminated most of the controversial provisions. The basic objective was to have Congress focus on statehood rather than the proposed constitution.

In 1987 this revised document was submitted to Congress for approval as the Constitution for the State of New Columbia Approval Act of 1987.[66] With the Democrats holding a seven to four majority on the District Committee, the statehood measure was expected to win approval in spite of a vigorous fight by Republican members.[67] The leading foe of the statehood bill was Representative Stan Parris, the new ranking minority member on the District Committee. Parris had previously operated largely as a gadfly on the committee but his views and actions took on added importance when he succeeded the late Representative Stewart B. McKinney as the ranking Republican member.

In June 1987, Representative Parris introduced a disapproval resolution (the second introduced in Congress dealing with statehood) designed to veto the Constitution for the State of New Columbia Approval Act. After more than a month of political skirmishes, postponed meetings, and debate over the measure's constitutionality, the District Committee approved the State of New Columbia constitution by the close vote of six to five. In the 1990 congressional elections, Parris was defeated by Democratic challenger James P. Moran, who was prepared to take up the gauntlet of ardent foe of District of Columbia statehood.[68]

CIVIL LIBERTIES AND RIGHTS

The major challenge in the area of civil liberties and rights dealt with the local attempt to revise the District of Columbia Criminal Code. This challenge resulted in a veto that will be discussed in the next chapter. The other two challenges under civil liberties and rights—affirmative action in employment and disinvestment in South Africa— were not serious ones and are discussed together below. They were among the challenges that did not generate hearings or further action after they were referred to the House District Committee.

The Affirmative Action in District Government Employment Act, enacted over Mayor Walter Washington's veto in 1976, required all District agencies to aim for a work force that reflected the racial and sexual makeup of the city's entire labor force.[69] In addition to dealing with the hiring of women and minorities in District government jobs, the act also covered the role of departmental equal employment opportunity (EEO) offices and specialists in deciding EEO complaints. The resolution to veto this act was introduced by Republican Representative James M. Collins of Texas.

Some members of Congress viewed the District as getting involved in foreign policy and attempting to regulate commerce with foreign nations when it took up the matter of human rights in South Africa. It was an issue with both international affairs and human rights dimensions. The District legislation to take city government funds out of firms doing business with South Africa, approved by the council in 1983, was a step that had already been taken by many states and local jurisdictions.[70] This act required the city to withdraw investments from banks, other financial institutions, or companies that operated in South Africa or made investment loans there.[71] A resolution to veto the District act was introduced by Representative Philip M. Crane (R-Ill.), with strong support from Representative Stan Parris (R-Va.). Surmising that a vote to overturn the measure would be viewed as a racist action, no Senate opponents of the measure came forward to lead the fight against the District of Columbia act.[72] Congressional leaders had expected the District of Columbia bill to spark intense debate on President Ronald Reagan's policy of "constructive engagement" with South Africa, but the measure made it through the review period with something more like a whimper of opposition than a bang of controversy. In the final analysis, Congress decided to back away from a civil rights/home rule/foreign policy debate, for little or no gain, and allow the local law to stand as enacted.[73]

PUBLIC WORKS AND TRANSPORTATION

In spite of a normal flow of new local policies dealing with public works and transportation, this was a relatively quiet policy area with respect to congressional disapproval resolutions. Only one local action—dealing with automobile service stations—has been challenged in this policy area during the current home rule era. It is noteworthy that the challenge to the local service station act was the only disapproval resolution introduced during the 95th Congress (1977–78).

Retail Service Stations

The Retail Service Station Act of 1976 contained three substantive titles, each involving a different form of regulation of the gasoline distribution/marketing industry. It prohibited any oil refining company from running its own station in the District after 1 January 1981. After this date, all stations were required to be owned by or leased to independent dealers. The act clarified the contractual relationship between gasoline distributors and dealers and placed various economic restraints on oil companies, including prohibitions against arbitrary canceling of sales arrangements with independent dealers. A two-year moratorium, until 1979, was placed on further conversions from full service gasoline stations to limited service (gas-and-go) stations.

Hit where it was likely to hurt most, in the cash flow artery, the oil companies struck back, spearheaded by a resolution to veto the District of Columbia law, introduced by Representative Bill Archer (R-Texas). His congressional district included the city of Houston, the nation's unofficial oil capital. In testimony on his resolution, Archer called the city measure "unnecessary, almost certainly unconstitutional and clearly anti-consumer."[74] The oil executives insisted that the District measure would prevent economies that are passed on to motorists in the form of lower gasoline prices than full-service dealers can give.

Hearings were held by the Subcommittee on Economic Development and Regional Affairs of the House District Committee. The committee, finding little or no federal interest in the District bill, voted to kill the veto resolution.

Challenges of District legislation began during the first year of home rule and have been a continuing activity ever since. A total of thirty-six disapproval resolutions on twenty different subjects had been introduced by the end of 1993. The subjects of the acts challenged ranged from public safety and revenue to natural death and the international issue of disinvestment of funds in South Africa. Failing congressional approval by just ten votes, the most serious challenge involved the public safety issue surrounding the early release of District prisoners. Although these perceived conflicts of interest by some of the lawmakers were not substantiated by Congress as a whole, they point up the disparate nature of the views of federal and local interests.

In light of the tremendous power and influence of Congress, any official action or attempted action in this body must be taken seriously. Even action by an individual member takes on added weight when it may determine the controlling policies for the hundreds of thousands of citizens who live in the nation's capital. Any congressional resolution of disapproval, like other public policies, may be introduced by a single member of Congress, but must be viewed in this context.

I have used the procedural step of congressional hearings as some indication of the comparatively serious challenges of District of Columbia legislation by Congress. With the exception of the District of Columbia Revenue Act of 1975, which generated the very first disapproval resolution on District legislation during the current home rule era, most of the congressional challenges were considered sufficiently serious to schedule public hearings on the disputed District legislation. There were challenges, however, that did not generate hearings. These challenges originated in the House and were referred to the District Committee where they were pigeonholed. None of the latter challenges made it to the floor, nor did they arouse much interest or support in Congress.

Whether successful or not, the challenges erode the freedom of action at the local level. Most of the challenges originated from sources other than a genuine national interest. Parochial interests were behind the actions of the congressmen from the neighboring states who sought to block certain revenue measures. Several local and national interest groups that were concerned about issues such as retail service stations, rent control, and a legalized lottery, sought to use Congress as an appeal body after losing at the local level. Elements of arrogance at the national level can be seen in the efforts to block local action on the issuing of general obligation bonds and on disinvestment in South Africa. The challenges contribute little support to the Rowat thesis of an inevitable conflict between federal and local interests.

NOTES

1. The second session of the 103d Congress (1994) is still in process but one challenge to District legislation has already been made by four Republican members of the House: Cass Ballenger (N.C.), Thomas J. Bliley (Va.), Dana Rohrabacher (Calif.) and Jim Saxton (N.J.). Introduced on 24 March 1994, their resolution challenged the action of the District Council in approving the Displaced Workers Protection Act of 1994 (DWPA). This act requires a contractor performing certain services in the District to retain employees of the previous contractor for a 90-day transition employment period. The challengers charge that the DWPA interferes with employers' rights to select their representatives and violates several national laws and the United States Constitution as well (art. 1, sect. 10). The DWPA is now effective law but the sponsors of the challenge have vowed to pursue this matter through a repeal of the statute.

House, J. Res. 345, 103d Cong., 2d sess., 24 March 1994; D.C. Act 10-193, Displaced Workers Protection Act of 1994, 36 *District of Columbia Register* 1011 (4 March 1994); C.H. Albright, Jr., minority chief counsel, House Committee on the District of Columbia, telephone interview by author, 23 June 1994, Washington, D.C.

2. Senator Eagleton introduced the veto resolution on behalf of himself and all six other members of the Senate District of Columbia Committee. *Washington Post,* 25 November 1975, C-6.

3. Ibid., 12 December 1975, A-1.

4. In actuality, the mayor's pledge of prior consultation was less of a concession to Congress than a statement of political reality about the power relationship between the city and Congress. Ibid., 12 December 1975, A-1.

5. Ibid., 12 December 1975, A-5; *Congressional Quarterly Almanac* 29 (1975): 441 ff.

6. A legal lottery had been in operation since 1973 in the neighboring state of Maryland. Many of the customers of the Maryland games came across the state line from the District of Columbia. *Washington Post,* 5 March 1981, C-1.

7. The city-run Blue Plains facility is the region's largest sewage treatment plant, serving two million people in the District, large parts of Prince George's and Montgomery counties, and some areas of Arlington, Fairfax, and Loudon counties. Ibid., 12 February 1992, D-5.

8. Ibid., 27 June 1992, A-18.

9. Ibid., 23 June 1975, A-1.

10. If all else failed, the AOBA threatened to seek an injunction against the rent control bill if it was enacted into law. Ibid., 11 July 1975, A-8.

11. Ibid., 7 October 1975, A-4.

12. Ibid., 16 August 1980, A-1.

13. Ibid., 16 August 1980, A-1.

14. Ibid., 30 August 1980, A-16.

15. The Firearms Control Act of 1975 amended the District of Columbia Police Regulations, articles 50 through 55, dealing with comprehensive firearms bans, registration, and licensing. Legal memorandum from Louis P. Robbins, Acting District of Columbia Corporation Counsel, to David A. Clarke, Chairman, Committee on the Judiciary and Criminal Law, Council of District of Columbia, 23 March 1976.

16. Memorandum from David A. Clarke, Chairman, Committee on the Judiciary and Criminal Law, to members of the Council, Council of District of Columbia, 21 April 1976.

17. The NRA challenged the 1975 District of Columbia gun control law in *McIntosh, et al., vs. Washington, et al.* The NRA sided with McIntosh and won an initial decision. In an appeal by Washington, however, McIntosh and the NRA lost. McIntosh claimed that the District of Columbia city government had overstepped their home rule powers in formulating the 1975 gun control law. The court disagreed; Washington won and the 1975 District of Columbia gun control law was upheld. In an appeal decision handed down on 24 October 1978, presiding judge George H. Goodrich stated that "the primary purpose of the Home Rule Act . . . was to relieve Congress of the burden of legislating

upon essentially local matters to the greatest extent possible." *McIntosh, et al., vs. Washington, et al,* District of Columbia Court of Appeals, no. 12073 (1978).

18. During the period from January 1988 to December 1990, the District of Columbia police had recovered approximately 8,500 guns, and had traced 70 percent of them to distributors in Maryland and Virginia. *Washington Post,* 13 December 1990, C-1.

19. By late December 1990, when the gun liability measure was being considered, a record 467 persons had been slain in the city during the year. Ibid., 19 December 1990, B-1.

20. These weapons included the Uzi, Beretta, and Tec-9 or Mac-10. Ibid., 19 December 1990, B-1.

21. The Gun Liability Act was transmitted to Congress on 11 January 1991, but before the congressional review period ended, which was to happen on 6 March the mayor and council had arranged a political solution with Congress—repeal of the act in order to gain additional funding. Accordingly, the council enacted an emergency repeal of the Gun Liability Act on 15 February 1991. *Bliley et al. v. Kelly et al.,* 793 F. Supp. 353; Ibid., 15 June 1991, B-6.

22. Ibid., 6 November 1991, A-27.

23. Ibid., 7 November 1991, D-1.

24. Representative Bliley indicated that he might introduce legislation to ban gun liability laws nationwide. Ibid., 22 November 1991, C-1.

25. Smith's measure was attached to a spending bill for the departments of State, Commerce and Justice, forcing the latter bill to be negotiated in a House-Senate conference committee, where it did not survive. Ibid., 27 January 1992, B-3; 28 July 1992, B-5.

26. Representative Bliley and three other Republican members of the House District Committee argued that the District was trying to create a loophole in Congress's power to oversee city matters. Ibid., 20 February 1992, B-4.

27. Ibid., 23 May 1992, F-3.

28. *Congressional Record,* 100th Cong., 1st sess., 14 October 1987, H8612.

29. According to the ACLU's National Prison Project, only eight states had not been subjected to major civil rights litigation due to crowding in their prison systems. Reported in *Washington Post,* 15 July 1987, B-1.

30. It was reported that the District had the third highest incarceration rate in the world—behind the Soviet Union and South Africa, where political prisoners comprise a large percentage of the total number. In addition to the number incarcerated, there were 13,000 people on probation, 2,500 on parole, and 9,000 more awaiting trial. House, Subcommittee on Judiciary and Education, Committee on the District of Columbia, *Prison Overcrowding Emergency Powers Act of 1987: Hearings and Markups on H.R. 2850 and H.J. Res. 341,* 100th Cong., 1st sess., September 10, 1987, 80. *Washington Post,* 5 July 1987, B-3.

31. In five separate court orders or consent decrees, the courts set the following limits on the prison population at: District of Columbia Jail—1,684 (limit); Maximum Security Facility at Lorton—536 (maximum); Central Facility at Lorton—1,166 (limit); Youth Center No. 1—406 (limit); Occoquan I, II, and III—1,281 (limit). *Congressional Record,* 100th Cong., 1st Session, 14 October 1987, H8612.

32. The mayor faced a 1 July federal court deadline to relieve crowding at three Occoquan prison facilities at the Lorton Reformatory. At that time these facilities housed 1,970 inmates, 689 above the court-ordered limit of 1,281. United States District Judge June L. Green proceeded to grant a second one-month reprieve from her court order on the Occoquan prisons. *Washington Post,* 1 July 1987, C-6.

33. The Home Rule Charter allows the council to act swiftly, sidestepping or deferring congressional review, in cases of emergency. If at least a two-thirds majority declares that an emergency exists, the council can pass a bill after a single reading and it becomes law for ninety days as soon as it is signed by the mayor. Because of excessive use of its emergency powers, the District of Columbia Court of Appeals ruled in 1980 that the council cannot pass more than one emergency law on any subject unless it has permanent legislation before Congress. Public Law 93-198, District of Columbia Self-Government and Governmental Reorganization Act 13; 87, *Statutes at Large,* 93d Cong., 1st sess. (1973): 774; *Washington Post,* 10 June 1980, A-19.

34. Four of Lorton's prisons—Central, Maximum, and the two youth centers—were under federal court-ordered inmate population ceilings. The imposition of the Occoquan limits left only two institutions—Minimum and a 400-bed modular facility—without population ceilings. Ibid., 4 July 1987, B-1; *Congressional Record,* 100th Cong., 1st sess., 14 October 1987, H8612.

The District's system of prisons—all of which are in suburban Virginia and Maryland—is designed to hold about 7,350 inmates. Some 7,950 inmates were held in prisons and halfway houses when the first emergency was declared on 3 July 1987. *Washington Post,* 5 December 1987, B-5.

35. District of Columbia Council, Committee on the Judiciary, Report on Bill 7-177, Prison Overcrowding Emergency Powers Act of 1987, (Washington, D.C., 17 June 1987).

36. The new law prohibited the mayor from reducing the sentence of any prisoner serving a life term or mandatory sentence or who was convicted of a violent felony. *Washington Post,* 6 December 1987, B-1.

Any District of Columbia act relating to the D.C. Code (Title 24) has a sixty-day review period in Congress (instead of thirty days) before it becomes law. The legislative review period for Act 7-56 was scheduled to expire on 13 November 1987.

37. On 30 June 1987 Parris introduced H.R. 2850 to repeal District of Columbia Council Act 7-40, the *District of Columbia Prison Overcrowding Emergency Powers Emergency Act of 1987.* On 22 July he introduced H.J. Res. 341 to disapprove District of Columbia Council Act 7-56, the *District of Columbia Prison Overcrowding Emergency Powers Act of 1987.*

38. House, Subcommittee, *Prison Overcrowding Emergency Powers Act of 1987,* v.

39. *Washington Post,* 25 November 1987, D-1.

40. The subcommittee attempted to meet in the morning and again in the afternoon, but with only one minority member present, Representative Thomas Bliley, there was no quorum at either meeting on 7 October; the full committee proceeded with its markup on 8 October with no minority members in attendance. House Subcommittee *Prison Overcrowding Emergency Powers Act of 1987,* 161–62.

41. The District of Columbia Charter allows a single member to offer a privileged motion to discharge the District Committee from further consideration of a disapproval resolution after twenty calendar days. Public Law, 93-198, *District of Columbia Self-Government and Governmental Reorganization Act,* sec. 604.

42. With between 2,400 and 2,500 District-sentenced prisoners housed in federal facilities, the Federal Bureau of Prisons had said there was no more space available to house District Columbia prisoners. The District had recently decided to construct a new 700-bed facility in the District with a special drug treatment center, but the Senate called for a delay (fiscal year 1988 appropriations bill) and the fiscal year 1987 appropriations bill prohibited further expansion of the facilities at Lorton. *Congressional Record,* 100th Cong., 1st sess., 14 October 1987, H8612.

43. United States Constitution, art. 1, sect. 8, clause 17; *District of Columbia Self-Government and Governmental Reorganization Act,* Public Law 93-198, 93d Cong., 1st sess., 24 October 1973, 50.

44. *Congressional Record,* 100th Cong., 1st sess., 14 October 1987, H8607.

45. *Washington Post,* 23 November 1987, D-1.

46. Ibid.

47. Parris had taken a random sample of over 100 of the approximately 978 inmates released under the 90-day emergency program and found that many of the inmates released had been convicted of a wide range of serious crimes including robbery, assault, illegal drug sales, and weapons violations. Many were not eligible for early release at all because they were serving mandatory drug sentences, an offense that was specifically banned from the early release program.

Representative Thomas J. Bliley, Jr. (R-Va.) took the floor to assist his colleague from Virginia by listing the names and giving a vivid description of the serious crimes committed by some of the prisoners who had been given early release. *Congressional Record,* 100th Cong., 1st sess., 14 October 1987, H8612.

48. *Washington Post,* 15 October 1987, A-1. A later *Washington Post* estimate placed the number at "about 20." 23 November 1987, D-1.

49. The final vote showed 207 Democrats and 3 Republicans voting in favor of the motion. A total of twenty-three members—Democrats and Republicans—did not vote on the measure. *Congressional Quarterly Almanac,* 43 (1987): 110-H.

50. *Washington Post,* 15 October 1987, A-1. The permanent legislation was implemented under tougher guidelines, prohibiting the release of certain categories of violent offenders. Inmates serving life sentences or mandatory minimum sentences were not eligible for release. Ibid., 7 December 1987, B-4.

51. Congressional criticism or mistrust of the District of Columbia government should not be confused with "District-bashing," which is criticism of the District government in the expectation of political gain. R. Kent Weaver and Charles W. Harris, "Who's in Charge Here? Congress and the Nation's Capital," *The Brookings Review,* 7, no. 3 (Summer 1989): 45; *Washington Post,* 23 November 1987, D-1.

52. District of Columbia Council, Notice of Public hearing on proposed Legislation, *Natural Death Act of 1981*, Bill 4-204; *Determination of Death Act of 1981*, Bill 4-206 (Washington, D.C., 28 May 1981).

53. After the act became law, the opposing Council member, H. R. Crawford (D-Ward 7), introduced repeal legislation at the request of some constituents. *Washington Post*, 8 March 1982, C-3.

54. Ibid., 4 October 1986, A-1.

55. Ibid., 12 August 1986, A-8.

56. Under Senate rules, a disapproval resolution can be passed as a rider to an unrelated bill. Ibid., 20 June 1986, B-1.

57. A local suburban group, the Committee to Protect the Family, based in Falls Church, Virginia, joined with the Moral Majority in active lobbying against the District of Columbia law. The insurance industry, which had spent $200,000 trying to defeat the bill, pinned its hopes on a judicial challenge to the law, which was not successful. Ibid., 4 October 1986, A-4.

58. Nothing had happened to the rider that was attached to the debt ceiling bill because, after several months, the latter measure had not gone to conference. Ibid., 11 October 1986, B-4.

59. This action took the form of a provision in the District of Columbia Appropriations Act for fiscal year 1989 which required the repeal or amendment of the AIDS insurance law of 1986 (D.C. Law 6-170) to allow testing for the AIDS virus as a condition for acquiring health, life, and disability insurance without regard to face value of such policies. Public law 100-462, *District of Columbia Appropriations, 1989*, 100th Cong., 2nd sess., 1 October 1988, 13; 102 *Statutes at Large* 2269-13

60. D.C. Law 7-208, *Prohibition of Discrimination in the Provision of Insurance Amendment Act of 1988* (16 March 1989); *Washington Post*, 5 October 1988, A-1.

61. Senator Trent Lott (R-Miss.) introduced a disapproval resolution in the upper chamber. *Congressional Record*, 102d Cong., 2d sess., 9 June 1992, S7697.

62. *Washington Post*, 11 June 1992, C-3.

63. Ibid., 4 October 1992, B-1.

64. Ibid., 26 February 1981, C-2.

65. Ibid., 11 March 1981, 3–5.

66. The revised District of Columbia Statehood Constitution was submitted to Congress as District of Columbia Act 7-19. House, *Admission of State of New Columbia Into the Union*, 102d Cong., 2d sess., 25 September 1992, H.Rept., 909.

67. The Democratic majority lost one of its allies during the struggle in 1987. Representative Romano L. Mazzoli (D-Ky.), who argued that Delegate Fauntroy and the council were wrong to have scrapped the constitution approved by the voters, sided with the Republicans on most key issues and joined with them in voting against the overall bill. *Washington Post*, 4 June 1987, D-1.

68. Representative Thomas J. Bliley, Jr., also of Virginia and a statehood opponent, became the senior Republican on the House District of Columbia Committee. Ibid., 6 October 1992, C-6.

69. Ibid., 9 April 1976, C-4.

70. Included were the states of Connecticut, Michigan, Delaware, Massachusetts, and Pennsylvania and approximately ten cities. Ibid., 29 January 1984, A-1.

71. The council enacted Act 5-76, *Prohibition of the Investment of Public Funds in Financial Institutions and Companies Making Loans to or Doing Business with the Republic of South Africa or Namibia Act of 1983.*

72. One of those willing to work to overturn the District of Columbia measure was Senator Steve Symms (R-Idaho), but he would not agree to lead the fight. *Washington Post,* 29 January 1984, A-1.

73. Ibid., 31 January 1984, A-14.

74. The constitutionality of laws similar to the District's Retail Service Station Act was being contested in three states: Florida, Maryland, and Delaware. Testimony of Jerry A. Moore, District of Columbia Councilman At Large, before the House Subcommittee on Economic Development and Regional Affairs of the Committee on the District of Columbia, *To Disapprove the District of Columbia Retail Service Station Act of 1976: Hearings on H. Con. Res. 144,* 95th Cong., 1st sess., 23 March 1977; *Washington Post,* 24 March 1977, G-10.

5

Congressional Vetoes

A look at the District legislation that has been formally vetoed by Congress provides the best insights into the nature and degree of conflict between federal and local interests in the District of Columbia. How far apart are the national and District governments in their perceptions and operational definitions of federal and local interests? The sheer execution of a congressional veto is evidence of intense conflict. But were these conflicts really between the federal interest and local city residents' desire for self-government, or were there other forces at work The existence of weighty encumbering factors in some of the cases discussed in this chapter makes it difficult to isolate the interests of the national and local levels, and suggests that far more than clear federal interests are involved in triggering congressional veto decisions. The encumbering factors include moral issues that divide the nation, parochial interests, and even arrogance at the national level.

Although some twenty acts of the District government have been formally challenged during the current home rule period, only three have been overturned: the Location of Chanceries Act of 1979, the Sexual Assault Reform Act of 1981, and the Schedule of Heights Amendment Act of 1990. Each of these acts will be discussed separately. The District government has enacted approximately one hundred statutes per year (council period) since home rule has been in effect.[1] Therefore, on the matter of vetoes per se, as distinct from congressional action through other channels such as appropriations (discussed in chapter 6), self-government under home rule seems to have a reasonably good record. On the other hand, the threat of the veto, as represented through challenges of District legislation, has cast a shadow over the ultimate freedom of locally elected officials to make policies on behalf of their constituents.

LOCATION OF CHANCERIES ACT OF 1979

Although several challenges had already occurred, home rule was in effect for nearly five years before the first congressional veto, involving foreign missions, was executed. The conflict over the location of chanceries represented differing perceptions of what each level of government viewed as its respective policy area. In light of the fact that the general area of foreign missions is in the federal domain, the city was left with a heavy responsibility to establish its claim to jurisdiction.

Background

It is an accepted fact that the nation's capital and its residents have a special obligation to the hundreds of ambassadors, diplomats, and employees of the more than 190 foreign governments and organizations with offices in the city.[2] They need guaranteed security and must have reasonably convenient places to live and work. This is what distinguishes a capital city, and both the federal and local governments have a special responsibility in this regard. The reciprocal requirements and security of our own diplomats in foreign lands are at stake. In 1979, when the problem arose over the location of chanceries, there were approximately 132 countries with governmental offices in the nation's capital and 17,500 foreign government employees competing with private industry, local residents, and the federal and local governments for living quarters and working space. By 1993 these numbers had grown to 163 foreign embassies and 21,832 foreign government employees. No other city in the United States copes with such a mass influx of foreign offices as Washington, D.C.

Now and then, despite everyone's awareness of the obligations, the interests of the diplomatic community collide with the interests of local residents.[3] Nowhere is this conflict more troublesome than in the area of land use policy and zoning. One of the most serious conflicts between the federal and District governments during the current home rule era was over the location of chanceries in the nation's capital.[4] As the issue was debated by the two governments and finally resolved at the national level, it was not so much a question of a liberal national policy versus a restricted local policy as it was a matter of who, national or local authorities, would determine what the policy would be.

Prior to 1958 chanceries were permitted in any and all zoning districts in the city as a matter of right. In fact, prior to 1957, a certificate of occupancy was not required for such chancery uses.[5] In 1958, however, as part of a comprehensive revision of the zoning regulations, chanceries were determined to be essentially business uses and, therefore, precluded from locating in any residential district as a matter of right. They were permitted in residential districts, however, by special exception approval from the District of Columbia Board of Zoning Adjustment (BZA).[6]

Fulbright Act

In 1964 Congress passed the Chancery Act, or the Fulbright Act as it is also known, which prohibited new chanceries in all residential zones except those classified as medium-high or high density residential apartment zones. They were permitted in these zones only by the special exception approval of the BZA under criteria set forth in the act.[7]

Diplomatic Overlay Districts

During 1977, pursuant to its statutory authority, the National Capital Planning Commission (NCPC), working in cooperation with the Department of State and the District of Columbia Municipal Planning Office (MPO), proposed a so-called Foreign Missions Element to the Comprehensive Plan for the National Capital.[8] Asserting that it was under pressure to find suitable locations for chanceries, the State Department was the prime mover in the NCPC action. Spokespersons for the State Department said that it was searching for a workable plan that would allow the United States to meet its obligations to foreign countries.[9] The Foreign Missions Element set goals, objectives, criteria, and policies to facilitate the future location of chanceries and included a diagram indicating those areas in the District which, in the NCPC's opinion, were suitable for the location of chanceries. Significantly, the element recommended that chanceries be permitted in lower density residential areas along 16th Street and Massachusetts Avenue, Northwest, in spite of the proscription of new chanceries in such areas by the Chancery Act of 1964. It was suggested that the Zoning Commission implement regulations to make zoning requirements consistent with criteria and plan policies of the element.[10]

Upon adoption of the Foreign Missions Element, the Zoning Commission directed the MPO to prepare proposed regulations and maps implementing the NCPC's recommendations.[11] The Zoning Commission's initially proposed regulations provided for Diplomatic Overlay Districts ("D" Districts) to be superimposed on existing zoning districts. Chanceries were to be permitted as a matter of right in areas designated for chancery use by the Foreign Missions Element.

The overlay zones would permit chanceries in strictly residential areas (zoned R-1 through R-5-B), while keeping underlying zoning in "full force and effect."[12] But serious questions were immediately raised regarding the legality of the proposed amendments/regulations in light of the congressional mandate in the Chancery Act of 1964.[13]

The Zoning Commission soon announced that it had decided to redraft its regulations and to permit chanceries in lower density residential areas only by special exception approval by the BZA, rather than as of right. In May 1978, the Zoning Commission published its second proposal to amend the zoning regulations and map relating to the location of chanceries, incorporating these special exception provisions. However, there were still concerns about a conflict between the proposals and the Chancery Act. In a legal memorandum, the District of Columbia corporation counsel concluded that "although it cannot be gainsaid that the creation of certain of these new [diplomatic] zones would create an appreciable legal question as to inconsistency with the Chancery Act, it is my opinion that their establishment is, at the least, legally defensible."[14]

In September 1978 the Zoning Commission adopted amendments to the zoning regulations and map, creating a new zoning designation, the Mixed Use Diplomatic (D) District.[15] In any area where the (D) District is mapped, a chancery is a permitted use if approved by the BZA. Some of the areas included in the new overlay districts were zoned for commercial activity and others were in residential zones that had been off limits since 1964.[16] The apparent design and only effect of the (D) District as applied to lower density residential areas was to permit chanceries where they had been prohibited by statute.

Although the Zoning Commission was authorized to "execute all the powers and perform all the duties with respect to zoning in the District . . .," including the adoption and promulgation of regulations, it did not have the power to modify a statute of Congress by regulatory fiat.[17] By giving the BZA the power to approve new chanceries in residentially zoned areas on a case-by-case basis, the Zoning Commission rejected efforts by the State Department and the NCPC to give foreign governments a legal right to locate in residential zones. The BZA was required to rigorously review plans for any new chanceries in the designated areas, whereas the State Department, backed by the NCPC, wanted foreign governments to automatically have the right to locate in the affected areas.[18]

Residents in the affected areas of Northwest Washington were very upset over the action of the Zoning Commission and appealed to the District Council for assistance and relief. The opposition to more chanceries was strongest among the affluent residents of the Embassy Row area of Massachusetts Avenue; other affected areas included sections of 16th Street and New Hampshire Avenue, around Logan Circle, 13th Street, and Rhode Island Avenue. The residents wanted new chanceries confined largely to areas already zoned for commercial activity. They objected to the noise, traffic, and other disruptions that would result from additional chanceries on their tree-lined streets. Moreover, the diplomatic community's traditional disregard for parking and traffic regulations served only to compound the problem. In an editorial entitled "Where Should the Chanceries Go?" The *Washington Post* sided with the local residents by responding that chanceries and international offices were better suited to commercial areas.[19]

The Council Acts

Spurning advice from the corporation counsel, the city's chief legal officer, the District Council decided to consider legislation intended to bar new chanceries from residential neighborhoods.[20] Fully aware of the implications of its actions, Council Chairman Sterling Tucker predicted that consideration of the proposed bill would represent a showdown between the council and the NCPC, which, under the Home Rule Charter, serves as the guardian of federal interests in the city. The prime movers in the council action were council members Polly Shackleton (D-Ward 3) and David Clarke (D-Ward 1), whose wards included the affected areas, and Marion Barry (D-At Large).

As the council moved forward with its bill to bar any more chanceries from residential neighborhoods, the State Department, asserting White House support, carried out an intensive lobbying effort on Capitol Hill, especially with the leadership of the powerful House Foreign Affairs and the Senate Foreign Relations Committees. In a statement circulated on the Hill, the State Department declared that the council bill represented excessive "interference with the conduct of foreign relations."[21]

While Congress was supporting the position of the State Department, the District Council, led by Shackleton and Clarke, built its case around carrying out the will and intent of Congress as expressed in the 1964 Fulbright Act, which had banned additional chanceries from residential areas. They argued that chanceries belonged in office buildings outside of residential neighborhoods. The only problem was that Congress did not view the council's action as carrying out congressional will and intent. At a hearing before the council, the State Department described the local legislation as interference with the conduct of foreign affairs, stating that it would make it more difficult for the United States to obtain suitable chancery sites and concessions in foreign capitals.

By a unanimous vote on 9 October, the council passed the Location of Chanceries Amendment Act of 1979, which outlawed all new or expanded chanceries in residential neighborhoods zoned for low and moderate densities. The act was signed by Mayor Marion Barry on 9 November and transmitted to Congress on 19 November 1979. This action overturned the less restrictive chancery regulations that had been adopted by the NCPC and the Zoning Commission.

Congress Reacts

Even before the act was officially transmitted to Congress for the thirty-day review period, veto resolutions had been introduced in the House and Senate.[32] Leading the action in the House were Representatives Fortney H. (Pete) Stark (D-Calif.), an author of the city's Home Rule Charter, and Clement J. Zablocki (D-Wis.), Chairman of the Foreign Affairs Committee. They were joined by Representatives Dante Fascell (D-Fla.), William Broomfield (R-Mich.), and Millicent Fenwick (R-N.J.), all members of the Foreign Affairs Committee, and Representatives Jack Brooks (D-Texas), chairman of the Government Operations Committee, and Charles Wilson (D-Texas), chairman of the House District of Columbia Appropriations Subcommittee. Senator Frank Church (D-Idaho), chairman of the Foreign Relations Committee, introduced the veto resolution in the upper chamber, joined by Senators Claiborne Pell (D-R.I.), Jacob K. Javits (R-N.Y.), and Charles H. Percy (R-Ill.).[23]

The congressional challenge to the council action was not led by traditional critics of the District but by some of its best friends. Among them were Senators Thomas F. Eagleton (D-Mo.) and Charles McC. Mathias, Jr. (R-Md.) and three House members—Pete Stark, Millicent Fenwick, and Stewart B. McKinney (R-Conn.)—who in the past had pushed to expand rather than restrain home rule powers.[24]

The crux of the State Department's argument was that the District action would create reciprocal problems for United States embassies in foreign countries.[25] Probably its most serious charge was that the District government had become "increasingly unresponsive to the needs of the federal government." Representative Stark and other House members said that the District had exceeded its authority in overturning the action by the NCPC and the Zoning Commission, to the detriment of federal interests.[26]

City officials argued that the council had the power to enact local policies under which the Zoning Commission must operate.[27] Referring to the actions of the two commissions as "an end run around the act of Congress [Fulbright Act]," council member David A. Clarke (D-Ward 1) insisted that the council, far from ignoring the needs of the federal government in passing the challenged legislation, actually "was propping up a standard that Congress gave us." Apparently, Congress did not share this view. During a spirited exchange between the corporation counsel, Judith Rogers, and Representative Fenwick, a member of both the District and the Foreign Affairs Committees, the District action was termed "preposterous . . . nonsense . . . maddening . . . incredible . . . ridiculous."[28] In a subsequent controversy on the chancery issue, the city's position was laid bare when the chairman of the District of Columbia Zoning Commission, Walter B. Lewis, called attention to the fact that the real issue was the location of office buildings. He added, "It's a lousy precedent to suggest that a foreign country should be treated . . . different [from American citizens]. We are doing enough as it is."[29]

During the five years of home rule, a total of eight congressional attempts had been made to veto District legislation, but this was by far the most serious and, if approved, it would be the first to succeed.[30] Representative Ronald V. Dellums (D-Calif.), Chairman of the House District Committee, was known to be opposed to the precedent of Congress vetoing city legislation. At the committee stage, he proposed that the veto effort be dropped and that Congress consider its own legislation on the location of chanceries. When the resolution reached the House floor, much of the debate centered on whether, instead of a veto, Congress should allow the city's bill to become law and then pass its own measure later to reverse it and permit chanceries in the affected areas. Dellums, the leader of the effort to turn back the veto, argued that the matter could be resolved in a different way, without a veto. After stating that the District government thought it had a "prerogative" in the matter, and that jurisdiction was a "debatable question," he urged his colleagues to consider a different route by going back to the organic acts (the Fulbright Act and the Home Rule Charter) to eliminate any ambiguities regarding federal and local interests and prerogatives.[31]

The debate on the veto resolution became highly emotional at times, with angry charges being hurled about. The scene in the cloakroom of the House might have been from the early 1960s, as opposing factions on the upcoming vote traded charges of "racism," "plantation mentality," and worse. Speaker Thomas P. (Tip) O Neill, Jr., said he understood the problem but wondered, "How in the hell did this thing become a racial issue?" In spite of the opposition of the chairman, the District Committee voted eight to six to send the measure to the floor, with all five black members, along with Representative Romano L. Mazzoli (D-Ky.), voting against the resolution. In their support of the District government on this issue, the members of the Black Caucus unwittingly came down on the side of the city's conservative white establishment, which had fought home rule every step along the way. It was mainly this same conservative element that was behind the District government action to curb the influx of chanceries into their neighborhoods. With reference to the overall chancery issue, some local residents felt that the countries to whom the chanceries belonged—Western European as opposed to Third World nations—made a difference to the conservative white Republicans in the city.[32]

Acting at the request of the State Department and with newly announced support from the White House, the Senate Governmental Affairs Committee approved a resolution (as recommended by its Subcommittee on Governmental Efficiency and the District of Columbia) to overturn the council action. On 19 December 1979 the Senate, by a voice vote and without debate, approved a resolution to veto the action of the District of Columbia Council. On the next day, by the same method of vote, the House approved the resolution passed by the Senate.[33]

With this action Congress had written a controversial page in the five-year history of home rule in the nation's capital. The State Department had mounted a strong lobbying effort and in the head-on clash in Congress between foreign affairs and District self-government, international diplomacy won handily. Cases of conflict between federal and local interests are usually characterized by encumbering factors that tend to muddle the issues that are in conflict. In this case, however, the respective interests remained sufficiently discrete to generally support

Rowat's theory concerning the inevitable conflict between national and local interests in federal capital cities.

A Continuing Controversy

The controversy regarding chanceries did not end with the congressional veto of the District legislation in 1979. Still dissatisfied with the procedure and the decision-making process regarding the location of foreign missions, the State Department was back on Capitol Hill in 1981 appealing to Congress for assistance. During its consideration of the Foreign Missions Act of 1982, the House Committee on Foreign Affairs inserted language which would have dramatically altered the way decisions are made regarding the location of foreign missions in the District and would have greatly expanded the areas where they could locate. In less than two years, the District was again caught in an international diplomatic crossfire that local officials saw as a threat to the city's hard-won powers of self-government. Essentially, it was a continuation of the issues of 1979. Would new chanceries be allowed in residential neighborhoods and which jurisdiction—federal or District—would decide on chancery sites?

The State Department convinced the House Foreign Affairs Committee that the federal interest would be better served if the decisions concerning chancery sites were made by a federal body. Consequently, in a bill authorizing a variety of diplomatic functions, including establishment of a foreign missions office, a provision (Foreign Missions Act, section 206) was included that would strip the city government of any control over the location of foreign chanceries.[34] This power would be transferred from the city's two zoning bodies (the Zoning Commission and the Board of Zoning Adjustment) to the NCPC, a federal body with both District and federal representatives.[35]

State Department officials made a number of points in support of their case. First, they said that they did not know of any foreign nation that required the United States to deal with municipal rather than national authorities in locating United States embassy facilities abroad.[36] Not only did the city put needless procedural roadblocks in the way of chancery-seeking governments, it was generally not responsive enough to the need for locating chancery sites. Its procedures were described as "too complex, too restrictive, and too time-consuming." The State Department also charged that the city did not adequately consider national interests when acting on chancery applications.[37]

Representative Dellums, chairman of the House District Committee, concurred with city officials in viewing the move by the State Department as a serious challenge to home rule powers and was
prepared to put up a strong fight against it. Insisting that this was a
home rule matter in which the local residents had a legitimate concern,
Dellums persuaded House officials to let his panel review the proposal
of the Foreign Affairs Committee before the full House acted on it.[38] At
his urging, State Department and city officials began negotiations in an
attempt to reach a compromise solution that would avert a congressional confrontation between the two committees.[39]

There was intensive behind-the-scenes maneuvering on the
chancery issue and it did no harm to the city's cause that some of the
most affluent white residents in the District of Columbia lived in the
turn-of-the-century mansions where new chanceries would likely be
located. In something of a surprise move the NCPC, by a nine to one
vote, adopted a resolution opposing the State Department's plan. In
objecting to the proposed role of monitoring chancery sites, its resolution declared in part, "It has not yet been demonstrated . . . that there
is a problem" with the current system.[40] Any belief State Department
officials had that the NCPC, because of its predominantly federal
makeup, would give rubber-stamp approval to their plan was dashed
by the resolution and by a vote on a chancery application taken the
same day.[41]

The negotiations between the State Department and the District
government were not successful and the District Committee, which
voted against the proposal, was put on a collision course with the far
more influential Foreign Affairs Committee. In mid-1981, after fruitless
efforts to reach a compromise, the House voted to go along with the
proposal of the State Department and the Foreign Affairs Committee.

When this issue reached the Senate, Mayor Barry, buttressed by
support from Senator Charles McC. Mathias, Jr. (R-Md.), stiffened his
resistance to the proposal. At the Senate Foreign Relations Committee
hearing chaired by Senator Charles Percy (R-Ill.), he testified that no
need had been shown for such a move, which would erode the city's
home rule powers, and stated his opposition to further efforts to reach
a compromise with the State Department concerning the matter.

City officials soon found that the power move by the State Department was national in scope. The proposed Foreign Missions Act
would preempt local zoning and compliance powers not only in the
District but in hundreds of local jurisdictions across the country. Sec-

tion 206 would abrogate home rule authority with respect to zoning for chanceries by creating a special federal zoning commission. In addition, section 207 of the bill would allow the secretary of state to preempt state and local regulations relating to zoning and land use, health, welfare, local taxation, and so on in the 213 major American cities where consulates were located. To the District's advantage, its plight got caught up in the growing resistance in the Senate to sections 206 and 207 of the Foreign Missions Act.[42] While both the State Department and the District claimed that international precedents were on their side in this issue, the Senate came down solidly on the side of the city and provided documentation for its case.[43]

Senator Mathias, a member of both the Foreign Relations and Governmental Affairs Committees, became a formidable ally of the mayor in the fight against section 206, characterizing it as further erosion of the limited home rule in the District. He argued that the District had "performed admirably under its home rule powers in granting benefits to chanceries and embassies," and there was no reason to challenge the District in circumstances where the federal interest was already protected by representation on local boards. Mathias characterized section 207 as a serious invasion of local government that was both inappropriate and unnecessary to accomplish the purposes of the Foreign Missions Act, which he supported. A number of other senators sided with Mathias against the State Department and the House-endorsed bill, and soon three powerful organizations joined the fray on their side: the U.S. Conference of Mayors, the National League of Cities, and the District of Columbia Bar Association.[44] Mathias concluded his debate on the Senate floor by urging his colleagues to vote for his amendments to the Foreign Missions Act which would alter the effects of sections 206 and 207. The Mathias amendment was approved on 27 April 1982 in a close vote of forty-nine to forty-three, across party lines. The Senate then passed the amended bill by a voice vote.[45]

Section 206 of the bill containing the chancery provision was changed substantially on the Senate floor. With the House having passed the original version of the bill, the matter was sent to conference, where the section was retained in altered form, settling the issue in favor of the District. Although some policy changes regarding chanceries were retained in the conference measure, the District, through its two zoning bodies, remained involved in the process of location, replacement, or expansion of foreign missions in the nation's capital.[46]

SEXUAL ASSAULT REFORM ACT OF 1981

Moral issues can quickly arouse strong feelings and reactions from concerned individuals and groups. No conflict between Congress and the District government has been more highly charged, politically, than that over sexual assault reform. There were schisms at both the local and national levels over this issue. With the precedent of casting a formal veto already set by the location of chanceries case, there was no longer a "first time" factor to weigh in on either side of District efforts at sexual assault reform.

Background

When home rule became effective in 1975, Congress retained control of the District of Columbia Criminal Code, which was to be turned over to the District at a later date.[47] The transition process began in 1974, when Congress created the District of Columbia Law Revision Commission. That commission conducted extensive public hearings in 1977 and 1978 on the criminal laws of the District of Columbia and then recommended that the criminal laws in the District be reformed and updated to conform with trends in other jurisdictions. The commission called for a change in the sexual assault laws to enable prosecution of serious sexual abuses that were not covered by existing laws. On the basis of that recommendation, the District of Columbia Council conducted further public hearings in 1980 and 1981, resulting in the adoption of the Sexual Assault Reform Act, which generally followed the Model Penal Code and was consistent with the laws of some twenty-five other states.[48]

The chief architect of the District of Columbia Sexual Assault Reform Act of 1981 was council member David A. Clarke (D-Ward 1), whose purpose was to draft a bill that would revise the city's criminal code, which contained many archaic statutes that were rarely enforced. Among other provisions, the new bill broadened the definition of rape and repealed the criminal penalties for fornication, adultery, bestiality, and sodomy between consenting adults.[49] It included criminal penalties for sexual offenses not specifically covered under the existing law, for example, sexual abuse of persons institutionalized in hospitals, juvenile detention facilities, or foster homes. It would have allowed wives to press rape charges against their husbands and would have removed all references to the gender of the victim.[50] One of the highly controversial provisions of the bill reduced the maximum penalty for forcible rape from life in prison to twenty years.[51]

The bill as a whole was generally aimed at broadening criminal penalties for sexual assault and diminishing penalties for sex between consenting adults. This bill was considered a major victory for many women's groups and especially for the city's politically influential gay community.

In its original form, the bill contained a provision that would have effectively lowered the age of consent for sexual acts between children to twelve years, but this provision caught the attention of the media and caused such an uproar among religious and other local groups that the council quickly backpedaled and agreed to let the age of consent remain at sixteen.[52]

After a week of emotionally charged debate that involved council members and religious and community groups, the council unanimously passed the bill over the protests of angry ministers who mobbed the District Building. Much of the debate centered on the council's role in moral issues. The mayor signed the bill on 21 July 1981, and it was submitted to Congress on the same day.

Local Reaction

As is often the case, lobbying groups that lose at the District Building try to win on Capitol Hill what they have lost at the local level.[53] Efforts by a coalition of community and religious groups to persuade Congress to overturn the Sexual Assault Act began as soon as the bill was signed by the mayor. Included were the mostly black District of Columbia Federation of Civic Associations; its mostly white counterpart, the Federation of Citizens' Associations; the District of Columbia Baptist Ministers Conference; and the Committee of 100 Ministers.

The groups complained to Representative Philip Crane (R-Ill.), who knew little about the sexual assault reform bill at the time but quickly introduced a resolution to disapprove it.[54] He admitted, however, that with the exception of "a few obnoxious features" in the bill, it was a good piece of legislation. As a former teacher, he was especially concerned about the provision that would have removed criminal penalties for teachers who have sex with consenting students, sixteen years or older. Catholic Archbishop James A. Hickey also attacked the bill, asserting in an open letter that many sexual acts legalized by the measure are immoral and "the withdrawal of civil prohibitions and penalties does not make them morally permissible. . . . The fabric of society is weakened when basic values of family life and human sexuality are no longer protected by law."[55]

The broadside attack on the measure came from the Moral Majority, under the leadership of Reverend Jerry Falwell, which conducted a nationwide crusade against what it termed sexual immorality in the nation s capital. Falwell made no bones of the fact that he considered the overturning of the Sexual Assault Act a key vote in Congress and vowed to campaign against any congressman "who failed to see the light."[56]

Congressional Action

As in the normal course of review for District legislation, council acts submitted to Congress are referred to the respective authorizing committees: the House District of Columbia Committee and the Subcommittee on Governmental Efficiency and the District of Columbia of the Senate Governmental Affairs Committee. Both committees held hearings on the Sexual Assault Reform Act and heard testimony from many groups and individuals. The discussion at the House hearings contained few hints of the emotions evoked by the bill. Rather, the hearings focused narrowly on whether the council, by passing the measure, had exceeded its legal authority and whether there was an overriding federal interest in the legislation.

In considering resolutions of disapproval of District legislation, the House District Committee applied its standard criteria, posited in the form of three primary questions: (1) Has an action of the city exceeded the powers granted to it under the Home Rule Act? (2) Has the city clearly violated any constitutional principle? (3) Has the city interfered in a federal question or obstructed the federal interest? Based on the application of the criteria, Committee Chairman Ronald V. Dellums ruled out testimony on the substance of the sexual assault bill itself.[57] The final vote in the House Committee was eight to three in opposition to the veto resolution. The Senate subcommittee, chaired by Senator Charles McC. Mathias (R-Md.), conducted a hearing on the resolution but adjourned without taking a vote.

As the momentum against the Sexual Assault Act grew, the sponsors of the veto resolutions, Representative Philip Crane (R-Ill.) in the House and Senator Jeremiah Denton (R-Ala.) in the Senate, sought to develop a strategy that would accomplish their objective. They began to focus on a provision in the Home Rule Act which allows a single congressman to offer a privileged motion to discharge a committee of further consideration of a resolution disapproving the action of the District of Columbia Council.[58] A few days after the committee's vote, Crane made good on his promise to go directly to the House floor to discharge the District Committee and proceed with the vote to veto the District of Columbia act.[59]

In spite of the intense action in process on the Hill, the city did very little toward mounting a campaign in defense of the Sexual Assault Reform Act. Many city officials seemed resigned to the fact that Congress would do as it pleased anyway. The mayor's chief lobbyist made only a handful of phone calls to explain the measure, stating: "No matter what we did on the sex bill, we questioned whether we could prevail."[60] While many District of Columbia officials and citizens viewed the unprecedented veto of a predominantly local policy matter as a serious threat to home rule, Mayor Barry tried to put the matter in perspective by insisting that the conflict with Congress over the sexual reform act was merely an aberration and that the overall relations between the District and Congress were good.[61] In recent months, however, the city had suffered a series of defeats at the hands of Congress, including House action that effectively outlawed a police hiring plan ordered by the mayor, thwarted a city proposal to ship sludge to Pennsylvania, temporarily sidetracked the city's efforts to run a gambling lottery, and prohibited a boycott of any state that had not passed the Equal Rights Amendment.[62]

Contrary to the avowed bipartisan approach in Congress on District issues, reaction to the Sexual Assault Reform Act came to be viewed in distinctly partisan terms. House Speaker Thomas P. (Tip) O'Neill (D-Mass.), Majority Leader James C. Wright (D-Tex.), Ways and Means Committee Chairman Daniel Rostenkowski (D-Ill.), and other Democratic leaders became convinced that the Republicans were trying to trap them into an embarrassing vote in favor of sexual perversion.[63] It appeared that self-government was being relegated to a secondary position, behind the manipulation to make liberals on the Hill appear to support sexual depravity. Democratic principles aside, many of the moderate members of Congress were unwilling to take the political heat on the city's behalf in the face of intense lobbying by a powerful interest group on a controversial issue.[64]

Although a disapproval resolution was introduced in the Senate, action by only one house of Congress was needed to kill the bill. On 1 October 1981 a group of conservative congressmen forced floor votes on both the discharge motion and the resolution.[65] In spite of the fight against the resolution on the House floor led by District Committee Chairman Dellums, the veto resolution was discharged from the committee by a vote of 279 to 126 and approved by a similar majority vote of 281 to 119.[66] As members filed in for the roll-call vote, most had little trouble in making up their minds. It was a cheap vote that could be given up without affecting the home district and would eliminate the possibility that one would have to do a lot of explaining at the time of reelection. Representative Thomas Foley (D-Wash.), later to become Speaker of the House, probably represented many colleagues when he said his gut feeling was that he could not trust the city.[67] Although the principle of home rule was not the target, it got caught in the middle of heavy political crossfire and suffered serious damage. As summed up by one committee staff person: "They just wanted to get the Moral Majority off their backs. They didn't care one way or another about the District."[68]

Intractable Differences

To the very end there were intractable differences between the opponents and supporters of the measure on the proper interpretation of certain provisions of the bill and what they would mean in terms of legal versus illegal behavior. In reference to some of the controversial provisions, opponents of the measure used the term "legalize," while supporters preferred "decriminalize," which conveyed significantly different impressions to the public.[69]

The media literally had a field day covering the deliberations and activities on the sexual reform act at both the local and national levels, causing one council member to angrily denounce the media reports as misinterpreting the council's intention. Since few persons studied cr analyzed the actual bill, their knowledge of its contents came from media reports. For example, The *Washington Post* headline "D.C. Panel Backs Bill to Legalize Sex Between Consenting Children," which referred to a single section of the bill (that was later deleted), conjured up a frightful impression in the minds of many people concerning the entire measure.[70]

The Federal Interest

A total of ten resolutions of disapproval had been considered by Congress since home rule had been in effect. Of this number, only the resolution on the location of chanceries, characterized as a matter with "a clear and compelling federal interest," had been passed by Congress.[71] Although some members tried to make a case for the federal interest in the sexual reform act, the law was generally viewed by members of Congress and the media as having no apparent bearing on the federal interest. Hardly any issue is one hundred percent in the federal or local interest category, but the Sexual Assault Reform Act dealt primarily with local policy. Those members who sought to link the issue with the federal interest did so in broad and general terms, such as the presumed protection of thousands of visitors in the nation's capital who are subject to its laws. In his role as chief spokesman for the opposition to the disapproval resolution, Representative Dellums asked: "Has the District Council engaged in an act that thwarts the capacity of the U.S. Congress to represent the American people in carrying out its responsibilities?" His response to this rhetorical question was a resounding "no."[72]

A much larger number of congressmen simply relied on the Constitution and the Home Rule Charter, which give Congress the authority to monitor and approve or disapprove laws passed by the District Council. They took issue with complete reliance on the three criteria established by the House District Committee as a basis for a congressional veto and they pointed to the provision in the charter that gives Congress the authority to act as a legislature for the District "on any subject, whether within or out of the scope of legislative powers granted to the Council by this Act."[73]

The defeat of the Sexual Assault Reform Act, a bill which originated from a request of two congressional subcommittees, left the city with a patchwork of antiquated sex laws, including statutes dating back to 1901, banning fornication, adultery, and sodomy between consenting adults.[74] Some thirteen years have elapsed since this action took place in 1981 and there has been no comprehensive statute overhauling the sexual assault laws of the city.[75] Changing the sodomy law continued to be one of the more sensitive political issues in the city, pitting gay rights leaders against highly influential ministers. Legislation to repeal the ban on sodomy between consenting adults was in the council's Judiciary Committee for years. In something of a surprise move, in late 1992, the council did vote on a change of the sodomy law, but it lost on a split vote of five to five.[76]

In the spring of 1993 the council again repealed the city's forty-five-year-old sodomy statute and sent the measure to Capitol Hill with some doubts that its action would survive the requisite sixty-day review by Congress. Although there was some critical response and action by local opponents, neither the House nor the Senate interfered with the council's repeal this time and it became effective law at the expiration of the review period in September 1993. It happened that this action came during the national controversy stemming from the move by President Bill Clinton to lift the ban against homosexuals in the military and may have profited from the atmosphere created by this larger national issue.[77]

The original congressional idea behind the Home Rule Charter was to allow the local government to act on purely local matters. The legitimate issue regarding congressional oversight was whether or not the city's enactment raised a federal issue or obstructed the federal interest. The Sexual Assault Reform Act may not have been a model piece of legislation, but it dealt with a policy area over which the city had a legitimate claim. In principle both liberals and conservatives subscribe to the view that the state should not intrude into the private lives of consenting adults. These may be valid principles in the majority of the states but here they could not prevail because politics rose above them in a unique fashion, peculiar to the status of the federal district.[78]

Powerful political and extraneous factors played a dominant role in the congressional decision to overturn the city's action. Although a local policy was overturned in this instance, this was not a bona fide case of conflict between federal and local interests and does not provide support for the Rowat thesis. The federal interest was so nebulous in this case that few members even tried to make the connection. With a powerful interest group such as the Moral Majority involved, most of the lawmakers apparently felt that it was not the time to take a stand for democratic principles in defense of a powerless unit. This case highlights some of the factors and conflicts, registered in the name of the national interest, that operate to defeat the democratic principle in the nation's capital.

SCHEDULE OF HEIGHTS AMENDMENT ACT OF 1990

Probably the best case for a congressional veto, from the standpoint of federal versus local interests, can be made in the conflict over height limitations. At least a clearly perceived national interest was at stake. This happens to be one policy area where the District has voluntarily conceded the primacy of the federal interest.[79]

Background

There were important points of difference in the congressional handling of the Schedule of Heights Amendment Act of 1990 and the two previous District of Columbia acts vetoed by Congress. First, consideration of the veto resolution on building height limitations centered mainly on the legal interpretation of the controlling statute, the Height of Buildings Act of 1910, rather than on political or other factors. Second, the final action taken by Congress followed the recommendations of the congressional authorizing committees (House District of Columbia and Senate Governmental Affairs). And third, the issue at hand was well within the purview of the federal interest.

Building height regulations are rooted in the advances of late nineteenth century commerce and technology. Demands for concentrated business space in city centers pushed building heights upward and drove the advances in building technology which ultimately made the skyscraper possible. By the turn of the century several American cities, including Boston, Chicago, and St. Louis, had adopted regulations limiting the height of building construction.[80] The primary purpose of these earliest regulations was to preserve surrounding light and air and to prevent construction beyond the limit of fire-fighting capability, thereby protecting property values and public safety and welfare. Fashioning laws and regulations to effect these goals was not such a simple proposition and, as experience showed in the nation's capital, a period of trial and error was required.[81]

Established in 1800, Washington is a relatively young city, but building height is one of the most sensitive topics associated with the historic environment in the nation's capital. Press accounts of the earliest limitations, which date from 1894, confirm the considerations of fire safety, light and air, and property values, but also reflect the aesthetic concern that would soon become the driving force behind Washington's height limitations.[82] The ideal of a lower skyline that protects the symbolic primacy of the national monuments and structures has since become the strongest influence on the shape and character of the capital city and one of its most valuable legacies.[83]

Height of Buildings Act of 1910

Although there was previous legislation in 1894 and 1899, the Height of Buildings Act of 1910 established the basic height restrictions gov-

erning all private construction in the city.[84] Throughout the years the
basic principle has remained unchanged—limiting building height to
protect the city's open and expansive quality, promote a harmonious
urban composition, and preserve the primacy of government buildings.[85] During the 1990 congressional debate on height limitations, the
city's design—especially the mall and surrounding landmarks—was
described as conveying not only a sense of beauty, calm, and strength
but also "promise and freedom."[86]

The 1910 act regulates the heights of buildings on business as
well as residential streets, based essentially on the width of the street
on which the building fronts. On business streets, the maximum
height is the width of the street plus 20 feet, not to exceed 130 feet.[87]
On residential streets, heights may not exceed the width of the street
less 10 feet or 90, whichever is less.[88] After establishing the general
regulations, the 1910 act recognized the need for Congress to be particularly mindful of regulating height and setback and certain aspects
of the design of buildings fronting on federally regulated sections of
the District. This authority was delegated to the District's three-member Board of Commissioners.

> On blocks immediately adjacent to public buildings or to the side
> of any public building . . . the maximum height shall be regulated
> by a schedule adopted by the Commissioners of the District of
> Columbia.[89]

This provision was implemented by the commissioners over a
period of time, and the authority for administering it passed to the District Council under the Home Rule Act of 1973. Under the Schedule of
Heights provision of the 1910 act, the commissioners exercised their
authority to set forth specific restrictions on the height of buildings adjacent to certain public buildings in fifteen different areas of the District.[90] Most of these limits apply to the blocks around the White House,
the Supreme Court Building, and the House and Senate Office Buildings. The limits set under the schedule are lower than would otherwise
be permitted under the Heights of Buildings Act. These height limits
for city blocks adjacent to public buildings are not contained in the
1910 act.[91] The primary issue in this conflict between the District and
the federal governments centered on the official terms and circumstances under which the city could regulate building height through
the Schedule of Heights.

Economics: A Living Downtown

The centerpiece of Mayor Marion Barry's administration was economic development, focusing on downtown revitalization. Working closely with the business community, the mayor was committed to bringing new life to the downtown area. In accordance with this objective, the council concluded that making an exception in the height limitation for the Market Square North project would have "a positive fiscal impact on the District of Columbia."[92]

Market Square North was to be located on the east side of 9th Street, between D and E Streets, Northwest, facing the FBI Building across the street. The District government agencies worked closely with the developers of Market Square North to formulate an agreement requiring certain development conditions that promised significant public benefits. Market Square North was presented as a unique development project, consisting of residential, office, retail, and arts space. In making an exception in the allowable height for the project, the council cited three points of justification including support from the Pennsylvania Avenue Development Corporation:[93]

1. Market Square North is sponsored and approved by a federal agency—the Pennsylvania Avenue Development Corporation.
2. There are special site and design circumstances resulting from the relationship of Market Square North to the 160-foot-high FBI Building.
3. The project included major residential development and other neighborhood serving uses that are essential to the Comprehensive Plan policy for a "living Downtown."

In spite of its interest in economic development, the council made it very clear that any proposal for an amendment to the Schedule of Heights should be reviewed very carefully from both planning and design perspectives to ensure that the basic purpose of the height act—preserving the horizontality of the Washington skyline—would not be undermined.

The Legal Context of City Action

Mayor Barry requested the Council of the District of Columbia to amend the Schedule of Heights to allow the Market Square North complex on square 407 to have a height of 130 feet.[94] The C-4 (central business) zoning designation for square 407 would otherwise limit the height of the proposed building to 110 feet, or about eleven stories. Square 407 is within the Pennsylvania Avenue area that was being planned and developed under the auspices of the Pennsylvania Avenue Development Corporation (PADC). The overall development was consistent with the Downtown Element of the Comprehensive Plan.[95]

The Council of the District of Columbia has had authority over the Schedule of Heights since 1975 through a transfer of the authority of the Board of Commissioners to the presidentially appointed District of Columbia Council in 1967 (Reorganization Plan Number 3) and by transfer of the pre-home rule authority of the appointed council to the present Council of the District of Columbia.[96]

At the public hearings conducted by the council on the bill to amend the Schedule of Heights, witnesses representing a number of well-known agencies and organizations presented testimony. The number of groups testifying in support of Bill 8-616 was about the same as the number in opposition.[97] From the vantage point of the city, it was significant that the project was being planned and developed under the auspices of a federal agency, the PADC, which the city said had requested the proposed legislation. The PADC support was included in the official statement of purpose for Bill 8-616, prepared by Council Chairman David A. Clarke, its chief sponsor. Another federal agency, the National Capital Planning Commission (NCPC), the official watchdog of the federal interest, took a strong position against the measure on the grounds that the council did not have authority to amend the Schedule of Heights as proposed in Bill 8-616. According to the NCPC, Congress alone had the authority to grant relief from the 1910 height act restrictions, not the local council.

It was generally agreed by all of the parties at both the local and national levels that the council had the authority to amend the Schedule of Heights. The question was whether it could amend the Schedule as proposed in the pending bill, that is, in a way that exceeded the limitations in the 1910 act that might otherwise appear to be applicable. The street "width plus twenty rule" was a case in point. Placing the weight of their argument on the provision of the 1910 act (District of Columbia Code, sec. 5-405) that made an exception for "blocks immediately adjacent to public buildings," the council's own general counsel and the District of Columbia corporation counsel gave a positive response to the above question.

Much of the city's case centered on the FBI Building, adjacent to the proposed project and standing 160 feet high.[98] The blocks adjacent to the FBI Building were not included in the Schedule of Heights, but this omission, according to the city, was simply a matter of timing. The fifteen sections of the schedule had been adopted by the Board of Commissioners at various times in the early 1900s and related to public buildings existing or planned at those times. The FBI Building was not completed until 1975, which was after the authority to adopt sections of the Schedule of Heights had passed to the home rule District Council. The council had the authority to amend the schedule, either by changing one of the fifteen existing sections or by adding a new section to deal with a new site, as was proposed in Bill 8-616.[99]

Relying on what it interpreted as the legislative intent and history of the 1910 act, one of the council's stated objectives in adding the respective section to the Schedule of Heights was to achieve harmony between the FBI Building and the property around it. Allowing the project facing the 160-foot-high FBI Building to rise to a height of 130 feet would help establish a more "harmonious relationship" between the buildings in that section and serve as a transitional height to the 110-foot-high buildings to the east of Market Square North. A further point in the city's case was that the provision authorizing the establishment of the Schedule of Heights was not subordinated to the authority contained in other sections of the 1910 act.

Conflicting Interests

Contrary to the situation with the Sexual Assault Reform Act, it was generally agreed at both the national and local levels that the height limitation issue was well within the federal interest. And though the Home Rule Act could have been clearer with regard to the Schedule of Heights and its inclusion in the 1910 act, there was little doubt that the intent of the act was to limit the authority of the council to legislate on height limitations.

In addition to its legal argument, the NCPC attempted to apply general logic in dealing with what it viewed as a conflict of federal and local interests. It pointed out that in providing for a separate schedule of heights on blocks immediately adjacent to or on the side of public buildings, Congress clearly intended to protect public properties above and beyond the general provisions of the Height of Buildings Act that would otherwise apply. With that being the case, even if the council had uncircumscribed authority to amend the schedule, it would be incumbent upon it to prove that a proposed amendment served a purpose to protect the federal property. Although it was assumed that the powers of the current council and those of the Board of Commissioners, who were given the original authority under the· Height of Buildings Act, are equivalent and interchangeable in function and authority, the NCPC argued that this assumption "must be tempered with logic."

Since the original commissioners were clearly a federal body, "appointed by the President and confirmed by the Senate," Congress had entrusted them with federal interests to be served by a schedule of heights. Whereas the goal of local self-government was generally served by the transfer of the original authority of the commissioners to the locally elected council, protection of federal buildings by restricting the height of adjacent private development might actually thwart local interests. Under such circumstances, the authority of the council must be carefully scrutinized for potential conflict between federal and local interests.[100]

Council Approval/Opposition

Based largely upon the legal advice that it received from its general counsel, the corporation counsel, the PADC, and other bodies, the council proceeded to enact Bill 8-616, the Schedule of Heights Amendment Act of 1990. It amended the Schedule of Heights by adding the following new paragraph 16 at the end:

> On the east side of Ninth Street, NW between D and E Streets, adjacent to the Federal Bureau of Investigation Building, no building shall be . . . higher than a horizontal line 130 feet above the top of the curb at the southwest corner of eighth and E Streets, ...[102]

This action was not unanimous in that four of the thirteen council members spoke and voted against it. Led by council member William P. Lightfoot (I-At Large), they argued that the amendment violated the height limitation and the horizontal character of the city. Since this would be the first time that the council had amended the Schedule of Heights to exceed the limitations in the 1910 act, the opposing members were concerned about setting a bad precedent, a fear later concurred in by members of Congress.[103] It would open the door to other buildings to exceed the height limitations. And besides, they wondered, why take such a risk for what they viewed as a small return?[104]

The Schedule of Heights Amendment Act of 1990 was approved by the council on 18 December, signed by Mayor Barry on 27 December 1990, and officially transmitted to Congress on 15 January 1991.

Congressional Action

With a constant stream of legislation being submitted by the District Council, it is not clear as to who sounded the alarm to Congress that the measure on building height limitation should be examined seriously. Certainly the preservationist groups, having lost at city hall, were not about to let this measure slide routinely through Congress.[105] Representatives Dana Rohrabacher (R-Calif.) and Larry Combest (R-Texas) introduced separate disapproval resolutions in the House and Senator Carl M. Levin (D-Mich.) introduced a disapproval resolution in the upper chamber.[106]

While the District Council interpreted its authority under the 1910 act as being the same as that of the Board of Commissioners, who had been delegated explicit authority to adopt a schedule of heights, Congress viewed the council's authority with regard to the 1910 act as having been circumscribed by the Home Rule Act. The council was prohibited from enacting any act which permitted the building of a structure that exceeded the height limitations in the 1910 act or the limitations in effect when the Home Rule Act was signed on 24 December 1973, including the Schedule of Heights as it existed at that time.[107] In other words, the council is not prohibited from amending the Schedule of Heights as long as the amendments do not allow any increase beyond the overall height limits set forth by the Height of Buildings Act of 1910, as amended. Also, the council's authority to amend the Schedule of Heights is subject to the other limitations of the Height of Buildings Act. In effect, this meant that both the Height of Buildings Act and the Home Rule Act prohibited the council from amending the Schedule of Heights as proposed in the pending act. Only Congress could grant relief from the 1910 act.

The congressional position on the pending disapproval resolution was heavily influenced by the legal counsel and policy arguments Congress received from a number of federal and private agencies, who shared the view that the legal interpretation of the Height of Buildings Act of 1910 upon which the council based its action was incorrect. The federal agencies included the General Accounting Office, the NCPC, the Department of Justice (Environment and Natural Resources Division), the Congressional Research Service, the Commission on Fine Arts, the Smithsonian Institution, and others.

It fell to the lot of Representative Ronald V. Dellums (D-Calif.), Chairman of the District Committee, to bring the resolution of disapproval to the floor of the House. Reaffirming his staunch commitment to home rule, Dellums declared that he had argued against every single resolution of disapproval of District of Columbia action that had come before the House and had never before voted in support of one. But if the District had violated the Height of Buildings Act of 1910, which was the position being taken by the District Committee, it had also violated the Home Rule Act. When the District Committee applied its three criteria for the consideration of a disapproval resolution, it found that two of the criteria had been met: violation of the Home Rule Act and violation of the federal interest. (The violation of the Constitution was not charged.)

After alluding to the need of the city to generate additional revenue and find increased housing for its residents, the House placed a strong disclaimer on any attempt to pass judgment on local land use policy or the merits of the Market Square North project.[108]

> Neither urban design nor land use issues are being considered here today. Only the legal authority of the D.C. Council with regard to the 1910 Height of Buildings Act is being decided.[109]

For the first time in the history of the current home rule era, Congress was at peace with itself on the veto of a District of Columbia act. The disapproval resolution had the unprecedented backing of both the chairman and the ranking Republican of the House District of Columbia Committee, Representative Thomas Bliley of Virginia. On the day following action by the Senate on a voice vote (5 March 1991), the House took Senate Joint Resolution 84 from the Speaker's table and approved it by the same method.[110]

District officials put forth very little effort to preserve the height exemption that had been granted to the Market Square North complex. Between the time of council approval of the Schedule of Heights Amendment Act in late 1990 and its subsequent disapproval by the Congress in early 1991, the officers of mayor, council chairman, and delegate to Congress had changed. The new officials kept their distance from this ill-fated amendment and simply expressed regret that a matter left over from the previous administration required a disapproval resolution.[111]

The issue of height limitations as defined in the relevant statutory law is well within the parameters of the federal interest. The council enactment and subsequent congressional disapproval of the Schedule of Heights Amendment Act was primarily a legal conflict, unencumbered by weighty political and extraneous factors. When the resolution of a legal question turns on a statute and the intention of the framing body, the first step is to study the language and then proceed to the legislative history if the language is unclear. Unfortunately, this was a case of first impressions with respect to interpretation of this statute. As such, there were no court decisions or administrative adjudications to serve as guidance and by which to resolve the issue definitively. When both the language and legislative histories were analyzed, the conclusion drawn by Congress, which has the last word, was that the District had overstepped its authority.

Although the District was generally viewed by federal officials as acting in good faith, it is unlikely that the ensuing rift between the two jurisdictions over height limitations would have become an issue except for the District's interest in economic development. Both local and national governments expressed fundamental concern about maintaining the city's unique design, but the federal position was unadulterated by the economic development motive. With the PADC on one side and the NCPC on the other, there was strong federal representation on both sides of this issue during the initial stages, but the case presented substantial differences in the interests that were in conflict.

The three cases discussed in this chapter present mixed signals concerning the Rowat thesis. The two cases involving land use tend to support the thesis, while the sexual assault measure does not. All three of the cases represented major conflicts of interests but the case on building height limitations was probably the clearest example of a conflict between genuine national and local interests, followed by the case on location of chanceries. A federal law to govern height limitations was on the books but the top legal experts at the national and local levels differed on how it should be interpreted. This case was unencumbered by other weighty forces.

The federal interest is so predominant in an area such as foreign missions that the city was at a serious disadvantage in trying to make its case. With the State Department as a prime mover in the chanceries controversy, the reaction at the national level reflected arrogance that the city would dare get in the way. The sexual assault reform legislation was not a legitimate federal interest and other forces were busy at work to dictate its outcome.

N O T E S

1. Information secured from the Legislative Services Unit of the District of Columbia Council which maintains an official record of all bills introduced in and the action taken on them by the council.

2. *Washington Post*, 22 February 1978, A-20. As of June 1993, the District of Columbia was home to 21,832 foreign government employees (including diplomats, staff, servants, and dependents), 163 foreign embassies, including one for the European Community (EC), and 27 foreign organizations. Lawrence Dunham, Office of Protocol, United States Department of State, telephone conversation with the author, 24 June 1993.

3. Offenses committed by members of the diplomatic community who are immune from local criminal laws are a recurring problem in the city.

4. A chancery is the site and any building(s) therein containing offices of a foreign mission and used for diplomatic, legation, or consular functions. The term includes a chancery-annex or the business offices of those attaches of a foreign government who are under the personal direction and superintendence of the chief of the mission and who are engaged in diplomatic activities recognized as such by the Department of State of the United States Government. The term does not include the business offices of nondiplomatic missions of foreign governments, such as purchasing, financial, education, or other missions of a comparable nondiplomatic nature. Embassies, as the official residences of ambassadors, are located among other residences and utilize the amenities of local neighborhoods. District of Columbia Zoning Commission, *Zoning Text Amendment for Chanceries and International Agencies*, case no. 77-45, 14 September 1978.

5. Memorandum of law from Wilkes & Artis, attorneys at law, to the Department of State regarding: Zoning Commission cases no. 77-45 and no. 77-46, *Text and Mapping Amendments to Zoning Regulations for Chanceries and International Agencies*, 16 January 1978.

6. The BZA consist of five members, including one alternate. Three members are mayoral appointees, one is a member of the National Capital Planning Commission, and one, the alternate, is a member of the Zoning Commission.

7. This act was sponsored by Senator J. William Fulbright (D-Ark.), who served as chairman of the Senate Foreign Relations Committee from 1959 to 1974. Medium-high and high density residential zones included R-5-C and R-5-D, W, C-R, and S-P districts, where chanceries were permitted by special exception from the BZA. Memorandum from Wilkes & Artis to the Department of State.

8. The NCPC, on 6 October 1977 formally adopted the Foreign Missions and International Agencies Element and Related Modifications to Other Elements of the Comprehensive Plan for the National Capital. Memorandum of law from Wilkes & Artis to the Department of State.

9. *Washington Post,* 1 August 1978, B-2.

10. D.C. Code, sec. 5-414, states, inter alia, that "zoning maps and regulations, and amendments thereto, shall not be inconsistent with the comprehensive plan for the National Capital."

11. Sponsored by the Zoning Commission, those proposed amendments to the zoning regulations and map were docketed as Zoning Commission cases no. 77-45 and no. 77-46.

12. R-1 through R-5-B zones are residential zones that are not medium-high or high density. Zoning Commission cases no. 77-45 and no. 77-46.

13. The Zoning Commission received letters from Senators J. William Fulbright (D-Ark.), author of the Chancery Act of 1964, and Thomas J. McIntyre (D-N.H.), conference chairman on the Chancery Act, both of whom advised the commission that the proposal to alter the zoning regulations applicable to residential areas was inconsistent with the Chancery Act of 1964 and would create confusion and instability in the areas concerned.

14. Memorandum from Louis P. Robbins, Acting District of Columbia Corporation Counsel, to Steven E. Sher, Executive Director, Zoning Secretariat, 7 July 1978.

15. District of Columbia Zoning Commission case no. 77-45, sec. 4602.

16. These areas included such lower density residence zones along Massachusetts Avenue, Northwest, from Dupont Circle to Observatory Circle and 16th Street, Northwest, north to Park Road. Zoning Commission case no. 77-46, Zoning Atlas Index Map; *Washington Post,* 14 July 1978, A-8.

17. The Zoning Commission vote (four to zero) was subject to concurrence by the NCPC, but in light of the fact that the impetus for this action originated with the NCPC, it was not likely that it would vote against it. Ibid., 14 July 1978, A-8.

18. Part of the argument was over what constituted a residential zone. The protesting homeowners contended that residential zones were all areas zoned by the city for residential purposes. Many embassy offices were already clustered in these specified areas prior to 1964, when the Chancery Act was passed. The NCPC contended that areas such as Embassy Row and 16th Street (above Scott Circle) were more "mixed" than "residential," and that it made sense to locate chanceries there. Ibid., 15 September 1978, C-1.

19. Ibid., 22 February 1978, A-20.

20. The top legal officer of the council disagreed with the ruling of the corporation counsel and concluded that the council had the authority to act, stating, ". . . I do not agree that all zoning matters involving chanceries directly are out of bounds to the Council, simply because chanceries are involved." Memorandum from James M. Christian, General Counsel, Council of the District of Columbia, to Chairwoman Willie J. Hardy, Committee on Housing and Economic Development, 17 September 1979.

21. *Washington Post,* 15 December 1979, B-1.

22. Congress has thirty legislative days to review and/or take action on acts passed by the District government. Resolutions to veto the Chancery Act were introduced in both houses on 14 December 1979. Ibid., 15 December 1979, B-1.

23. S. Con. R. 63 and H. Con. R. 228 were introduced in the Senate on 19 December 1979 and in the House on 20 December 1979, respectively, *To Disapprove the Location of Chanceries Amendment Act of 1979 Passed by the City Council of the District of Columbia.* House, 96th Cong., 1st sess., 1979, H. Rept. 728; Senate, 96th Cong., 1st sess., 1979, S. Rept. 533.

24. *Washington Post,* 20 December 1979, B-1.

25. At the time that the veto resolution was being considered, American hostages were being held by Iran at the United States Embassy in Tehran. The State Department cited this situation to demonstrate the need for cooperation from foreign governments. Ibid., 20 December 1979, B-1.

26. Ibid.

27. Memorandum from James M. Christian to Chairwoman Willie J. Hardy; memorandum from Louis P. Robbins, to Steven E. Sher.

28. *Washington Post,* 20 December 1979, B-1.

29. Ibid., 9 June 1981, C-3.

30. *Congressional Quarterly Almanac* 35 (1979): 550.

31. In an effort to stave off this unprecedented veto, Representative Dellums and Delegate Walter Fauntroy (D-D.C.) sought more time to work out a compromise and made an extraordinary but unsuccessful trip to the District Building to try and persuade the District Council to delay the effective date of its bill. In rejecting this appeal, one council member asked, "What are we going to do? Every time we pass something (Congress doesn't like)[*sic*], are we going to pull it back and veto it?" *Washington Post,* 21 December 1979, B-1.

32. The chanceries were being located mainly in the affluent white neighborhoods of the city. Ibid., 23 December 1979, B-1.

33. Ibid., 21 December 1979, B-1; *Congressional Quarterly Almanac* 35 (1979): 198H.

34. These changes were contained in S. 854, *The Foreign Missions Act of 1982,* which would repeal the 1964 Fulbright Act that limited chanceries to high-density residential and commercial zones in the city. *Washington Post,* 19 June 1981, B-2; *Congressional Record,* 97th Cong., 2d sess., 15 April 1982, 6907.

35. Federal representatives, including two from Congress, have eight of the NCPC's twelve votes.

36. This point was more or less refuted during floor debate when this conflict reached the Senate. See p. 111 n. 43.

37. Mayor Barry testified that city zoning officials had denied only two of fifteen chancery applications—from Iran, prior to the hostage crisis of 1979 to 1981, and one from Bangladesh. Opposed by neighbors complaining that their neighborhood was already overburdened by chancery traffic and parking problems, Bangladesh was refused permission to occupy a three-story former residence on Massachusetts Avenue. *Washington Post,* 9 June 1981, C-3.

In 1978 Iran applied for the re-zoning of a property adjacent to their chancery to allow for building an annex to their existing chancery. Iran wished to change the zoning designation from residential to diplomatic. Iran's representative to the proceedings claimed that Iran's chancery functions had increased beyond the level foreseen when built in 1960. Subsequent to the filing of the application, Iran's government changed and the future uses of the chancery fell into question. In September 1979 the District of Columbia Zoning Commission unanimously voted to deny Iran's chancery annex application, stating that Iran had neither proven it needed the extra space nor justified the annex's potential encroachment into a residential area. District of Columbia Zoning Commission order no. 294, case no. 78-29, 13 September 1979.

38. Because of its direct relationship to the District of Columbia and its government, the District Committee requested and was provided sequential referral of the bill. House, *Activities and Summary Report of the Committee on the District of Columbia for the 97th Congress*, 97th Cong., 2d sess., H. Rept. 999, 22.

39. Under a compromise proposal being considered, the State Department made concessions on the transfer of all zoning power to the NCPC. The District of Columbia Board of Zoning Adjustment would be required to pay greater attention to the "federal interest" in finding sites for chanceries. If the BZA turned down a foreign government's application for a chancery site, the denial could be appealed to a new seven-member panel, made up of five members of the Zoning Commission plus two federal government representatives. *Washington Post*, 11 June 1981, A-18.

40. Ibid., 13 June 1981, A-21.

41. The NCPC gave advisory opinions on chancery sites but it refused to endorse an application/proposal by the Philippine government, pending before the District of Columbia BZA, to build a new chancery at the corner of 17th Street and Massachusetts Avenue, Northwest, due to an inadequate number of off-street parking spaces. Ibid.

42. During floor debate in the upper chamber, Senator Thomas Eagleton (D-Mo.) reported that seven members of the Foreign Relations Committee and five members of the Governmental Affairs Committee concluded that the case for removing the city from the chancery zoning process was not convincing. *Congressional Record*, 97th Cong., 2d sess., 15 April 1982, 128, pt. 6: 6920-21.

43. A survey conducted by the Congressional Research Service of the Library of Congress revealed that in twenty-five overseas capitals, local zoning procedures were adhered to in all but the totalitarian nations. Ibid., 6921.

44. Other members of the upper chamber who sided with Mathias against sections 206 and 207 of S. 854 included Senators Thomas Eagleton (D-Mo.), Warren Rudman (R-N.H.), Carl M. Levin (D-Mich.), James Sasser (D-Tenn.), and others. *Congressional Record*, 97th Cong., 1st sess., 15 April 1982, 6908.

45. The Mathias amendment reversed the effect of Section 207 by reaffirming the authority of state and local jurisdictions regarding zoning, land use, health, or welfare except where there has been a denial to a foreign mission by the Secretary of State. Public Law 97-241; 96 *Statutes at Large* 288.

46. House, *Activities and Summary Report of the Committee on the District of Columbia*, 22.

47. When Congress passed the Home Rule Act in 1973, it withheld from the local government the transfer of authority over its criminal laws. That authority was transferred to the city in 1979, enabling the District government to enact new criminal laws. *Congressional Record,* 97th Cong., 1st sess., 1 October 1981, 127, pt. 18: 22750.

48. Ibid.

49. *Washington Post,* 25 June 1981, A-1.

50. Although not a part of the explicit statutory requirements, a husband cannot be charged with a rape of his wife by operation of a common law tradition known as spousal immunity. District Council, Committee on the Judiciary, Report on Bill 4-122, *District of Columbia Sexual Assault Reform Act of 1981,* 4.

The existing law presumed that women would be the victims of all sexual assaults. *Washington Post,* 15 July 1981, B-1.

51. In testimony before the District Council, women's rights organizations proclaimed that a sentence of life imprisonment for rape dissuaded most people from convicting a person for rape. *Congressional Record,* 97th Cong., 1st sess., 1981, 22770.

52. In 1981 sex between consenting teenagers was permitted in twenty-six states unless there was a significant age difference. Statistics compiled by the National Legal Resource Center for Child Advocacy and Protection, American Bar Association, Washington, D.C. This provision brought opposition from the mayor and council chairman and outrage from local groups. *Washington Post,* 26 June 1981, B-1.

53. In taking the matter to the Hill, the ministers' group was calling on Congress to play the "overlordship" role that is so vehemently opposed by most District officials. The ministers, led by the Reverend John D. Bussey, pastor of the Bethesda Baptist Church in Northeast Washington, said they saw nothing wrong with taking their complaints to Congress: "Going to Congress is a part of home rule, and we hope it stays that way." Ibid., 26 October 1981, A-1.

54. Ibid.

55. Letter from James A. Hickey, Archbishop of Washington, in the *Catholic Standard,* 16 July 1981, 3.

56. Spearheading opposition to the effort to veto the legislation was a newly formed coalition, Citizens for Home Rule, composed of leaders of civil rights, religious, and citizen groups. This group sought to enlist support from conservative as well as liberal organizations, but was no match for the efforts and momentum on the other side. *Washington Post,* 26 October 1981, A-1.

57. Two opponents of the Sexual Assault Reform Act, Representatives Thomas J. Bliley (R-Va.) and Romano L. Mazzoli (D-Ky.), took issue on the proper interpretation of the committee's criteria. They contended that the thousands of visitors to the nation's capital constituted a strong federal interest in the legislation. Ibid., 25 September 1981, B-1.

58. Under the Home Rule Charter, an individual member may make a motion to discharge the District Committee from further consideration of a disapproval resolution dealing with an act of the District Council; and a majority is all that is needed to sustain this action. With other standing committees, a petition signed by 218 members is necessary to discharge a committee. Public

Law 93-198, Sec. 604; *Congressional Record*, 97th Cong., 1st sess., 1 October 1981, 22768.

59. In the floor debate, Delegate Walter E. Fauntroy (D-D.C.) brought out the point that the House was being asked to discharge a committee from a responsibility which it had already carried out and that this action with regard to House Resolution 208 would dismiss the proper and careful considerations that the committee had given to the subject matter. *Congressional Record*, 97th Cong., 1st sess., 1 October 1981, 22758-59.

60. The mayor did not try to buttonhole any members of Congress and said that the city did not have the resources to mount a campaign against the activities of the Moral Majority. *Washington Post*, 26 October 1981, A-1.

61. Ibid., 25 October 1981, A-1.

62. All of these defeats were executed through the congressional appropriations process. Ibid.

63. The sexual assault reform measure drew strong opposition from congressmen, even though many of its provisions were identical to—and in some cases less liberal than—those in their home states. Ibid., 2 October 1981, A-1.

64. Ibid., 15 October 1981, A-1.

65. The outcome of the 1 October 1981 vote was loudly cheered by the Moral Majority, which had sent out more than 800,000 mailing alerts all over the country and vowed to inform constituents on how their representatives voted on the resolution. Ibid., 2 October 1981, A-1.

66. There were thirty-two members not voting and one member voted "present." *Congressional Record*, 97th Cong., 1st sess., 1 October 1981, 22779; House District of Columbia Committee, unofficial records of congressional resolutions disapproving District of Columbia legislation.

67. *Washington Post*, 26 October, A-2.

68. Ibid., 3 October 1981, B-1.

69. Ibid., 5 October 1981, A-12.

70. Ibid., 1 July 1981, B-1.

71. *Congressional Record*, 97th Cong., 1st sess., 1 October 1981, 22774.

72. *Ibid.*, 22765.

73. Ibid., 22770

74. *Washington Post*, 3 October 1981, B-1.

75. Telephone interview with Attorney David A. Clarke, former chairman of the District of Columbia Council and chief sponsor of the Sexual Assault Reform Act of 1981, 10 November 1992. In a special election in the fall of 1993, Clarke was returned to the chairmanship to complete the term of the late John A. Wilson who committed suicide on 19 May 1993.

76. Some of the council members who voted against the measure in December 1992 said they supported it in principle but voted in the negative because standard council procedures, involving committee consideration and public hearings, had been ignored. *Washington Post*, 2 December 1992, D-1.

77. Until 1961 every state had a law making sodomy a criminal offense. In repealing its statute against sodomy, the District joined twenty-seven states that no longer penalize this conduct. The neighboring state of Virginia is among fifteen states that outlaw both heterosexual and homosexual sodomy.

Nine others, including the adjacent state of Maryland, have revised their laws to prohibit only homosexual sodomy. Ibid., 8 April 1993, A-l; 11 April 1993, A-20; 18 September 1993, B-3.

78. Ibid., 8 April 1993, A-1.

79. Emphasizing the historic and scenic importance of air rights over the nation's capital, District Delegate Eleanor Holmes Norton amended the District of Columbia statehood bill in 1993 to allow the federal government to take an aerial easement over New Columbia by eminent domain before statehood takes effect. This action means that District of Columbia statehood would not interfere with the national preservation of the unique view of the monuments in the capital city. Ibid., 8 November 1993, A-20.

80. Wilkes, Artis, Hedrick & Lane, attorneys at law, memorandum of law, attachment E, in re: Authority of the City Council Under Schedule of Heights Authority Provided in the 1910 Height Act, Washington, D.C., 12 September 1990.

81. Memorandum of law from the Department of Justice to the National Capital Planning Commission, Washington, D.C., 6 November 1990.

82. Wilkes, Artis, Hedrick & Lane, memorandum of law.

83. Ibid.

84. There are various exceptions to the basic limits, as well as instances where District of Columbia zoning regulations are more restrictive. Ibid.

85. Ibid.

86. This description of hope for local residents and the nation as a whole was given by Senator Carl Levin (D-Mich.) in floor debate. *Congressional Record,* 102d Cong., 1st sess., 28 January 1991, S2527.

87. Except between 1st and 15th Streets on the north side of Pennsylvania Avenue, where buildings may be erected to a height of 160 feet. Wilkes, Artis, Hedrick & Lane, Memorandum of law.

88. Where the width of the street is 60 feet or less, the building height may be equal to the width of the street and, for streets 60 to 65 feet in width, a height of 60 feet is permitted. 36 *Statutes at Large* 452 (1910), Sec. 5-405(a)-(e); D.C. Code Sec. 5-405(a)-(e).

89. *Congressional Record,* 102d Cong., 1st sess., 1991, S2529.

90. By 1930 the commissioners had expanded the Schedule of Heights to cover more than a dozen locations. District of Columbia Council, David A. Clark, Chairman, memorandum to members of the council, subject: Bill 8-616, Schedule of Heights Amendment Act of 1990, 27 November 1990.

91. The Schedule of Heights is found in appendix G of the District of Columbia Zoning Regulations.

92. It was estimated that the development of the project would generate approximately $2.4 million in annual property tax revenues, or about five times the revenue currently generated on the site. Additional revenues would include an undetermined amount of income tax revenue from persons living in the residential units and from District residents employed on the site and an undetermined amount of new revenue from franchise and sales taxes associated with retail and parking services on the site. The Market Square North developer estimated that the project would provide approximately 300 construction jobs and 1,700 permanent jobs and at least 51 percent of the jobs under his control in each of these categories would be filled with residents of the District of Columbia. District of Columbia Council, memorandum from Clarke to the members of the council.

93. The PADC Design Committee felt that the increased height for Market Square North was acceptable and, in fact, had positive urban design values in view of the height and setback of the FBI Building. District of Columbia, testimony of Fred L. Greene, Director, Office of Planning, before the Committee of the Whole, Council of the District of Columbia on Bill 8-616, *Schedule of Heights Amendment Act of 1990,* 18 September 1990.

94. This project was deemed important to the rejuvenation of the Pennsylvania Avenue corridor. It was designed to include 201 residential units, 394,000 square feet of office space, and 27,000 square feet of retail and arts space, including a grocery store and a restaurant. The height increment requested would boost the allowable floor area ratio (FAR) on the property from 8.5 to 10.0. *Washington Times,* 26 February 1991, B-10.

95. District Council, memorandum from Clarke to the members of the council.

96. This authority was contained in paragraph 120 of section 402 of Reorganization Plan no. 3 of 1967, and in section 404(a) (D.C. Code, section 1-144(a)) of the *District of Columbia Self-Government and Governmental Reorganization Act of 1973.* Section 602(a) (6) of the Home Rule Act (D.C. Code, section 1-233(a) (6)) proscribes any council act permitting the building of any structure in the District "in excess of the height limits contained in the 1910 Act."

97. Presenting testimony in support of Bill 8-616 were the following: the PADC, the District of Columbia Office of Planning, the District of Columbia Office of Corporation Counsel, and Square 407 Limited Partnership (developer). The following presented testimony in opposition to Bill 8-616: the National Capital Planning Commission, the District of Columbia Preservation League, the Committee of 100 on the Federal City, and the Residential Action Coalition; the Commission on Fine Arts sent comments in opposition to the measure. District Council, memorandum from Clarke to the members of the council.

98. This exception to the height limitation was permitted by the 1910 act for all buildings located on the north side of Pennsylvania Avenue.

99. District Council, memorandum from Clarke to the members of the council.

100. Ibid., attachment B.

101. Some of the other organizations that supported the council's legal authority to enact Bill 8-616 included the District of Columbia Office of Planning, the counsel for the developer, and Wilkes, Artis, Hedrick & Lane, Chartered. District of Columbia Council, memorandum from Clarke to the members of the council.

102. District Council, memorandum of law from S.M. Jones, general council, to David A. Clarke, chairman, 27 November 1990.

103. The Schedule of Heights Amendment Act of 1979 (D.C. Law 3-43) changed one of the existing fifteen sections of the Schedule of Heights to allow

an increased height for Metropolitan Square. District Council, memorandum from Clarke to the members of the council.

It would be the first time in which a nonfederal building was allowed to exceed the limitations contained in the 1910 act. *Congressional Record,* 102d Cong., 1st sess., 6 March 1991, daily ed., H1439-40.

104. They maintained that the District was not getting additional housing in the project; the units planned for this site represented exactly what PADC required in the first place. District Council, period 8, 47th Legislative Meeting, 4 December 1990, 190–91.

105. Both the District of Columbia Preservation League and the Committee of 100 on the Federal City presented testimony against the height amendment when it was being considered by the council. District of Columbia Preservation League, Testimony Before the Committee of the Whole, District Council, on Bill 8-616, Schedule of Heights Amendment Act, 18 September 1990; District Council, memorandum from Clarke to the members of the council.

106. The cosponsors of S. J. Res. 84 were Senators John Glenn (D-Ohio), John Heinz (R-Pa.), Daniel P. Moynihan (D-N.Y.), William V. Roth, Jr.(R-Del.), and Jim Sasser (D-Tenn.).

107. D.C. Code 5-405 (a) through (h).

108. *Congressional Record,* 102d Cong., 1st sess., 6 March 1991, daily ed., H1435.

109. Ibid.

110. Ibid., H1445.

111. The new officials were Mayor Sharon Pratt Dixon, Council Chairman John Wilson, and Delegate Eleanor Holmes Norton. *Washington Times,* 7 March 1991, B-3.

6

Appropriations

Politics is largely a contest over whose preferences will prevail in the determination of public policy. The budget records the outcome of this struggle. In a democracy, the budget is supposed to represent the will of the citizens who provide revenues for programs and services. But this is hardly the case with the District of Columbia budget, where the real battles are removed from the elected representatives of the local citizens.

The conflicts of interest between the federal and District governments have found primary expression in the congressional appropriations process. This chapter examines the nature of these conflicts, their underlying causes, the means by which they are resolved, and the outcomes of these disputes. After a brief explanation of the emergence of home rule and the institutional framework of the District budget, the chapter proceeds with a discussion of the ways in which congressional budget mechanisms have been used to influence District policies and decisions, including two condensed case studies of attempts to enact major public policies through the appropriations process.

HOW HOME RULE BUDGET POWERS CAME TO BE

The budget authority for the District is contained in the District of Columbia Self Government and Governmental Reorganization Act, better known as the Home Rule Charter.[1] The charter provisions left the District budget in the hands of Congress, thus setting the stage for decision-making that is characterized by the mingling of local policy issues and congressional politics and parochial interests.

During the crafting of home rule legislation in 1973, a strong home rule bill was reported out of the House District Committee.[2] This bill would have transferred line-item budget control, as well as the authority to levy taxes and issue bonds, from Congress to the local government. But, when it appeared that this bill would be difficult to pass, home rule advocates in the House worked out a compromise at the last minute which left budget authority with Congress. It boiled down to a matter of making concessions on the budget issue to prevent passage of a gutted substitute measure by opponents of home rule. The agreement demonstrated the power and influence of the House Appropriations Committee and its senior members. The member who would have been most affected by a change in local control of the budget was Representative William H. Natcher (D-Ky.), the powerful chairman of the District of Columbia Appropriations Subcommittee. Although the appropriation of the federal payment to the District would have remained with his subcommittee, his power would have been greatly diminished. In fact, this change would have diminished the power of the entire Appropriations Committee and its members. Faced with this critical situation, key home rule advocates in Congress agreed to leave budget control with Congress in return for Natcher's support.[3] His support carried not only many members of the Appropriations Committee but a large number of Southern congressmen and various other members who did not want to undercut the power of the Appropriations Committee and, moreover, did not really trust elected District officials to spend wisely the money of their constituents.[4]

The Senate proposed and passed a much stronger bill than the House. It not only granted budget autonomy, but also gave the local government power to issue general obligation bonds without the approval of Congress, established a formula-based federal payment, and delegated other powers not included in the House bill. The only District of Columbia budget responsibility that Congress would have retained was appropriation of the federal payment.

With different versions of home rule passed by the House and Senate, a conference panel was necessary. The conference version of the bill adopted the House budget provisions so that all District government expenditures, including those funded by local revenues, would have to be appropriated by Congress. The relevant provision in the Home Rule Charter states:

> No amount may be obligated or expended by . . . the District of Columbia government unless . . . approved by Act of Congress, and then only according to such Act.[5]

This means that the District budget has to make the same rounds through the executive branch, via the Office of Management and Budget (OMB), as all other federal agency budgets and must be submitted to Congress by the president. Congress also retains a number of additional levers of influence over the District government, including unrestricted power to legislate on all District matters and to veto all legislation enacted by the District government.[6]

Many members predicted that the city would enjoy a kind of de facto budgetary autonomy. Representative Joel T. Broyhill (R-Va.), an opponent of home rule for the District, said that he did not think that the appropriations committees would change much, if anything, in city budgets.

> I think that the people of the District can make the point that self-government means they control the budget and it's tough to go against that because it would be like opposing the flag and America.[7]

According to Broyhill, that was the very point behind congressional approval of home rule and, "It's tough to have to explain why you oppose self-government."

The fact that full budget autonomy was not conveyed, however, has made a major difference in the political life of the District. Although there is little or no indication that Congress planned that the budget would be an instrument for regular intervention in District of Columbia affairs, leverage tends to be used when it is available.[8] Certainly the budget process that was adopted has not allowed the de facto autonomy referred to by Broyhill.

THE HANDLING OF THE DISTRICT BUDGET

The mayor is required to submit an annual budget to the District Council, which must hold public hearings on the proposed budget and adopt, by act, an annual budget for the District. Extensive hearings are conducted at the local level and estimates are reviewed, modified, and approved by the mayor and staff, the various council committees, and the full council. The budget is then reviewed by OMB and submitted by the president to Congress.

As a matter of practice, OMB and the president usually do not get involved in the District of Columbia operational budget except in a very general way. When transmitting the budget to Congress, the president may direct attention to certain issues which bear on operating funds. For example, when the fiscal year 1990 budget was submitted, President George Bush encouraged Congress "to continue the abortion funding policy," established in fiscal year 1989, "which prohibits the use of both federal and local funds for abortions."[9] OMB does scrutinize the basis upon which the District prepares the federal payment estimates, with the stated objective of recommending a payment that is both "complementary and compatible" with the operational budget. During 1991, the first year of Mayor Sharon Pratt Kelly's administration, Congress authorized a formula-based federal payment for the District for fiscal years 1993 through 1995. It was to be equal to 24 percent of the local revenues collected two years prior to the respective budget year as reviewed by the comptroller general of the United States.[10]

Congress has the authority to conduct a comprehensive line-item review of the District's appropriated budget. In spite of the rigorous review of the District budget at the local level, the process essentially starts all over again when it reaches Congress. Public hearings are held to ascertain the views of local citizens and groups who wish to be heard. In recent years, however, only larger agencies and/or agencies with major policy issues have presented testimony. This congressional review encompasses the revenues the city anticipates collecting, the expenditures it wants to make, and the appropriate size of the federal payment. Congress may cut or increase any amount and add or delete any item.

The thoroughness of the congressional review of the District's budget during the early years of home rule is brought out in the following statement by Senator Patrick J. Leahy (D-Vt.) during his chairmanship of the District of Columbia Appropriations Subcommittee (1977–1981): "The final . . . review of the [District of Columbia] budget is both awesome and complete . . . any line item can be changed . . . and Congress can in fact dictate policy by either approving or denying specific program requests."[11] Yet many members of Congress are troubled by their role in the District budget process. In floor debate on the District budget in 1979, Representative Stewart B. McKinney (R-Conn.) asked his colleagues, ". . . aside from the federal payment, what right should the Congress have to a line-item review over a budget in which the citizens most directly involved have no legitimate vote?"[12]

The chairmen and members of the appropriations subcommittees along with their staffs play a key role in the review process. Because the subcommittees devote a great deal of time and attention to the review of the budgets under their jurisdiction, there is a tendency for the full appropriations committees and the respective chambers as a whole to respect their recommendations and to go along with them in the final analysis. Of course, there are exceptions to this practice, as will be shown in the next section. During floor debate on the fiscal year 1989 District budget, the recommendations of the subcommittee and also the conference committee, concerning the funding of abortions, were successfully challenged.

One of the problems in the handling of the District budget is that the chairmanship of the Senate subcommittee has changed fairly often (see table 6.1). Of course, this turnover can work for and against District interests. For example, Senator Leahy was fairly rigid in his scrutiny of the District budget and relations between him and District officials were often strained. For years the senator posed a virtual single-member barrier to the District's plans to build a convention cen-

TABLE 6.1 Chairmen of the District of Columbia Appropriations Subcommittees 1975–94

Congress	House	Senate
94th (1975–76)	William H. Natcher (D–Ky.)	Lawton Chiles (D–Fla.)
95th (1977–78)	William H. Natcher (D–Ky.)	Patrick J. Leahy (D–Vt.)
96th (1979–80)	Charles N. Wilson (D–Texas) Julian C. Dixon (D–Calif.)	Patrick J. Leahy (D–Vt.)
97th (1981–82)	Julian C. Dixon (D–Calif.)	Alfonse M. D'Amato (R–N.Y.)
98th (1983–84)	Julian C. Dixon (D–Calif.)	Arlen Specter (R–Pa.)
99th (1985–86)	Julian C. Dixon (D–Calif.)	Arlen Specter (R–Pa.)
100th (1987–88)	Julian C. Dixon (D–Calif.)	Tom Harkin (D–Iowa)
101st (1989–90)	Julian C. Dixon (D–Calif.)	Brock Adams (D–Wash.)
102nd (1991–92)	Julian C. Dixon (D–Calif.)	Brock Adams (D–Wash.)
103rd (1993–94)	Julian C. Dixon (D–Calif.)	Herbert Kohl (D–Wis.)

ter.[13] The District was probably quite willing to take its chances with any replacement for Leahy.

District officials generally felt that they had a difficult time in the short period that Representative Charles H. Wilson (D-Texas) chaired the House District of Columbia Appropriations Subcommittee, not so much in terms of his defense on the House floor, but rather in terms of what was brought to the floor. When Wilson was leaving the chairmanship of the subcommittee, Mayor Marion Barry said that he did not understand the city's problems, adding, "Charles Wilson was too tough and too rough and not quite together on what our problems were."[14] Representative Julian Dixon (D-Calif.), current chairman of the House District of Columbia Appropriations Subcommittee, has established good rapport with city officials and is considered an ally of the District. He has chaired the subcommittee for over thirteen years and has stated that his objective is to bring to the floor a bill that protects the federal interest, while at the same time preserving the integrity of home rule.[15]

There are three possible mechanisms for federal influence on the District budget through the appropriations process: (1) the amount of the federal payment, (2) control of line items, and (3) general provisions and legislative language. The greatest influence on the District budget has been exercised through general provisions and legislative language.

DISTRICT APPROPRIATED FUNDS AND THE FEDERAL PAYMENT

Generally, over 80 percent of congressional appropriations for the District are derived from local revenues—taxation, fees, and charges.[16] The main portion of federal funds is appropriated in the form of the federal payment. Other federally appropriated funds are contributions to the District pension system for firefighters, police officers, teachers, judges, and coverage of water and sewer services furnished to federal facilities by the District. The federal payment is not a gift or subsidy to the city but rather compensation for federal and foreign tax-exempt land in the District and for services rendered by the city to those interests. The payment was intended as a means for the national government to carry a fair share of the fiscal burden that it creates in the District, a unique jurisdiction with city, county, and state functions.

The federal payment has been the source of considerable controversy since the capital was established in the District in 1800. Congress has undertaken comprehensive, formal reviews of the payment at least seven times in the past one hundred years, and it thus far has reached one consensus: the extraordinary federal presence imposes costs on the District for which the federal government acknowledges a financial obligation.[17]

In the history of the capital city, the federal payment has been as low as 8.5 percent and as high as 50 percent of the local budget.[18] For approximately ninety years (1835–1925) the payment level was set according to a formula which ranged from 40 percent to 50 percent of the District budget. In 1925, however, the formula approach was abandoned in favor of a "lump sum" concept, with the payment set each year based on negotiations between the District and Congress. This negotiated approach remained essentially unchanged from 1925 to 1991. During this time the federal share of the District budget ranged from less than 9 percent to about 30 percent of actual appropriations.[19]

Although the advent of home rule brought two new features to the federal payment process—the authorization of payment levels in advance (through fiscal year 1980), and a formal justification format— the amount of the payment since home rule has provided less than one quarter of the funds needed to finance the city's programs (see table 6.2). In fact, the payment has represented a fluctuating but declining share, from 26.7 percent in 1975 to 13.9 percent in 1990. Between 1981 and 1985 the federal payment authorization was increased annually, going from $300 million in 1981 to $425 million in 1985. Between fiscal year 1985 and fiscal year 1990 there was hardly any increase in the federal payment, which averaged $428.9 million per year during this period. In fiscal year 1990 President Bush proposed a payment of $430.5 million for the District in his budget, which was approved by Congress. During fiscal year 1991 Congress and President Bush provided an additional $103.6 million supplemental appropriation for a total federal payment of $534.1 million.[20]

In 1991 legislation was enacted for a formula-based federal payment authorization for the District. This formula tied the level of the federal payment to the general fund local revenues collected by the District government and provided the District with a predictable estimate of the payment it would receive to support its annual budget. For fiscal years 1993, 1994, and 1995, the authorized level of the federal payment was set at 24 percent of the "general revenue local collections" of two years prior to the respective budget year.[21] Problems arose during the Bush administration, however, with regard to implementing this for-

TABLE 6.2 The Federal Payment in Relationship to the District of Columbia General Fund Fiscal Year 1975 – Fiscal Year 1993[a] ($000's)

Fiscal Year	Total Appropriation	U.S. Share	%	U.S. Share in 1987 Constant $[b]
1975	845,617	226,200	26.7	475,410
1976	1,042,143	248,949	23.8	488,327
1977	1,130,506	276,650	24.5	500,905
1978	1,260,791	276,000	21.9	465,587
1979	1,335,746	250,000	18.7	388,138
1980	1,426,093	276,500	19.4	389,327
1981	1,457,887	300,000	20.6	383,779
1982	1,587,298	336,600	21.2	402,199
1983	1,792,104	361,000	20.1	411,349
1984	1,897,285	386,000	20.3	423,014
1985	2,076,246	425,000	20.5	449,640
1986	2,247,906	412,388	18.3	423,614
1987	2,461,113	444,500	18.1	444,500
1988	2,701,265	430,500	15.9	415,500
1989	2,862,130	430,500	15.0	398,132
1990	3,107,833	430,500	13.9	381,514
1991	3,204,698	530,500	16.6	449,652
1992	3,310,623	630,500	19.0	519,443
1993	3,574,111	624,824	17.5	499,899

[a]Excludes one-time special payments in the following years ($000's): 1979 ($9,900), 1983 ($2,300), 1984 ($3,200), 1985 ($25,100), 1990 ($46,772), 1991 ($814,440), 1992 ($13,280), 1993 ($33,315).
[b]Office of Management and Budget, *Budget Baselines, Historical Data and Alternatives for the Future*, Table 1.3—Summary of Receipts, Outlays, and Surpluses or Deficits (–) in Current Dollars, Constant (FY 1987) Dollars, and as Percentages of GDP: 1940–1993 (January 1993), 282.
Senate, *District of Columbia Appropriations Bill, 1993*, 102d Cong., 2d sess., 1992, S. Rept. 102-333, 23-24.

mula. In the fiscal year 1993 District of Columbia budget request submitted to Congress, OMB froze the federal payment at the level of the previous year without mentioning the legislation that created the formula. Although District officials tried to fight this action, the ultimate payment received was only about $625 million, which was roughly $30 million less than the amount they had counted on getting, as calculated by the formula.[22] There is usually very little difference between the

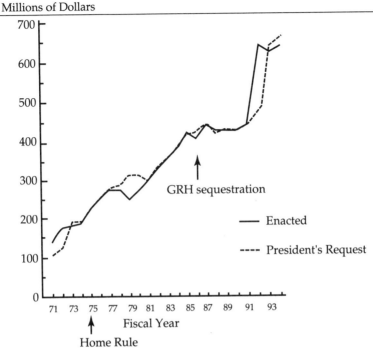

Millions of Dollars

Figure 6.1 Federal Payment to District Government Fiscal Years 1971–94

amount for the federal payment that is requested by the president and the amount enacted by Congress; fiscal years 1992 through 1994 represented exceptions to this pattern (see figure 6.1).

CONTROL OF LINE ITEMS

In order to evaluate the role of Congress in dealing with line items in the District budget, the District of Columbia appropriations bill and other documents for the entire home rule period were studied with special attention to selected years. Three fiscal years were selected for in-depth inventory: 1980, 1988, and 1992. Fiscal year 1980 was the first budget presented by the administration of Mayor Marion Barry; 1988 came late in his twelve-year term in office, when relations between the federal and District governments were at a low point. Fiscal year 1992 was the first budget presented by the administration of Mayor Sharon Pratt Kelly. Of these three fiscal years, only fiscal year 1980 showed a reduction in the District of Columbia estimates (see table 6.3).

TABLE 6.3   Increase/Decrease in Appropriations over District of Columbia
Budget Estimates
(in thousands of dollars)

	Federal Funds	District Funds	Total Appropriations
1980	– 113,192	– 115,412	1,915,834
1988	+ 42,930	+ 7,127	3,077,347
1992	+ 52,070	+ 15,905	3,895,772

In light of the comparatively heavy cuts in the District estimates for fiscal year 1980, we wanted to see what some of the line items looked like before and after congressional action. Representative items were chosen from the main budget categories: governmental direction and support, economic development and regulation, executive office, public safety and justice, and human support services.

The eleven items selected ranged from the fire department, under public safety and justice, to the Minority Business Opportunity Commission, a new agency under economic development and regulation (see table 6.4). The eight line items that appeared in the previous fiscal year budget showed an increase in funding for fiscal year 1980, and all eleven, except the National Guard, showed a cut in the requested amount. The largest cut in dollars was absorbed by the Department of Human Resources, which had $20 million cut from a request of $291.8 million; the largest percentage cut—56 percent—was made in the budget of the Minority Business Opportunity Commission. On balance, there was a greater tendency to cut the amounts for operational agencies in the executive branch and in "governmental direction and support" than in areas such as public safety and justice. The amount for the latter category, which includes the police and fire departments and the courts, was more likely to be increased; such was the case for fiscal year 1992, when $75,000 was added to this line.

A review of the main budget categories for fiscal years 1988 and 1992 did not show reductions in District of Columbia estimates. And the full survey of the treatment of line items by Congress during the other home rule years generally showed minimal changes in the District of Columbia estimates. The amounts of federal funds appropriated were increased by $42.9 million in fiscal year 1988 and $52.1 million in fiscal year 1992.

TABLE 6.4 District of Columbia Appropriations for Fiscal Year 1980:
Selected Line Items ($000's)

Item	District of Columbia Estimates	Appropriation	Compared to FY 1979	Estimates
Public Education System	326,162	312,494	+2,930	–13,668
Department of Human Resources	291,814	271,830	+4,781	–19,984
Fire Department	55,018	54,312	+3,634	–706
Department of Corrections	55,389	53,491	+959	–102
Council of the District of Columbia	3,917	3,455	+738	–462
Department of Housing and Community Development	6,197	6,169	+473	–28
Minority Business Opportunity Commission	175	77	—*	–98
Office of Secretariat	1,305	1,252	+548	–53
Office of Inspector General	612	560	—*	–52
Office of Communications	213	191	—*	–22
National Guard	359	359	+11	—

*New or reorganized office.
Sources: P.L. 96-93, *District of Columbia Appropriation Act, 1980,* 93 *Statutes at Large* 713,
96th Cong., 1st sess., 30 October 1979; House, Committee on Appropriations, *District of
Columbia Appropriation Bill, 1980,* 96th Cong., 1st sess., 1979, H. Rept 294; Senate, Committee on Appropriations, *District of Columbia Appropriations Bill, 1980,* 96th Cong., 1st
sess., 1979, S. Rept. 257.

One factor that helps to explain the minimal changes in the District
of Columbia budget estimates is that District officials have learned to
play the budget game fairly well. During budget preparation, District
budget staff members spend days on the Hill working with the staff
members of the appropriations committees to develop a mutually acceptable document from the standpoint of format, justification, and
numbers. The local officials have developed a sense of "what will go."
Members of the mayor's budget staff feel that they have developed a
good working relationship with the staffs of the appropriations committees but, with reference to the subcommittee members, they were quick
to add, "You can't second-guess them. They will turn right around and
go in the opposite direction from what you expected."[23]

The media also play a prominent role in the District budget process and agencies are sometimes affected by emergent problems and current events which cannot be predicted ahead of time but may radically alter budgetary prospects for some programs. For example, in approving the District's fiscal year 1988 budget, the Senate voted to put on hold the construction of a new $50 million District of Columbia prison in the southeast section of the city while three alternative sites were examined. Extensive media coverage of "archaeological findings" on the initial 10.5-acre plot, along with coverage of complaints from residents near the site, was a factor in this sudden decision which caught District officials by surprise.[24]

LEGISLATIVE LANGUAGE

A third form of congressional intervention through the appropriations process is the introduction of legislative language in appropriations bills that forbids or requires the District government to undertake specific actions. In theory, legislating in an appropriations bill is prohibited by the rules of the House of Representatives, but this rule is often ignored and Congress has intervened in a variety of policy areas, including personnel, public safety, education, land use, and public works.[25] Although Congress is ostensibly protecting the federal interest in the nation's capital when it intervenes in local policy matters, examination of several examples of appropriations language fails to reveal any criteria for carrying out this responsibility, and tends to suggest more provincial motives behind much of the congressional intervention (see table 6.5).

For many years Congress maintained a ceiling on the number of employees that could be hired by the District government. This cap was raised or lowered for a respective fiscal year, and under the general cap there were often subceilings on the maximum number of permanent employees that could be hired by specified institutions such as the District of Columbia General Hospital and the public schools (fiscal years 1980–83). The ceiling on District employees originated out of concerns of Congress that the District government employed too many people for a city of its size. Congressional studies were conducted and statistics compiled comparing the District on a per capita basis with other jurisdictions of similar size. Although these studies attempted to allow for the lack of state, county, or special jurisdictions in the case of the District, local officials and some members of Congress challenged their validity.[26]

TABLE 6.5 Selected Riders and Budget Provisions: Excerpts from District of Columbia Appropriations Documents

Personnel

1. None of the funds in this Act shall be available to pay the salary of any employee whose name, title, grade, salary, past work experience, and salary history are not available for inspection by the House and Senate Committees on Appropriations, the House District of Columbia Committee and the Subcommittee on General Services, Federalism, and the District of Columbia of the Senate Committee on Governmental Affairs, and the D.C. Council.

2. The City Administrator shall be paid, . . . a salary at a rate established by the Mayor, not to exceed the rate established for level IV of the Executive Schedule. . . .

3. Appropriations in this Act shall not be available, . . . for the compensation of any person appointed to a permanent position in the District of Columbia government during any month in which the number of employees exceeds 39,262 (FY 1991–P.L. 101-518, 100th Cong. 2d sess., 1990).

4. None of the funds appropriated in this Act may be used for the implementation of a personnel lottery with respect to the hiring of firefighters or police officers (FY 1991. Ibid).

Human Support Services and Education

5. None of the funds contained in this Act shall be used to perform abortions except where the life of the mother would be endangered if the fetus were carried to term.

6. *Provided further*, That this appropriation shall not be available to subsidize the education of nonresidents . . . at UDC unless the Board . . . adopts . . . a tuition rate schedule . . . for nonresident students. . . .

7. No funds made available pursuant to any provision of this Act shall be used to implement or enforce any system of registration of unmarried, cohabiting couples whether they are homosexual, lesbian, or heterosexual. . . .

Public safety, Justice, Corrections

8. The District of Columbia shall place on the ballot, without alteration, at a general, special, or primary election to be held within 90 days after the date of enactment of this Act, the following initiative: Mandatory Life Imprisonment or Death Penalty for Murder in the District of Columbia.

9. None of the funds made available in this Act may be used by the District of Columbia to operate, after June 1, 1993, the juvenile detention facility known as the Cedar Knoll Facility.

10. *Provided*, That the Metropolitan Police Department (MPD) shall maintain a force of not less than 4,889 officers and members.

TABLE 6.5   *cont.*

11.   *Provided further,* That the Metropolitan Police Department shall provide quarterly reports to the Committees on Appropriations of the House and Senate on efforts to increase efficiency and improve the professionalism in the department.

12.   . . . the conferees direct District officials to keep Engine Company No. 3 open for the 12 months of FY 1992 and to absorb the total operating costs . . . within the existing appropriation (FY 1992. 102d Cong., 1st sess., H. Rept. 102-181, 1991)

Governmental Direction and Support

13.   None of the funds provided in this Act may be used . . . to provide for the salaries, expenses, or other costs associated with the offices of U.S. Senator or . . . Representative. . . .

14.   No sole source contract with the D.C. government . . . may be renewed or extended without opening that contract to the competitive bidding process as set forth in section 303 of the District of Columbia Procurement Practices Act of 1985.

15.   The Mayor shall not expend any moneys borrowed for capital projects for the operating expenses of the D.C. government.

16.   The conferees direct District officials to consult with the House and Senate Committees on Appropriations prior to making any changes to the budget documents for the FY 1994 budget (FY 1993. 102d Cong., 2d sess., H. Rept. 102-906, 1992).

Public Works

17.   *Provided,* That this appropriation shall not be available for collecting ashes or miscellaneous refuse from hotels and places of business.

18.   Appropriations in this Act shall not be used for or in connection with . . . any regulation or order of the Public Service Commission requiring the installation of meters in taxicabs, . . . (FY 1986. 99th Cong., 1st sess., D.C. Appropriation Bill, 1986, H.R. 3067, committee print, 1985).

Source: *All items are from District of Columbia Appropriations Act, 1993* (P.L. 102-382, 102d Cong., 2d sess., 1992) unless a different year and source is indicated after the item.

The personnel ceiling cap last appeared in the District of Columbia appropriations bill for fiscal year 1991. Elected on a campaign pledge to cut the size of the city's bureaucracy and faced with major budget deficits since taking office in 1991, Mayor Sharon Pratt Kelly, along with the District Council, has been forced to deal with hiring freezes and layoff plans for government workers. The local budgetary situation and employment trends have rendered congressional action unnecessary in controlling further increases in the size of the District bureaucracy. For a similar reason, the usual budgetary limitation on the costs of overtime and temporary positions has not appeared in the District of Columbia appropriations act since fiscal year 1991.

In an effort to meet its affirmative action goals in 1981, the District sought to implement a personnel lottery system in the hiring of fire fighters and police officers. This action was blocked initially through congressional budget action (fiscal year 1982), and was banned in every appropriations act through fiscal year 1991.

Congress has repeatedly used appropriations bills to require the District to maintain a specific minimum number of uniformed police officers. For many years this number was 3,800 sworn officers, backed by the stipulation that no appropriated funds would be available if the officer ranks fell below this number. The fiscal year 1993 appropriations act states that the Metropolitan Police Department (MPD) "shall maintain a force of not less than 4,889 officers and members."[27]

Several examples indicate that Congress has used the appropriations process to move from oversight to micromanagement of District affairs. After heavy lobbying by the city's fire fighters' union, the fiscal year 1986 appropriations bill blocked the closing of Engine Company No. 3, the firehouse nearest the Capitol. Union leaders argued that increased terrorist threats made it necessary to keep the station open. Even after the threat of terrorist activities subsided, this prohibition of closing was renewed annually. For years, the District had asked permission to redeploy the men and close down the building, whose doors were barely large enough for the new fire trucks to squeeze through. Besides, a brand new station sat two blocks away. For fiscal year 1992 the Senate approved an increased appropriation of $799,000 in federal funds to cover most of the estimated operating costs of keeping the station open. Initially the House did not approve such an increase. After citing congressional support for other cost-saving measures in the District appropriations act, District officials were "directed" to keep the station open and "to absorb the total operating costs including overtime pay within the existing appropriation."[28]

Finally, in the fiscal year 1994 appropriations, Congress agreed not to block the plans of the District to shut down the Capitol Hill fire station. Although House members traditionally had not been as devoted to the firehouse as senators, they had never before succeeded in changing the Senate's position. The key lawmaker in the debate over the fate of Fire Station No. 3 was Senator Herbert H. Kohl (D-Wis.), the new chairman of the Senate District Appropriations Subcommittee in the 103d Congress (1993–94). His predecessors in the position had insisted on legislation to keep the station in business, whereas Kohl, after an evaluation, did not foresee any diminution in service if it closed.[29]

Another example of micromanagement is the requirement that the University of the District of Columbia (UDC) adopt an out-of-state tuition rate for nonresident students. It is required that this rate be at least equal to that of other area public universities, presumably to prevent UDC from poaching students.[30]

At times Congress has intervened in local policies to protect its own collective interest.[31] Until fiscal year 1986 the District was required to keep the taxicab zone fare system in effect, rather than shift to meters which would have resulted in higher fares. The ban on taxicab meters dates back to the 1930s and local lore has it that members wanted to be certain that the rides from their Capitol Hill offices to downtown restaurants were billed at the lowest, one-zone fare. Even after this restriction was removed from the District of Columbia appropriations act, other micromanagement clauses on taxicabs followed. The fiscal year 1992 House/Senate conference report "directed" the District Taxicab Commission to complete its comparative study of the zone and metered taxicab systems and to issue a report no later than 1 June 1992.[32] The commission met the above deadline but the Senate Appropriations Subcommittee, after reviewing the report, was unhappy with it. Its official assessment, as stated in the fiscal year 1993 Senate District of Columbia appropriations bill, characterized the study as "inappropriate and unresponsive." During fiscal year 1993, the commission was instructed to submit quarterly reports detailing the "type of data collected, summaries of commission meetings, and expected timetable for making a final decision on zones versus meters."[33]

Abortion is another issue that has been fought through the budget process. During the House debate on the fiscal year 1980 appropriations bill, Representative Robert K. Dornan (R-Calif.) sought to amend the bill so that no appropriated funds, federal or District, could be used to pay for abortions except to save the life of the mother. Representative Charles Wilson (D-Texas), chairman of the District of Columbia Appropriations Subcommittee, objected on a point of order—that the amendment violated House rules because it was legislation on an appropriations matter. He argued that the amendment would impose additional duties on District officials to make new determinations and judgments not required by existing law as to the danger to the mother in each individual case. His point of order was sustained.[34]

When Dornan offered a revised amendment on the abortion issue that would not violate House rules, Wilson also disagreed with it on the grounds that it restricted the use of local revenues for programs which locally elected officials had decided to fund. He added that he did not believe that Congress should prohibit a local government from using its own funds for public policies which it had made a conscious decision to fund.[35]

The sponsor and supporters of the amendment argued that because District funds were commingled with federal money, Congress had a right and responsibility to act. A compromise was eventually reached which banned the use of federal, but not District, funds for abortion. The abortion controversy resurfaced with each annual appropriations measure until in fiscal year 1989, during President Ronald Reagan's final year in office, the District was prohibited from using its own funds for abortions. With either a veto or the threat of it, the latter prohibition was maintained throughout the administration of President George Bush (fiscal year 1990 through fiscal year 1993). With the election of President Bill Clinton, a Democrat who favors abortion rights, it was expected that Congress would relax its restrictions on abortion and no longer bar the use of District funds for this purpose. In spite of President Clinton's position on the issue, the House debate and vote on the city's appropriations bill was another battle in a long-running political war over abortion in the District. Ending a five-year ban on the use of any public money to pay for abortions for poor women in the District, the fiscal year 1994 appropriations bill allows the city to finance abortions with local tax money but not with federal revenue.[36]

MAJOR PUBLIC POLICY MAKING THROUGH THE BUDGET

Two selected cases illustrate the propensity of Congress to intervene in District policy making through restrictions on the use of funds. The effort to regulate the lottery by means of the appropriations process was successful, but a similar attempt to place limits on the Washington Convention Center was not. The arguments used in each case reveal the concerns of members of Congress. This section concludes with a discussion of high visibility riders attached to the appropriations acts of 1989 and 1993.

The Lottery.

The idea of a lottery in the nation's capital was controversial from the outset, and the city council decided that the question should be settled by a voter initiative. The authorizing measure for the lottery (District of Columbia Law 3-172) was adopted by a 64 percent majority of District residents voting and became effective 10 March 1981. A Lottery and Charitable Games Control Board was appointed to establish and regulate its operation.[37]

The initial request of the board for $628,000 in start-up operating funds, included in the fiscal year 1982 District budget, was rejected by the House District of Columbia Appropriations Subcommittee, which believed that "revenues to finance District programs should be provided through sources other than gambling." It urged the authorizing committees to consider increasing the federal payment to a level of revenue comparable to the projected first-year income from the lottery, which was $25 million.[38]

The Senate approved the budget request for start-up lottery funds and the matter was sent to conference for resolution. Many members were less than enthusiastic about having a lottery in the capital, expressing concern about the impression the lottery would make on those who visit the District.[39] In order to ameliorate some of the concerns, a Lottery and Charitable Games Enterprise Fund was established to operate the lottery and the District was required to "identify the source of funding for this appropriation from its own locally generated revenues."[40]

Along with appropriation of initial operating funds for the lottery, Congress prohibited advertising, sale, operation, or playing of the lotteries, raffles, bingo, or other authorized games within the federal enclave (the monumental core of city area around the Mall) and in adjacent public buildings and land controlled by the Shipstead-Luce Act,[41] as well as in the Old Georgetown Historic District. Advertising of the lottery on public transportation and at stations and stops was also prohibited.[42]

The board appealed to the appropriations subcommittees to lift some of the limitations in the restricted areas, and proposed amendments to the District's appropriations bills that would accomplish this objective. These amendments, submitted to the appropriations subcommittees in the House and Senate, have been rejected and the restrictions are still in effect.[43]

The Convention Center.

The District's appropriations bill for fiscal year 1983 became a battleground for clarifying policies concerning the use and operation of the city's convention center, which was nearing completion at the time. The House Appropriations Subcommittee approved requests for operating funds and for additional seating equipment but used the occasion to "direct" the board of directors, in their booking policy, to limit the center's use to national and regional conventions, trade shows, and product exhibitions. Section 123 of the fiscal year 1983 House appropriations bill stipulated that the center "was not to be used for entertainment purposes and was not intended to compete with existing facilities in the Washington area for entertainment and cultural events."[44] With members of the Maryland congressional delegation as the prime movers behind section 123, it was clear to almost everyone involved that this section of the budget was designed to prevent the convention center from competing with the privately owned Capital Center in nearby Prince George's County, Maryland, and that it originated with Abe Pollin, owner of the Capital Center.[45] There were strong objections to this provision. Representative Stewart B. McKinney (R-Conn.), who led the fight, believed there was "certainly no congressional intent that such a restriction should be in place" and there was no rational or legal basis for enacting such a restriction. To impose such restrictions on the city through an appropriations bill was called a devious strategy, led by a few members in the name of "congressional intent." Representative Doug Bereuter (R-Neb.) called it "incredible" that Congress would seek to pass a bill designed to restrict the District from getting the maximum return from its investment, funded by its taxpayers without a penny from the federal treasury.[46]

The convention center restrictions were removed from the District's appropriations bill on a point of order, challenging section 123 as violating House rules. First, it constituted legislation on a general appropriations bill and, second, it placed conditions on the expenditure of funds appropriated in other acts. Senate rules do not provide the convenient remedy of a ban on legislation in an appropriations bill. Senator

Thomas Eagleton (D-Mo.) found that the restrictions were not supported by the original legislation nor the hearing record on the creation of the center. There was no indication that Congress ever contemplated any statutory use restrictions and the record gave no justification for such restrictions. Decrying what he called the unbounded arrogance of some of his colleagues vis-à-vis the District of Columbia and the "outright greed" of Abe Pollin, Senator Eagleton fought the convention center restrictions to a standstill and the District of Columbia appropriations bill passed without the proposed restrictions.[47]

HIGH VISIBILITY BUDGET YEARS: FISCAL YEARS 1989 AND 1993

The fiscal year 1989 appropriations represented a considerable departure from previous practice. Rather than use the process to nudge the District in the desired direction, Congress seemed inclined to take bold actions to challenge local policies, backed up with threats to freeze both federal and local funds. Considered separately from other spending bills for the first time since 1983, the District's appropriations bill was more vulnerable to a veto than in past years; and with national elections a little more than a month away, the political stakes in some of the social issues being considered were extremely high. The range of social and political issues challenged by Congress included the city's residency rule, insurance regulations, prison construction, gay rights, and abortion.

The District was told to revise its residency rule (requiring most employees hired after 1980 to live in the city) by September 1989 or face a cutoff of funds to enforce the rule.[48] In addition, Congress stiffened its position on abortion. In the past, Congress had prohibited the use of federal revenue for abortions but had always stopped short of barring the use of local funds. Spurred on by threats from the Reagan administration of a presidential veto, the District's fiscal year 1989 appropriations act barred the city from using either federal or local revenues to fund abortions.

The city's human rights law prohibits discrimination on the basis of sexual preference. Under this law, a student group at Georgetown University, a Catholic institution, was successful in gaining funding support for homosexual student organizations. Led by Senator William L. Armstrong (R-Colo.), a provision was added to the appropriations bill freezing all operating funds after 31 December 1988, unless the city amended its human rights law to allow religious institutions to discriminate against homosexual groups. Charging infringement of its First Amendment right of free speech, the city council successfully challenged this provision in federal district court.[49]

The District's 1986 insurance law pertaining to AIDS had been a bone of contention for many members of Congress due to continuing pressure from the insurance lobby. Utilizing the threat of a total freeze on federal funds by December 31, 1988, Congress directed the city to amend its insurance law to eliminate that section which barred companies from denying coverage to those who test positive for exposure to the AIDS virus.[50] When the District's fiscal year 1989 appropriations bill finally became law, four local laws had been overturned and it was clear that the federal and local relationship on Capitol Hill was in trouble.

Congress has used the appropriations process to set conditions for the District that are intrusive, condescending, and often in conflict with policies adopted by the local government. Although the appropriations for 1990 were relatively quiet, 1991 produced a prime example of Congress rushing in where local officials—city or county—normally would tread. The city was prohibited from using a certain property in Georgetown as a home for mentally troubled young people until a lawsuit by neighbors was adjudicated.[51]

The Georgetown property in question was the Henry and Annie Hurt Home, which was purchased by the District in 1987 with federal grant funds at a cost of $2.9 million to establish a youth residential treatment program for children ages six to twelve at the time of admission. The main issue was whether or not District officials had followed proper procedures and obtained the necessary permits to establish the facility at the respective location. Community residents appealed the trial court's decision with regard to the latter issue. Congress included language in the District of Columbia appropriations act which prohibited the District from using the Hurt Home for either residents or day patients until a final decision was rendered by the District of Columbia Court of Appeals.[52]

The prospect of emotionally disturbed children wandering around the neighborhood was a bit disturbing to some of Georgetown's well-connected residents. So the Citizens' Association of Georgetown took the case to court in 1988 where it was stuck for a number of years.[53]

In 1991 the Court of Appeals partially reversed the decision of the trial court, requiring the city to obtain special permission from the Board of Zoning Adjustment to establish a residential-care home for twenty-four emotionally disturbed children, thus rejecting the arguments of the Citizens' Association of Georgetown. Nevertheless, the latter group persevered in its long legal and regulatory fight against the Hurt Home. The facility had been in operation for some thirteen months when on 26 May 1994 a three-judge panel of the District of Columbia Court of Appeals ruled against the city by rejecting the decision of the zoning board that allowed the District to open the controversial home for emotionally disturbed children.[54]

Congressional mistrust of the local government has been a factor in interventions throughout the current home rule era, beginning with certain provisions in the Home Rule Charter itself, for example, the provision on the National Capital Service Area. This lack of trust probably originates from several different sources: two different levels of government are involved and, although there are white and black members in both the national and local governments, the predominant racial makeup of the respective bodies is a likely source of mistrust. During the period of the fiscal year 1989 appropriations, however, there was an additional source of general mistrust, originating from the administration of Mayor Marion Barry.

Amid frequent press reports of alleged abuses or administrative problems in the District government and the criminal convictions of a number of top aides, the mayor himself was finally arrested and convicted by a federal jury of one misdemeanor count of cocaine possession. Long before the mayor was arrested in an FBI sting operation in January 1990, however, unsupported allegations swirled about the city concerning his appetites for alcohol, drugs, and women, and about his overall personal conduct. With the mayor's arrest and conviction, convenient reasons could be cited by members of Congress for voting against the District.[55] By late 1994 it appeared certain that ex-Mayor Barry and Congress would have another try with their relationship in 1995. The former mayor and ex-convict, representing Ward Eight on the District Council, stunned the political world by winning the Democratic nomination for mayor in September 1994, defeating incumbent Mayor Sharon Pratt Kelly and rival council member John Ray (D-At Large). With its predominantly Democratic electorate, a victory in the District primary is tantamount to election.[56]

It is neither coincidental nor surprising that national election years often produce some of the most striking forays into District affairs. Although the top micromanagement provisions of fiscal year 1989, such as the ban on funds for abortions, were reinserted in the budget in each succeeding year, District of Columbia appropriations for fiscal year 1993 lived up to election-year standards by producing more high visibility intrusions into local policies.

Led by Senator Trent Lott (R-Miss.) in the Senate and Representative Tom DeLay (R-Texas) in the House, Congress inserted language in the fiscal year 1993 District of Columbia appropriations act that forbade the use of any of the appropriated funds to implement the so-called "domestic partners" act, which would have enabled city employees to register a domestic partner and obtain health insurance for that person.[57] The measure was strongly supported by the city's gay community. DeLay is what city officials call a "District-bashing" member of Congress. Up for reelection, the conservative congressman apparently seized a unique opportunity to come out firmly against the sin of "homosexual marriage."[58]

Both the House and Senate District of Columbia appropriations bills for fiscal year 1993 included two proposals backed by lawmakers from suburban Maryland and Virginia. One would prevent the District from collecting a controversial sewage treatment fee in the suburbs. The other would force the District to close its troubled Cedar Knoll Juvenile Detention Center, located in Maryland, by 1 June 1993. Both riders were enacted into law as a part of District appropriations for fiscal year 1993, approved in October 1992.[59]

Spawned by the District's crime problem, probably the heaviest appropriations rider of the current home rule period involved the reinstatement of the death penalty in the District. Scaling back his initial request to the Senate to directly impose a death penalty in cases of first-degree murder in the District, Senator Richard C. Shelby (D-Ala.) sponsored a budget provision to force the District to hold a citywide referendum on this issue. Shelby was prompted to act by the slaying earlier in the year of one of his staff members, outside of the man's Capitol Hill apartment. Congress approved Shelby's proposal by a lopsided margin and the District was required to schedule a referendum on the death penalty no more than ninety days after the measure became law. The twin defeats for the District—the referendum and the domestic partners bill—came on the same day and were viewed by some veteran members of Congress as the city's worst day in memory.[60]

Mainly on the grounds of congressional meddling in local affairs, District officials and community leaders carried out an intensive campaign against reinstatement of the death penalty in the District. The measure was defeated at the polls in the November 1992 elections by a large margin. It passed in only 11 of the city's 140 precincts, all of which are west of Rock Creek Park in largely white, affluent communities such as Georgetown and Tenley Circle. Approximately 67 percent of District voters rejected the death penalty measure.[61]

PROPOSED RIDERS/MICROMANAGEMENT PROVISIONS

The full story of congressional interference in District affairs is not told through the riders and provisions that Congress approves. The policy matters that are approved in the House or the Senate appropriations bills, yet not accepted in conference, also impact District policymakers. The House and Senate reports are a part of the appropriations literature that is carefully studied by District officials. Policy matters that are passed by either chamber provide a clear warning signal to the District. Examples from the House and Senate, involving the Eastern Market on Capitol Hill, the George Washington University and the effort to legalize tear gas, make this abundantly clear.

In 1991 plans were under way to renovate historic Eastern Market, located on Capitol Hill. There was concern by preservationist groups and others that the historic character of the market might not be preserved. Consequently, Representative James M. Inhofe (D-Okla.) introduced an amendment to the District of Columbia appropriations bill, prohibiting the use of funds for the renovation of Eastern Market. People on all sides of the controversy, however, felt that federal intervention in the project was too draconian, even for those ardent in their desire to keep the market completely unchanged. Stating that the District government was proceeding by law and should be allowed "to continue in an orderly manner," the conferees eliminated this legislation from the District of Columbia appropriations act.[62] District officials will proceed, however, with the full knowledge of congressional interest.

During the same year as the Eastern Market controversy in the House (fiscal year 1992), the Senate appropriations bill for the District included $50 million for renovations at the George Washington University (GWU) Medical Center, a private institution. Senator Daniel K. Inouye (D-Hawaii), an alumnus of the GWU law school and a former university trustee, used his position on the Senate Appropriations Committee to attach this item to the District budget at the last minute. But the House voted unanimously to fight this effort and, after delaying District budget approval for several weeks, the Inouye amendment was dropped.[63]

Prodded by denunciations of the District as unsafe and morally suspect, the Senate inserted a provision in the fiscal year 1993 District of Columbia appropriations bill that would legalize personal tear gas canisters, commonly known by the trade name Mace. Introduced by Senator Mitch McConnell (R-Ky.), this legislation would have amended District laws, making it legal to purchase and carry tear gas devices. The District had banned Mace for years and local police officials were opposed to any change. This Senate legislation was deleted in conference with the explanation that a bill had been introduced in the District Council by the chairman to legalize the purchase and possession of Mace and similar compounds. The chairman indicated that he expected to transmit this legislation to Congress for review before the end of the year (1992).[64]

AREAS OF CONFLICT

If the frequency of congressional intervention through appropriations may be used as an indication, conflicts of interest between the national and District governments have occurred most often in the areas of public safety, personnel, general government, human services, and education. In most cases the city is simply told what to do, backed up by the threat of freezing its operating funds.

Federal intervention into District of Columbia decisions has clearly gone beyond the areas in which the federal interest is clearest: public safety and land use. And even within these situations, some congressional interventions have involved areas where the federal interest is questionable, such as firehouse closings and precise targets for uniformed police personnel. As shown in table 6.5, interventions have also occurred in virtually all other sectors of District affairs. When Congress finished with the fiscal year 1993 District of Columbia appropriations, the caption of a *Washington Post* article on the handling of the District budget read: " . . . How Congress Plays With The District."[65]

MECHANISMS OF CONTROL

Although the Home Rule Charter provides a variety of mechanisms for exerting federal influence, some have been used much more than others. The provisions for a legislative veto (now legislature plus executive) have been used very sparingly. While some thirty-eight resolutions had been introduced by the end of 1993, on twenty different subjects, only three had been adopted. And in one of the three cases, it was over the objections of the House District Committee, while the full Senate did not act at all.

A more general finding is that very little of the federal intervention in District affairs goes through the authorizing committees. They are rarely successful channels for assertion of federal interests, whether they truly be national interests or disguised parochial interests. The Democratic majorities on the House District Committee have for the most part been strong proponents of increased District autonomy in the home rule period. The role played by the committee results in large measure from the identification of its black chairmen (1973–92) and members with the self-government objectives of the District's black majority.[66]

The success of the House District Committee in defending District interests has forced critics of the District government to find other channels to override District government decisions. The appropriations process has been pressed into service and has taken up the slack as a channel of control. The District of Columbia budget has proven to be an effective device for congressional intervention in District affairs. The most intense budget battles are not about dollars and cents or the control of line items, but about riders and budget provisions that give detailed instructions to local officials and, in recent years, overturn District of Columbia laws. When these appropriations battles take place, the elected officials of the people who provide most of the revenue are like spectators, hoping that some member(s) will step forward to support their cause. Their own nonvoting delegate is like a player who is allowed into the game but is required to wear fetters during the competition.

Using the appropriations process has several advantages for interests seeking to influence or overturn actions of the District government. It does not require going through the House District Committee, which is dominated by members favorable to District interests. A legislative vehicle does not have to be created; the annual District appropriations bill provides a ready-made vehicle. Specific provisions that do not arouse opposition from interest groups or threaten members' interests can be buried in big packages that are unlikely to be challenged on the floor.

LEGITIMATE NATIONAL INTERESTS

Although District appropriations were not designed to reject general public policies, there are a few cases where there appears to be an assertion of legitimate national as opposed to local interests through the appropriations process. Congressional pressure to increase public safety personnel and certain aspects of the lottery restrictions are perhaps the best examples of this type of motivation. This does not mean that federal interests are especially narrow, just that they are generally well protected by existing procedures and have not required special interventions.

In terms of separating federal and local interests, full acceptance of the criteria established by the House District Committee would be a good starting point: Does the action by the District government violate the Constitution, the Home Rule Charter, or the federal interest? The residual powers of the states represent a model that could be followed for the District. Although it is not a state, why not treat it as a state with respect to its powers, except where this would clearly interfere with its mission and function as the seat of the national government? This is already being done in a number of areas.

In addition to the Twenty-third Amendment, there is a series of cases in which the Supreme Court has interpreted the word *state* to include the District.[67] The interstate commerce and extradition clauses of the Constitution have been extended to include the District, and Congress has treated the District as a state in major grant legislation and in other statutes.[68] The burden of proof would be on the national government to indicate by statute those areas or shared areas where it must retain control. As will be shown in chapter 9, this system seems to be working satisfactorily in several foreign countries with federal districts.

The case of the District of Columbia budget illustrates the difficulties of balancing federal and local interests in a federal capital city. The examples in this chapter indicate no clear trend toward general consensus on an appropriate federal role, but rather demonstrate how current institutional arrangements enable Congress to maintain the probability of intervention in policy making in an area it clearly regards as one of special interest.

Since effective democratic government in the capital of the nation is a clear national interest, there are some steps that might be considered by the national and local governments to improve the present home rule situation. Rather than continue its annual forays into District affairs via the appropriations process, Congress might develop statutory criteria for intervening in District policy matters. The House

District Committee criteria or similar guidelines could be made a prerequisite not only for formal veto action but for all congressional intervention into District policy matters. Congress would intervene only if District action violated the Constitution, the Home Rule Charter, or a clear federal interest.

The matter of determining the federal interest would continue to pose a problem in close cases. But where there is flagrant interference in local affairs, the District could at least ask the courts to require Congress to follow its own rules. Admittedly, the protection offered by this approach would be limited: first, because the courts might be reluctant to rule against Congress and, second, Congress could easily adopt a new policy that would legitimize its action. But establishment of such criteria would create an operational hurdle as well as a moral injunction against illegitimate congressional behavior.

The most forthright way to terminate inappropriate interference in District affairs would be to grant it statehood. Until that happens, the most effective way to cut down on the interventions in District policy matters would be to eliminate the mechanism most frequently used by Congress for this purpose—District of Columbia appropriations. As has been often suggested, why not transfer budget authority to the local government where the revenue is collected, leaving Congress responsible for appropriating the federal payment?

District officials might find ways to keep before Congress the need for more budget autonomy in making policies for the District. The gamut could range all the way from insertion of requests in the budget estimates, asking that certain restrictions be removed, as has been done on occasions, to effective networking in Congress by the nonvoting delegate, mayor, and other officials. In a continuous lobbying effort, the many restrictions on items in the budget might be targeted for systematic and organized requests for release.

One of the reasons for recommending that Congress relinquish its powers over the District budget (with the exception of appropriating the federal payment) is the presence of abuse in its exercise of them. With only the federal payment to appropriate, the present appropriations subcommittees for the District of Columbia, in the House and Senate, would not be necessary. Most of the other oversight of the District could be handled by authorizing committees or subcommittees. One reason why the use of these committees would probably lead to more restraint with regard to intrusions in local affairs falls into the area of operating procedures. Their assessments, including the use of hearings, would not necessarily be linked with budget considerations. Many of the riders and micromanagement decisions by the appropriating committees are enacted with little or no study of the item or question at hand, which is not the standard operating procedure for the authorizing committees.

NOTES

1. Public Law 93-198, *The District of Columbia Self-Government and Governmental Reorganization Act of 1973,* 93d Cong., 1st. sess., 1973; 87 *Statutes at Large* 774.

2. "Home Rule for District of Columbia is Approved by House," *In Common* 2 (19 October 1973), 1–4.

3. The leader in this effort was Representative Charles C. Diggs, Jr. (D-Mich.), chairman of the House District Committee that wrote the strong home rule measure. Ibid.

4. Ibid.

5. Public law 93-198, *District of Columbia Self-Government and Government Reorganization Act of 1973.*

6. Most council-passed legislation must "lay over" for thirty days before it goes into effect, giving Congress an opportunity to veto it. Changes in criminal law face a sixty-day waiting period. If two-thirds of the council determines that an emergency requires immediate attention, a simple majority may then pass legislation, effective for ninety days, that is not subject to congressional veto. R. Kent Weaver and Charles W. Harris, "Who's in Charge Here? Congress and the Nation's Capital," *The Brookings Review* 7, no. 3 (Summer 1989): 40–41.

7. Charles W. Harris and Alvin Thornton, *Perspectives of Political Power in the District of Columbia* (Washington, D.C.: National Institute of Public Management, 1981), 91.

8. Ibid., 45–46.

9. The White House, Office of Press Secretary, Release to the Congress of the United States, Washington, D.C., 9 May 1989; see also House, *Making Appropriations for the Government of the District of Columbia and Other Activities Chargeable in Whole or in Part Against the Revenue of Said District* 100th Cong., 2d sess., 1988, H.Rept. 1013, 3.

10. House Committee on Appropriations, *District of Columbia Appropriations Bill, 1993,* 102d Cong., 2d sess.,
1992, H. Rept. 638, 4.

11. *Congressional Record,* 96th Cong., 2d sess., 17 September 1980, 126, pt. 22: 29762.

12. Ibid. 96th Cong., 1st sess., 11 July 1979, 125, pt. 14: 18088.

13. *Washington Star,* 2 November 1978, A-1.

14. *Washington Post,* 5 March 1980, A-1.

15. Ibid., 28 June 1989, B-1.

16. The general fund of the District of Columbia government is the principal operating fund for government activities. During most of the current home rule era, federal funds have comprised less than 20 percent of the total general fund. Between fiscal year 1986 and fiscal year 1990, the federal percentage of total general fund revenue declined from 20.0 percent to 16.8 percent. Since fiscal year 1991 the trend has reversed, with federal support increasing to a planned level of 20.0 percent for fiscal year 1993. District of Columbia, *Fiscal Year 1993 Budget and Revised Fiscal Year 1992 Request* (Washington, D.C., 1992), B-3.

17. District of Columbia, *Fiscal Year 1993 Budget,* (Washington, D.C.), A-2.

18. *Washington Post,* 11 June 1991, A-21.

19. District of Columbia, *The Federal Payment—Fiscal Year 1981,* (Washington, D.C.: October 1979), 1.

20. The sum also included a one-time special payment of $3.6 million to offset costs associated with Operation Desert Shield/Storm. District of Columbia, *Fiscal Year 1993 Budget and Revised Fiscal Year 1992 Request,* A-3.

21. House Committee, *District of Columbia Appropriations Bill, 1993,* 4.

22. *Washington Post,* 30 January 1992, A-10.

23. Confidential interview with executive officer, District of Columbia Budget Office, 24 August 1988; see also *Washington Post,* 18 September 1987, A-1.

24. Ibid., 18 September 1987, A-1. On 8 June 1989, the District of Columbia Court of Appeals cleared the way for the building of the prison by refusing to prevent the demolition of a former hospital on the site, under historic preservation laws. Construction of the prison, first proposed in 1986, has been blocked repeatedly by court suits, congressional intervention, and community opposition. Ibid., 9 June 1989, A-1.

25. The prohibition against "legislation on a general appropriations bill" is contained in rule 21, clause 2 of House Rules (*Deschler's Procedure* 26 11.11 and 11.16), cited in *Congressional Record,* 97th Cong., 2d sess., 30 September 1982, 128, no. 133, daily ed.: H8145; also 96th Cong., 1st sess., 1979, 125, pt. 15: 19059–63.

26. A study conducted by the Congressional Research Service in 1979 of full-time equivalent employment of state and local governments showed the District as having the highest per capita employment in the country—708.4 employees per 10,000 population; counting temporary workers, the District had about 813 workers per 10,000 population. The District work force was 47,000, including 8,000 federal grant positions. With a population of 674,000 in 1979, the chairman of the House District of Columbia Appropriations Subcommittee, Charles Wilson (D-Texas), said that he did not believe 47,000 positions could be justified. *Congressional Record,* 96th Cong., 1st sess., 11 July 1979, 125, pt. 14: 18087 ff.

27. Public Law 102-382, *District of Columbia 1992 Supplemental Appropriations and Rescissions and 1993 Appropriations,* 102d Cong., 2d sess., 1992; 106 *Statutes at Large* 1424.

28. In making the decision to keep Engine Company No. 3 open, the House and Senate conferees said they were reluctant to overrule the city administration on this matter but they were not convinced that the decision to close the station was based solely on operational considerations. House committee of conference, *Making Appropriations for the Government of the District of Columbia and Other Activities Chargeable in Whole or in Part Against the Revenues of Said District for the Fiscal Year Ending September 30, 1992, and for Other Purposes*, 102d Cong., 1st sess., H. Rept. 181, 11.

29. *The Washington Post*, 15 October 1993, A-1.

30. House Committee on Appropriations, *District of Columbia Appropriations Bill*, 1994, 103d Cong., 2d sess., 1992, H. Rept. 152, 60.

31. Ibid., 27 September 1992, B-1.

32. The District of Columbia Taxicab Commission, established pursuant to D.C. Law 6-97, effective 25 March 1986, regulates the public vehicles for hire industry which includes taxicabs, limousines, sightseeing vehicles, tour buses, funeral cars, and private limousines. House Committee, *District of Columbia Appropriations Bill, 1993*, 56; *Making Appropriations for the Government of the District of Columbia and Other Activities Chargeable in Whole or in Part Against the Revenues of Said District for the Fiscal Year Ending September 30, 1992, and for Other Purposes*, 4.

33. Senate Committee on Appropriations, *District of Columbia Appropriations Bill, 1993*, 102d Cong., 2d sess., 23 July 1992, S. Rept. 333, 63.

34. *Congressional Record*, 96th Cong., 1st sess., 17 July 1979, 125, pt. 14: 19060–62.

35. Ibid.

36. Since 1977 the Hyde Amendment (Representative Henry J. Hyde (R-Ill.)) has made it illegal nationwide to pay for abortions with federal funds except in cases of rape, incest or where the life of the mother is in danger. All fifty states are free to make decisions concerning the use of their funds for abortions. *Washington Post*, 28 July 1993, A-1.

37. *Law to Legalize Lotteries, Daily Numbers Games, and Bingo and Raffles for Charitable Purposes in the District of Columbia, 28 District of Columbia Register*, 8 May to 12 June 1981, 2001.

38. House, *District of Columbia Appropriations Bill, 1982*, 97th Cong., 1st sess., H. Rept. 235, 35.

39. House. *Making Appropriations for the Government of the District of Columbia for Fiscal Year 1982*, 97th Cong., 1st sess., 1981, H. Rept. 327, 5.

40. Ibid.

41. The Shipstead-Luce Act (1930) provided for the Commission of Fine Arts to review building permits for new construction adjacent to or abutting existing or proposed public buildings and parks to insure against negative effects on these public properties. The area defined for review covered the whole of Rock Creek Park in the District; the Potomac Parkway; and the monumental core of Mall, White House, and Capitol. With later expansion of federal government facilities, the geographic boundaries of Shipstead-Luce Act jurisdiction were partially expanded. National Capital Planning Commission, *Worthy of the Nation* (Washington, D.C.: Smithsonian Institution Press, 1977), 200–01.

42. H. Rept. 327, 5.

43. An amendment to lift the restrictions was included in the District of Columbia appropriations bill for fiscal year 1987. For further discussion of the lottery with regard to the formal congressional challenge of its establishment, see chapter 4, pp. 73–74.

44. H. Rept. 235, 69.

45. *Congressional Record,* 97th Cong., 2d sess., 30 September 1982, 128, no. 133, daily ed.: H8141–49; see also 7 December 1982, 128, no. 142, daily ed.: S13992.

46. *Congressional Record* 97th Cong., 2d sess., 30 September 1982, 128, no. 133, daily ed.: H8146.

47. Senate, *District of Columbia Appropriations Bill, 1982,* 97th Cong., 1st sess., 1981, H. Rept. 254; see also *Congressional Record* 97th Cong., 2d sess., 7 December 1982, 128, no. 142, daily ed.: S13991–93.

48. *Washington Post,* 28 September 1988, A-1.

49. Ibid., 14 December 1988, A-1.

50. *New York Times,* 1 December 1988, A-28.

51. Located at 3050 R Street, Northwest, the Hurt Home was constructed in 1939 and served as a residence for the blind. It was purchased by the District because of its prior institutional use, location, and usable floor space. The suit against the Hurt Home as a residential-care facility was brought by the Citizens' Association of Georgetown. The Association's appeal in *Speyer vs. Barry* was to the District of Columbia Court of Appeals (Appeal No. 88-958). Public Law 101-518 (5 November 1990); 104 *Statutes at Large* 2224.

52. Ibid.

53. A ten-member advisory board, composed of a diverse group of Georgetown residents supported the project and served as a link between the home and neighbors. Some members of the advisory board were targets of hate mail and other forms of harassment and the chairman of the board linked the spray painting of his home to his civic activities involving the Hurt Home. *Washington Post,* 7 April 1992, B-3; 18 October 1992, C-1.

54. The city's options in dealing with the court's decision included asking the panel to reconsider the ruling, requesting the full court to hear the case, requesting special legislation from the District Council, etc. *Georgetown Current,* 1–14 June 1994, 1; *Washington Post,* 28 May 1994, B-5.

55. *Washington Times,* 6 October 1988, A-1,; *Washington Post,* 19 January 1990, A-1.

56. After his indictment (15 February 1990) and conviction (10 August 1990), Barry lost no time in trying to hit the political comeback trail with the ultimate goal of regaining the office of mayor of the city. In November 1990 he ran unsuccessfully as an independent (temporarily abandoning his life-long affiliation with the Democratic Party) for an at-large seat on the District Council. After completing his six-month jail term (26 October 1991 to 23 April 1992), Barry returned to the District and, *later in the year,* ran successfully as a Democrat for a seat on the council, representing Ward Eight, the poorest section of the city. In 1994 he made the ultimate move for an unprecedented fourth term as mayor. His main opponent in the general election will be former council member Carol Schwartz (R-At Large). David Remnick, "The Situationist," *New Yorker,* 5 September 1994, 87–88; *Washington Post,* 14 September 1994, A-25.

57. The law was left on the books but the District was barred from spending appropriated funds during fiscal year 1993 to implement it. Ibid., 23 September 1992, B-3.

58. Ibid., 1 October 1992, C-1.

59. The Senate District of Columbia Appropriations Subcommittee reported that in recent years Cedar Knoll had been plagued by numerous breaches of security, with more than twenty occurring in 1992. Senate, *District of Columbia Appropriations Bill, 1993,* S. Rept. 333, 59.

District officials gave a different assessment, saying that recent changes in operating procedures and the installation of a fence had improved security at Cedar Knoll. In late June 1992 they said that for the first time in its thirty-five-year history, "there had been no escape from Cedar Knoll over several months." *Washington Post,* 24 June 1992, A-1; 31 July 1992, C-1.

60. Ibid., 25 September 1992, A-1.

61. Ibid., 5 November 1992, C-1.

62. Ibid., 18 July 1991, A-16.

63. The $50 million item for the GWU Medical Center reappeared in the fiscal year 1993 Senate appropriations bill but, again, it was dropped from the final measure. Senate Committee on Appropriations, *District of Columbia Appropriations Bill, 1992,* 102d Cong., 1st sess., 1991, S. Rept. 105, 7–8; ibid., *District of Columbia Appropriations Bill, 1993,* 102d Cong., 2d sess., 1992, S. Rept. 333, 12–13.

64. House, *Making Appropriations for the Government of the District of Columbia and Other Activities Chargeable in Whole or in Part Against the Revenues of Said District for the Fiscal year Ending September 30, 1993, and for Other Purposes,* 102d Cong., 2d sess., 1992, H. Rept. 906, 24.

65. *Washington Post,* 1 October 1992, C-1.

66. This role has not been without costs for the committee. Like other committees that are seen as "captured" by the interests they oversee, the House District Committee has had difficulties in winning floor approval for its own agenda. See pp. 57–58; also Kent Weaver, "Congressional Politics and Local Autonomy in Washington, D.C.," unpublished paper, 18 January 1989, Brookings Institution, Washington, D.C.

67. See Judith Best, *National Representation for the District of Columbia* (Frederick, Md.: University Publications of America, Inc., 1984), 26.

68. Ibid.

7

Land Use: Techworld and Metropolitan Square

Whenever two jurisdictions have authority over the same territory, conflict and disagreement are almost inevitable. While control over land use policy may represent the most fundamental attribute of an autonomous local government, the national stake and interest are substantial in a federal capital city. Consequently, land use and the exercise of planning and zoning powers have been highly controversial policy areas in the federal district, placing them on the cutting edge of the relations between the District and national governments. As discussed in chapter 5, only three statutes have been rejected through formal congressional vetoes. Two of these dealt with land use policies. There have been conflicts over land use between the national and District governments other than vetoed measures, however, and these have been resolved or dealt with through other means.[1]

This chapter examines conflicting federal and local interests that arose over the construction of two mixed-use projects by private developers in the downtown area: Techworld and Metropolitan Square. The Techworld case centered on the city's stewardship responsibilities for the original Pierre L'Enfant Plan, as well as its power to close federally owned streets and alleys (those falling within the original L'Enfant city plan). The central issue in the Metropolitan Square case was building height limitation, which was greatly intensified by its connection with White House security. Each of these projects was approved and strongly supported by the city which, along with the developers, became the main defendant in both cases.

Two preservationist groups, the Committee of 100 on the Federal City (Committee of 100) and the District of Columbia Preservation League (DCPL), were tenacious opponents of Techworld and Metropolitan Square. When they lost at the local level, they sought a remedy through an appeal to national authorities. Although Congress was involved to a limited extent, these cases provide an opportunity to analyze conflicts that for the most part were not resolved through congressional vetoes, challenges, or appropriations. This chapter examines national and local interests as interpreted and articulated mainly by the representatives of the executive branches of the United States and District of Columbia governments, including their interactions with interest groups, community organizations, and the media. In order to analyze adequately the Techworld and Metropolitan Square controversies, it is necessary to review briefly how the current planning and zoning powers developed in the Home Rule Act.

THE PLANNING AND ZONING PROVISIONS OF THE HOME RULE ACT

Congress clearly wrestled with the issue of delegating comprehensive planning authority in the District when it considered home rule legislation in 1973. It faced the question of whether this authority should remain at the federal level in the hands of the National Capital Planning Commission (NCPC) or should be transferred to the local level and vested in the mayor and the city council. To some extent, congressional debate reflected this schism. It was more or less accepted that the planning for federal lands and projects would remain with the national government.

Federal and local leaders strenuously debated local planning and zoning issues both during the passage of home rule legislation and ten years later during the Techworld planning process. Although most of the personalities had changed, the focal point of the debate remained the same: Should federal or local authorities determine land use policy for the District of Columbia?[2]

The Committee of 100 and the Wisconsin Avenue Corridor Committee (WACC), citizens' groups composed primarily of residents from the far northwest portions of the District of Columbia, were outspoken advocates of retaining federal control over all planning within the District. The Coalition for Self Determination for the District of Columbia, another citizens' group, worked closely with Mayor Walter Washington and the District government and urged Congress to give control of local comprehensive planning to the home rule government.[3]

Both of the city's major newspapers, the *Washington Post* and the *Washington Star-News,* favored local control of the nonfederal aspects of comprehensive planning for the District of Columbia. These newspapers produced a series of editorials in defense of their positions, and sharply criticized the NCPC both as a comprehensive planning agency and as protector of the federal interest.[4]

The Senate sought to continue federal control of all planning in the District by refusing to amend the powers or composition of the NCPC. Conversely, the House of Representatives strongly favored relinquishing control of the nonfederal aspects of planning to the District. The ultimate resolution of this controversy granted the local government authority over the nonfederal aspects of planning for the first time in the history of the nation's capital. Under the final provisions of the Home Rule Act the NCPC continues as the central planning agency for the federal government in the region, while authority over planning functions for the District is delegated to the mayor.

Because the Home Rule Act changed both the mission and the membership of the NCPC, its effect was to redefine planning in the District of Columbia.[5] The local government is charged with the duty to prepare the District's elements of the comprehensive plan including land use; urban renewal; redevelopment; social, economic, transportation, and population distribution; and public works programs. The residual, non-District elements fall under the jurisdiction of the NCPC, which was required to prepare the comprehensive plan for federal activities in the national capital.[6] Furthermore, the act grants the NCPC veto power over the District elements of the plan if the NCPC finds that these elements impact negatively on the "interests or functions of the federal establishment." While veto power serves as a check on District planning activities, the increased District representation on the NCPC guards, to a certain degree, against arbitrary exercise of federal veto authority.

Finally, the act allows the NCPC to make nonbinding recommendations to the District of Columbia Zoning Commission on all proposed zoning map or text amendments. The NCPC's advisory role extends to making a determination as to whether a specific proposal comports with the comprehensive plan. This provision of the act ensures that the NCPC will exert influence over both planning and zoning activities in the District. While the NCPC's opinion is not binding on the Zoning Commission, it is accorded substantial weight. Both the Techworld and Metropolitan Square cases tested this elaborate system of checks and balances, which Congress "painstakingly and carefully" drafted to foster responsible land use policy in the District of Columbia.[7]

TECHWORLD

One of the most intense conflicts between federal and local interests during the home rule period involved the authorization to build the World Technology Trade Center for High Technology and Information Industries, better known as Techworld. The conflict that raged during the project's approval process consumed more time than was originally projected for construction. The Techworld saga lasted approximately three years (from 1983 to 1986) and is an important part of the history of the nation's capital, with special significance for the home rule period. In addition, the case contributed toward fleshing out the skeletal design for balancing federal and local interests that was created by the Home Rule Act.

Physical Design and Land Assembly

Techworld is a mixed-use project on a four-acre site comprising two city blocks, adjacent to the District of Columbia Convention Center. Working quietly between 1979 and 1982, the developer,[8] International Developers, Incorporated (IDI), assembled most of the land on the block bounded by K, Eye, Eighth, and Ninth Streets. Realizing later that one block was insufficient space to achieve his objectives, the developer contacted landowners in the block east of the proposed site, between Eighth and Seventh Streets. Through a joint venture arrangement, the developer gained control of most of that block. Final acquisition, however, was contingent upon the closing of Eighth Street and merging the two separate blocks into one parcel (see figure 7.1).

With a total net rentable area of 1,087,502 square feet in the three completed office buildings and the hotel, this property represents one of the largest commercial land assemblages in the city's history. The cost of the land alone was approximately $73 million and the cost of the total project, to be built in stages, was estimated at $300 million. Even after assembling most of the land for the project, the developer made it clear that the entire project remained in doubt without permission from the city to close Eighth Street, Northwest.[9]

Approval to Build

In order to integrate Eighth Street into Techworld, the developer petitioned the District government to permanently close the street to traffic and transfer the street title to the corporation. The developer planned

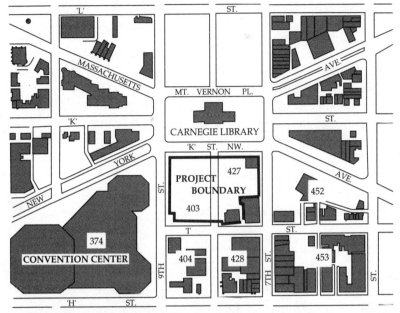

Figure 7.1 Street Map: Techworld Project

to convert a portion of Eighth Street running through the middle of the project into a pedestrian plaza; approximately 75 feet above this plaza, a five-story span would connect the top stories of the main structures, creating one large building. The entire structure would stand 130 feet high. From the time it first unveiled its proposal, IDI met with vocal and tenacious opposition, mainly from District preservationist groups.

The Committee of 100 on the Federal City, founded in 1923 by Frederick A. Delano, is the oldest planning organization in the District. It was created "to restore and promote sound city planning for Washington," and is dedicated to safeguarding the original street pattern for the city as embodied in the L'Enfant Plan for the federal city. The Committee of 100 objected to the closing of Eighth Street and entered the Techworld debate on behalf of its members, whose goal is to preserve the use and enjoyment of the open streets and vistas in the national capital.

The District of Columbia Preservation League (DCPL), a nonprofit corporation, is dedicated to the protection of landmarks in the District of Columbia. Part of its mandate includes preserving the original street patterns in the L'Enfant Plan for the federal city. As a result, the DCPL also became involved in the Techworld controversy on behalf of members who alleged injuries to the federal city landscape similar to those attacked by the members of the Committee of 100.

The preservationists' efforts centered on the developer's plan to close Eighth Street between Eye and K Streets.[10] The United States government held title to Eighth Street and IDI filed application with the city surveyor to close the street. As required by District law, the surveyor solicited comments from the NCPC, the District of Columbia Historic Preservation Review Board, the fire and police departments, the Office of Planning, the Department of Planning and Community Development, and the Department of Environmental Services. With the exception of the Historic Preservation Review Board, each agency recommended approval of the application with some modifications or adjustments that were designed to ensure that the street closing and the project as a whole would be advantageous to the city. The developer repeatedly changed and modified the project to address the concerns of the reviewing bodies.[11]

The Committee on Public Works of the District Council considered the proposal and submitted its final report, recommending the closing of a portion of Eighth Street and declaring that Techworld would have "a positive fiscal impact" on the District economy. The full council voted unanimously to close the specified block of Eighth Street and to transfer title to the developer. As required by the Home Rule Act, the mayor forwarded the measure to both houses of Congress for the mandatory thirty-day review period. Congress failed to exercise its veto power and the legislation became law in December 1984.

Both the NCPC and the Zoning Commission ultimately agreed that the project's design regarding Eighth Street did not substantially impair the vista that the preservationists sought to protect. These conclusions, however, ran contrary to the position of the NCPC staff, which recommended denial of the plan on the grounds that it would interfere with the landmark vista between the Carnegie Library in Mount Vernon Square and the National Portrait Gallery. The staff also stated that the project's proposed 130-foot height violated District of Columbia law. It further noted that Techworld's size would literally and figuratively overshadow Mount Vernon Square. By and large, these comments concurred with the preservationist groups' testimony at hearings before the NCPC.

In recommending denial of the Techworld project proposal, the NCPC staff equated the federal interest with the historic Eighth Street vista. In spite of the staff recommendation, the NCPC voted seven to four to approve what had become an intensely controversial proposal. Philosophical differences split the NCPC. While the commission was bound by its mandate to protect the federal interest in planning decisions affecting the national capital region, there were divergent perceptions among its members as to what constituted the federal interest within the context of the project being considered. Some members viewed the Eighth Street vista in historic context, emphasizing the original design of Pierre L'Enfant and focusing on the architectural splendor and aesthetic ambience of the city. Others purportedly accepted the full importance of the vista but recognized the overriding importance of supporting and nurturing development in the downtown area.

By endorsing the proposal, the NCPC showed support for the mayor's efforts to bring jobs to the city. Actually, the NCPC statement of approval was no more than an endorsement of Deputy Mayor for Economic Development Curtis McClinton's prodevelopment stance. Deputy Mayor McClinton had defended the project, including the proposed bridge over Eighth Street, and stated that Techworld required the open, continuous floor space that the span would create. He further expressed the belief that the project would bring needed business to the District's convention center.

While the Council of the District of Columbia is not bound by the recommendation of the NCPC in deciding a rezoning petition, the NCPC report can be a key factor in the council's deliberations. The Eighth Street Closing Act in some respects presaged the division that was later voiced at the NCPC hearing on the rezoning. The council approved the street-closing legislation conditional on the developer's promise to maintain the view along Eighth Street. Thus, the council attempted to placate the developer and the District government by granting the street closing, while simultaneously seeking to appease preservationists by restricting the project's encroachment into L'Enfant's prized vista.

The Legal Battle

Both the DCPL and the Committee of 100 are concerned with the protection of landmarks and the historic character of the federal district. In October 1985 they wrote to the director of the National Capital Region of the Department of the Interior, arguing that the Eighth Street Closing Acts were an unlawful appropriation of United States property.[12]

Their letter demanded that the Department of the Interior immediately move to reclaim the street and threatened a mandamus action if the department refused. The preservationists also persistently threatened the developers and District government officials with legal action to halt the development of Techworld.

Three months later, their demands still unmet, the preservationists filed suit in the United States District Court for the District of Columbia seeking declaratory and injunctive relief against IDI, Mayor Marion Barry, the District Council, several District officials, and the NCPC. The preservationists also sued the Department of the Interior for mandamus relief. On the same day, IDI brought an action against the DCPL, the Committee of 100, and the District of Columbia, seeking a declaration as to the legality of the transfer of the Eighth Street property.

Responding to the mandamus petition, the United States Department of Justice filed a quiet title action with respect to the Eighth Street property on behalf of the Department of the Interior, the Smithsonian Institution, and the NCPC.[13] The Justice Department also asked that IDI be required to shave twenty feet from the planned height of the two-square-block project. While some viewed the entrance of the United States government into the case as a challenge to home rule, the government emphasized instead that the issue was the preservation of Pierre L'Enfant's city street plan. Later, the preservationists consented to dismissal of the mandamus action, and the title action was consolidated with the other two actions.[14]

The preservationists and the federal government set forth numerous substantive and procedural arguments attacking the validity of the closing and bridging of Eighth Street.[15] Initially, the preservationists argued that the District Council exceeded its authority in the Home Rule Act when it purportedly ceded the Eighth Street tract to the developer under the Eighth Street Closing Acts. Next, the preservationists argued that the enactment of the closing acts was itself flawed for failing to meet the procedural requirements of the National Historic Preservation Act (NHPA). Because the Eighth Street vista was an historic landmark, the preservationists claimed that all previously granted excavation permits issued in connection with Techworld were illegal for failing to conform with District of Columbia historic preservation legislation. Finally, the preservationists argued that the proposed 130-foot height of Techworld violated the District of Columbia Height of Buildings Act. After an analysis of the issues, the court rejected each of these arguments.

Although the Home Rule Act prohibits the District government from enacting legislation which concerns the functions or property of the United States, the United States District Court's first inquiry was whether Congress, by the provisions of the Home Rule Act, intended to abrogate the District's power to close streets. Congress first delegated street-closing power to the District government in 1932. Each time Congress reorganized the structure of the District government, the power to close streets was passed on to the reorganized District government, along with all other previously held powers.[16]

The court reviewed the purpose of the Home Rule Act, which was to free Congress from the onus of administering the local concerns of the District by giving the District government most of the powers of other municipalities. Thus, the court concluded that to retrieve the street-closing power from the District would achieve a result in direct conflict with the act's stated purpose. As additional evidence of Congress's intent, the court noted that not only had Congress reviewed and not vetoed the closing acts during the thirty-day review period, but Congress also failed to veto a District statute changing the street-closing procedures.[17]

The preservationists also argued that even if the District government had the authority to close and transfer the Eighth Street property, the exercise of that authority was void for failure to comply with the procedures of the National Historic Preservation Act (NHPA).[18] The NHPA requires that the Advisory Council on Historic Preservation (ACHP) be allowed to make recommendations to any federal agency involved in an "undertaking" that affects historic areas. The NCPC was the only federal agency involved in the Eighth Street closing. The preservationists maintained that the Eighth Street closing was a "federal undertaking" within the meaning of this statute and that, since the ACHP was not given an opportunity to comment to the NCPC, the closing procedures were thereby flawed.

The court looked to the NHPA itself and found that the role of the NCPC did not rise to the level of an "undertaking," which exists "where a federal agency has direct or indirect control of a project involving the expenditure of federal funds, or the issuance of a federal license."[19] Here, the only NCPC involvement was to provide the District Council with a nonbinding recommendation. The NCPC itself did not believe that its limited role created an "undertaking." The court concluded that the Eighth Street closing was not a "federal undertaking" and, therefore, the relevant provisions of the NHPA were not triggered by the NCPC's involvement in Techworld.

Another of the preservationists' arguments alleged that the procedures used by the mayor in issuing the excavation permit for Techworld were flawed because the mayor failed to allow the District of Columbia Historic Preservation Review Board to comment on the permit applications as required by the Historic Landmark and Historical District Protection Act (HLHDPA). Like the National Historic Preservation Act, the HLHDPA requires a comment period by an independent historical preservation committee before the city may take action altering an historic landmark. Among the landmarks listed in the District of Columbia Inventory of Historic Sites is the "Eighth Street Vista from Mt. Vernon Square to National Archives."[20]

The court summarily rejected the preservationists' argument on the grounds that the vista described in the inventory did not in fact exist. It pointed out that interrupting the view between Mount Vernon Square and the National Archives is the Old Patent Office Building. Noting that the creators of the inventory "were not always able to exercise a constant degree of care," and without trying to resolve the ambiguity created by the inaccurate listing, the court concluded that there was no vista. Therefore, the HLHDPA comment provisions did not apply to Techworld.

The preservationists argued that an authorized height of 130 feet for the Techworld project violated the District of Columbia height limitation law. The Height of Buildings Act of 1910 provides that buildings may have a maximum height equal to the width of the street on which they front plus an additional 20 feet. Where a building fronts on a public space at the intersection of two or more streets, calculation of the width of the street may include any public space (a traffic circle or square) adjoining it, provided that the public space does not interrupt the course of the street.

The ultimate issue was whether or not Mount Vernon Square interrupted the respective courses of K Street, New York Avenue, and Massachusetts Avenue. The government (Department of Justice) argued that the project interrupted the course of each of these streets and, for this reason, the special "widest street" rule did not apply. Noting that the interpretation and application of the Height of Buildings Act was within the province of the District of Columbia corporation counsel, the court deferred to the counsel's ruling, which had authorized a height of 130 feet based on the District of Columbia surveyor's opinion that Mount Vernon Square did not interrupt the respective courses of the above three streets.[21]

Delivering its opinion on 5 August 1986 the court rejected all arguments made by the opponents of Techworld and confirmed the propriety of the Eighth Street closing and transfer. Some of the representatives of the preservationists and the national government said they expected to lose at the district court level, but were prepared to appeal and were optimistic about their chances of winning the next round.[22]

Making the Run to the Hill

The persistent threat of an appeal was a cause for worry on the part of the developer—a constituent of northern Virginia. After consultations with District officials within the offices of the mayor, council chairman, and corporation counsel, IDI sought insurance against further legal action by opponents of the project. Congressional action would bring permanent closure to the matter. Initially, the developer's overtures to Capitol Hill met with resistance from some District officials, who saw the move as undermining home rule. But when the preservationists filed their appeal on 25 September 1986 and the 99th Congress prepared to adjourn, IDI perceived an urgent need for action, lest the Techworld project be lost altogether.

Tapping his political contacts on Capitol Hill and relying on at least acquiescence from local government officials, the developer sought a joint resolution from Congress to reaffirm the city's action to close Eighth Street. Working mainly through members of the Virginia delegation in Congress (Republican Senators John Warner and Paul Trible and Representative Stan Parris) and Delegate Walter E. Fauntroy (D-D.C.), the developer intensified his efforts to obtain passage of this special legislation. Representative Parris introduced the legislation with Delegate Fauntroy as a cosponsor—one of the few times these members of Congress agreed on a District of Columbia issue. The District's fiscal year 1987 appropriations bill included a rider supporting Techworld that was attached during the final hours of the appropriations debate.[23]

The Techworld controversy centered around a conflict between local actors who sought to shift the arena. Congress, the usual intervenor in District affairs, did not get involved officially in the legal conflict, and when it finally entered the case, it sided with the local government. Congress's policy action originated from the parochial interests of members of the Virginia congressional delegation. There is no evidence that the rank-and-file members cared much about the conflict or its outcome.

In the split between the executive branch and Congress in the Techworld controversy, the executive agencies apparently assigned no great importance to this case. Agency interest appeared mainly among middle level rather than top executives, such as Attorney General Edwin Meese III and Secretary of the Interior Donald Hodel. Had there been strong interest from the executive branch, Congress probably would not have entered the case on the side of local government and the developer. In the final analysis Congress, with local acquiescence, was willing to rubber-stamp parochial concerns. It intervened for reasons other than protection of a national interest.

Land use policy continued to be at the cutting edge of the conflicts between the national and District governments. The next land use conflict—Metropolitan Square—focused on different issues and was resolved in a different way.

METROPOLITAN SQUARE

Although both Techworld and Metropolitan Square resulted in protracted conflicts between the national and District governments over land use policy, there are significant differences between these two disputes. While the central issue in the Techworld case focused on the original Pierre L'Enfant Plan for the city, the focal issue in the Metropolitan Square dispute was building height limitation. When the height of a building in the nation's capital poses a threat to White House security, there is due cause for alarm—especially if there is a possible misinterpretation of the controlling law.

A judicial remedy was sought and rendered in the Techworld case, but not in Metropolitan Square, since the court refused to get involved. The battle raged at the approval-to-build stage with Techworld, whereas the building was virtually up for everyone to see its height before the critical stage of conflict was reached in Metropolitan Square. A negotiated settlement was reached in the latter conflict and has worked reasonably well so far (1994) but still leaves some apprehension on the national side.

Both cases were driven by interest groups, joined by aspects of the national government. Although it was not a clear winner, the local government prevailed in both instances. Except when the threat to White House security came up in the Metropolitan Square case, the overall interest of Congress in these cases was relatively low.

Physical Setting

Metropolitan Square is a twelve-story office complex located across the street from the United States Treasury Department and one block from the White House grounds. When it was completed, its rooftop offered an unobstructed view of the North Portico of the Executive Mansion.[24]

The beginning stage of negotiations to arrive at a redevelopment concept for square 224 dates back to the administration of Mayor Walter Washington (1975–1979), the first mayor of the current home rule period. The process of review of plans for this square was probably the most comprehensive coordinated effort yet undertaken by the District of Columbia government over a specific piece of property. It involved one of the city's leading developers, the Oliver T. Carr Company, and many District and federal government agencies, including the District of Columbia Planning Office, the Economic Development Office, the NCPC, the United States Commission on Fine Arts, Don't Tear It Down, Incorporated, and other agencies and organizations.[25]

Emerging Issues: Development, Preservation, Security

The Metropolitan Square project was endorsed by Mayor Marion Barry in 1979 as a joint effort by public and private sectors and community groups that was important to the development and preservation programs in the downtown area. From a development standpoint, however, Metropolitan Square had its problems and risks. It was close to but not quite in what was the top location in the city for most office tenants and it contained four registered national landmarks: the Keith Theatre/Albee Building, the National Metropolitan Bank Building, Rhodes Tavern (all category II landmarks), and the landmark interior of the Old Ebbitt Grill.[26] When the developer began exploring the opportunity for a development project on the square, the Keith-Albee Building at the corner of 15th and F Streets was vacant and deteriorating, as was most of the block, with the exception of the Garfinckel Department Store at the corner of 14th and F Streets (see figure 7.2).[27]

The Metropolitan Square development and the conflicts that surrounded it went on for nearly ten years—from 1977 to 1986. The deci-

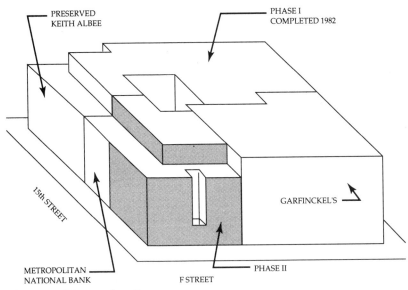

PRESERVED
KEITH ALBEE

PHASE I
COMPLETED 1982

15th STREET

GARFINCKEL'S

METROPOLITAN
NATIONAL BANK

F STREET

PHASE II

Figure 7.2 Metropolitan Square

sion of the District government to allow increased building height for the Metropolitan Square project became the focal point of conflict.

The Council of the District of Columbia gave enthusiastic support to the Metropolitan Square development. Its primary responsibility in this project, which it promptly assumed, was to enact legislation to increase the height limitation for this development.[28] The council took special note of the fact that the project was consistent with the goals of the overall economic development program for the District. Moreover, it was the first private redevelopment project in the downtown area outside of the work of the Pennsylvania Avenue Development Corporation (PADC). Since public funds for downtown development were not available in the amount required, the position of the council was that private redevelopment of downtown east of 15th Street "must be encouraged rather than hindered" if that area was to be revitalized.[29]

At the outset the main participants in the project—the developer, the District government, and the preservationists—were by and large a "consensus group," motivated by the common goal of improving and developing the capital city. With the exception of the profit motive, all of the parties were concerned about the same things, though not in the same order of priority: promoting economic development, preserving landmarks, revitalizing downtown, creating jobs, and, of course, maintaining strong White House security.

In time, the presence of the historic landmarks on the square made its development extremely complicated. The two prime movers in the project, Mayor Barry and the developer, both emphasized their concern for the District's preservation program. But both had items on their project agenda of higher priority. Developers, along with other entrepreneurs, must realize financial profit to remain afloat. A top priority with the mayor was to implement his perceived mandate from the people, which involved such items as revitalizing downtown, increasing the housing supply, improving the status of traffic and transportation, and generally expanding the tax base. The preservationists were concerned with architectural heritage, so the aesthetics of their community and the historic landmarks were the focus of their interest and attention.

In February 1978 the Carr Company applied for demolition permits for three landmarks: the Keith/Albee Building, the National Metropolitan Bank, and Rhodes Tavern. Although the permits were forthcoming, several delays were sought and granted in order that funds might be secured for preservation.[30] The initial estimated cost to save the three landmarks was placed at $5.9 million, with a later estimate at $7.2 million.

At this early stage, amid amicable relations among the parties, it seemed that the city's best response to the preservationist cause was to find the necessary funds to preserve the landmarks. Consequently, in late 1979 when the staff members at two federal agencies were writing letters and issuing reports opposing the proposed District Council action to amend the Schedule of Heights, several top staff members of Mayor Barry were engaged in a search to identify and commit funds to save the Keith/Albee facade. A wide-ranging search was carried out by the city and the preservationist groups but no commitment of adequate funds was found.

The local media were deeply involved in the project. For over a three-month period they had given almost continuous coverage to the cause of saving the Keith/Albee facade from destruction. Numerous editorials and feature articles appeared in both the *Washington Post* and the *Washington Star*. As efforts to save the facades intensified, increasing pressure was being placed on the Barry administration for help in achieving this goal. A total of nine design proposal alternates were prepared by the Carr Company for the development on square 224; some called for retaining the facades of the landmark structures and some did not.

In spite of the highly publicized efforts by the District government and others, commitments of actual funding to save the Keith/Albee facade were not made before a court-imposed deadline. By this time, the position of the District government was that all three of the landmark structures could not be saved, given the limited public funding available. District officials regarded the retention of the facades of the Keith/Albee and the National Metropolitan Bank to be of higher priority for preservation than the retention of Rhodes Tavern because of the relationship of the first two to the White House precinct and the Treasury Building in particular. Consequently, the city accepted the developer's proposal to remove Rhodes Tavern from its site by demolition or to allow its relocation to another site by a nonprofit organization. These decisions by the city were concurred with by Don't Tear It Down.

In July 1979 a District of Columbia Superior Court order was issued that finally permitted the developer to proceed with demolition of the Keith/Albee facade. Two days later the developer publicly offered to preserve the facade without public funding if a number of conditions and assurances of support for the Metropolitan Square project were agreed to by the District and federal governments. The District government was the point of contact and a list of some twenty-four conditions and/or items was communicated to Assistant City Administrator for Planning and Development James O. Gibson. One of the key conditions on the list was that the District government would amend the Schedule of Heights and give expedited assistance in the closing of the alleys on the square. Additionally, the Department of the Interior and the NCPC were to interpose no objection to the amendment to the height schedule by the District Council, and the White House was to support the total Carr project. Other demands included such items as

    a) Support approval of total Carr project before the following:
        Historic Preservation Review Board
        National Capital Planning Commission
        Any other District or Federal board or agency with approval or recommending authority.
    b) Vigorously oppose any actions which will impair, delay or prevent the development of the total Carr project.[31]

When a design was first being conceptualized for Metropolitan Square back in 1977, the Carr Company was planning to rehabilitate Rhodes Tavern as a part of its project. As late as September 1978, the company still intended to preserve Rhodes Tavern. By July 1979 Carr had changed its position and demanded the support of the city to eliminate Rhodes Tavern either by moving or demolishing it.

If the conditions were not met, Carr stated, "new construction" would be substituted for the Keith/Albee facade. Action was already under way in the District Council to amend the Schedule of Heights before the demands to the District government were put in writing. In light of the overall agenda of the Barry administration, including pressure from interest groups on Metropolitan Square, the council was inclined to move forward with the legislation to amend the Schedule of Heights.

The city accepted the terms of the Carr package. Indicating that the details would be conveyed by the assistant city administrator, Mayor Barry declared to the developer: "I am personally committed to working with you to complete your exciting project. . . ." On the same day, Gibson wrote to Carr assuring him that the Office of Planning and Development would "support approval of the total Carr project before reviewing boards and commissions," and would "oppose actions that would delay, interfere with, or prevent completion of the total Carr project."[32]

As public concern mounted to save the landmark buildings, Carr was well aware of the increasing pressure on the mayor and the city administration. It was a political situation that could be used to his advantage and he did a good job of exploiting it. What had been largely a consensus group, working together to revitalize downtown and preserve the city's landmarks, began to fall apart over disagreements about the strategies that should be followed to achieve the goals to which all of the parties were committed. The preservationists thought that the city was giving away too much to the developer for what it was getting in return. As the conflict intensified, the behavior of the respective parties began to be controlled increasingly by their top priorities. For the mayor, this was economic development; for the preservationists, it was the city's history and architectural heritage; and for the developer—a sound business investment.

In an exhaustive agreement, representing a hard-won compromise with the local preservationists and District government officials, Carr promised to incorporate the beaux arts facades of two nearby buildings—the Keith/Albee and the National Metropolitan Bank—and relocate the interior of the Old Ebbitt Grill in the Metropolitan Square project, which would retain a sense of the area's context. This agreement was concurred with by the main preservationist group, Don't Tear It Down. No provision to save Rhodes Tavern was included and the agreement later came unravelled when an eleventh-hour campaign was mounted by a citizens' committee to prevent its demolition.[33]

By this time the struggle over the Metropolitan Square project had become so bitter that conflicts were erupting within the ranks of the preservationists. Bob Peck, president of Don't Tear it Down, expressed sympathy for the developer who, in his view, had negotiated in good faith. After years of litigation that pitted hard-core preservationists against one of the city's leading developers, a bulldozer began knocking down historic Rhodes Tavern in September 1984. The District of Columbia Court of Appeals lifted an injunction that had blocked the District government from issuing a demolition permit for the building. The tavern's supporters accused the mayor and other city officials of letting Oliver T. Carr and his company "pull the strings" in the city. The seven-year struggle over Rhodes Tavern had managed to divide preservationists, politicians, and the general public and had written a classic chapter in the development and preservation records of the District.

District Council Action

When it was made clear by the District of Columbia corporation counsel that the Board of Zoning Adjustment had no jurisdiction to consider a "variance" from the Schedule of Heights, it was up to the District Council to consider the developer's request for a height increase. This legislation was approved by the council on 9 October and signed by the mayor on 3 November 1979. Apparently, the council had no warning of the storm of protest, particularly at the federal level, that would later erupt over its enactment of legislation amending the Schedule of Heights.

The council was not contacted nor did it receive any correspondence or information from any federal agency or source which mentioned the fact that raising the height limitation for a building on 15th Street would pose a threat to White House security. In fact, neither the matter of security nor any other concerns were raised with the council during the pendency of the act to amend the Schedule of Heights. The council did hear from preservationist groups expressing their concerns about granting a setback and height increase at a site opposite the United States Treasury Building. Among other objectives, the primary purpose of the Height of Buildings Act of 1910 (and adoption of the Schedule of Heights which it mandated) was to control the height of buildings on blocks immediately adjacent to public buildings or "to the side of any public building. . . ."[34]

Chairwoman Elizabeth Rowe of the Committee of 100 wrote to the District Council expressing the concern of her committee and recommending that it not grant exceptions to the 1910 height act without requiring certain review procedures, similar to those followed by the Zoning Commission and the Board of Zoning Adjustment when they consider the height exceptions within their jurisdiction. The Committee of 100 did not challenge the authority of the council to amend the Schedule of Heights, only its procedure for taking this action.[35]

Correspondence available to the council from Assistant City Administrator Gibson suggested that the federal executive branch was in support of the Metropolitan Square project, including the bill to alter the height limitation schedule. The letter from the assistant city administrator stated:

> The Federal Executive Branch has been responsive to all District efforts to date regarding Square 224, and its interest and assistance are expected to continue.[36]

Some four years after the Schedule of Heights Amendment Act of 1979 had been passed by the council, the above statement would take on added significance as Congress began to make inquiries into the circumstances under which the threat to White House security developed.

What was to become the critical point in the council's action did not surface officially until after the bill was passed. Did the council know about the security issue? In response to an inquiry from the NCPC concerning the council bill to amend the Schedule of Heights, the United States Secret Service officially communicated its concerns to the NCPC regarding the proposed council action. On 18 October 1979, a little over a week after the council had enacted the height bill, Executive Director of the NCPC Reginald Griffith wrote to Mayor Barry, conveying the Secret Service concerns. Two weeks later the mayor signed the measure and it went to Congress for the required thirty-day layover period before it became effective law.

Reginald Griffith sent the Secret Service letter to Mayor Barry under a cover letter which suggested that in light of the security concerns that had been raised, alternative height and setback modifications might be more acceptable in the area overlooking the White House. The executive director did not present the matter to the commissioners of the NCPC and this body never met to consider the Secret Service concerns.[37]

After the District government enacted the Schedule of Heights Amendment Act of 1979, the matter was more or less dormant for nearly four years, while phase I of Metropolitan Square was under construction. As long as the complex had not reached its ultimate height, no actual threat to White House security existed and not much attention was focused on it. But as the building neared completion, its period of "benign neglect" came to an end.

Making Security Adjustments

The United States Treasury Building across the street from Metropolitan Square is only 80 feet high and many of the buildings in the vicinity are limited to 95 feet. The authorized height of phase I of Metropolitan Square was 130 feet at the cornice line. The rooftop vantage point, however, topped by an equipment house containing machinery, raised the total elevation to 148 feet, affording a commanding view, over the Treasury Building, of the north side of the White House mansion. Metropolitan Square advertisements for tenants touted "an unobstructed view of the White House." As the building neared completion, the White House ceased the customary practice of having President Ronald Reagan greet visiting heads of state in the North Portico. Instead, the first family received the visitors inside.[38]

There were a series of meetings between the Secret Service and the Carr Company to decide upon a course of action to mitigate the security problem posed by phase I, and later these discussions included future precautionary measures for phase II. The Secret Service will not discuss the specific details of their security plan, but government officials familiar with the issue say that the plan included stationing agents on the building rooftops during special White House events and overseeing the Carr Company security system. The developer bore the costs of required modifications in the buildings and, apparently, the Secret Service quietly resolved most of its concerns about the security threat posed by the height of Metropolitan Square and the vantage point it provides onto the White House complex. In spite of all the precautionary steps that have been taken, Secret Service officials state unequivocally that White House security has been impaired by the height of Metropolitan Square.[39]

In 1983 the entire controversy took on new life and began to mushroom. How did it all happen? Who was looking out for the federal interest? How adequate is the system for keeping abreast of District government actions that might affect the federal interest? These were some of the lingering questions being raised by members of Congress, executive branch officials, local organizations, and citizens.

Congressional Inquiry

As the news of a possible breach in White House security, brought on by local action and/or federal inaction, began to circulate broadly in the media it would be expected that congressional concerns would lead to an investigation. The matter was receiving almost daily coverage in the local press and articles about the threat to White House security appeared in papers as far away as New Orleans and Los Angeles.[40] Considering the fact that only two years earlier (30 March 1981) President Reagan had been shot in the nation's capital, the security issue was touching a sensitive nerve in the federal establishment.

An initial congressional inquiry by the Subcommittee on Governmental Efficiency and the District of Columbia of the Senate Committee on Governmental Affairs was conducted in 1983, and two years later, in 1985, Senator Frank R. Lautenberg (D-N.J.) made a formal request to the United States General Accounting Office (GAO) for a full investigative report on height limitations in the District of Columbia. The chairman and ranking member of the subcommittee were Senators Charles McC. Mathias (R-Md.) and Thomas F. Eagleton (D-Mo.), who were mainly responsible for the investigation.

The respective inquiries from Mathias and Eagleton focused mainly on the security of the White House and its grounds as well as the invasion of privacy of the president and his family. Some of the specific questions raised in the Mathias and Eagleton inquiries centered on whether or not the District Council, prior to its enactment of legislation to change the permitted height for Metropolitan Square, was aware of Secret Service concerns about the security of the executive mansion complex. Was the council aware of questions concerning its legal authority, under the Home Rule Act, to pass the Schedule of Heights Amendment Act of 1979?

In his response to the congressional inquiries, District Council Chairman David Clarke explained that the body was unaware of any concerns about White House security when the bill to amend the Schedule of Heights was approved. With regard to their authority to amend the Schedule of Heights, Clarke stated that the council relied on a legal opinion from the District of Columbia corporation counsel which stated that the council had "explicit authority" to amend the schedule. The basis of this opinion was that the council, in passing the act in question, was exercising authority over the Schedule of Heights inherited from the pre-home rule government and that its action did not contravene "the plain meaning" of the Home Rule Act and its restriction on the power of the council to act in the area of building height limitation.[41]

In effect, the District Council had been able to give categorical responses to two of the main questions raised in the congressional inquiries: It was not aware of any security concerns of the federal government prior to its action amending the Schedule of Heights; it had abided by its legal authority under the Home Rule Act as interpreted by the corporation counsel.

The central question put to Mayor Barry by Senator Mathias was why had he signed the bill into law if he knew of security concerns or questions about the authority of the District government to alter the Schedule of Heights? The mayor's response included a number of points, emphasizing numerous contacts with the White House and many other federal agencies regarding the Metropolitan Square project. The mayor referred to a meeting of federal officials (including NCPC staff) that had been convened in April 1979 by the assistant city administrator to discuss the matter. A question about the project and a possible threat to White House security had been raised by the treasurer of the United States, Mrs. Azie Morton, who agreed to check into the matter. Her findings, according to the mayor, were that the matter had been discussed with the general counsel of the Treasury, and with the Secret Service and "there did not seem to be a concern."[42] The mayor confirmed one aspect of White House involvement that had been largely hearsay up to that time—that First Lady Rosalynn Carter was "interested in the preservation of the building facades" and that he had spoken with her about the matter on several occasions.[43]

Although he was not contacted through the congressional inquiry, developer Oliver T. Carr, Jr. decided to respond voluntarily. He said that visual access to the White House grounds "is provided by many buildings of even modest height that exist near 17th Street, Lafayette Park and the 15th Street financial district." Carr cited his own headquarters building at 17th and Pennsylvania Avenue as an example. He called attention to over twenty years of effective cooperation between his company and the Secret Service on security matters and expressed optimism that proper White House security could be provided in "a reasonable and professional manner" as it had in the past.[44]

There are different versions of the reason why Secret Service concerns about the proposed height of Metropolitan Square were not presented to the NCPC, guardian of the federal interest. One of the reasons given by the NCPC executive director, Reginald Griffith, was that he did not want to raise the security issue with NCPC Chairman David M. Childs because that would have possibly created "accusations of conflict of interest." Childs, who had hired Griffith as executive director in 1979, was the presidentially appointed chairman of the NCPC from 1976 to 1980. He was also the chief architect at the Oliver T. Carr Company for the Metropolitan Square project. Explaining that he wanted to avoid "even the appearance of conflict of interest," Griffith took up the matter with the vice chairman of the NCPC, who happened to be James O. Gibson, the assistant city administrator for the District of Columbia.

The final aspect of the congressional inquiry was to ask the NCPC to conduct a comprehensive internal investigation of its involvement in Metropolitan Square. The formal response of the NCPC to the congressional inquiry was that its staff had "acted responsibly in the matter" of the Metropolitan Square development project. It found "no impropriety" on the part of any staff or commission member. It did discover, however, that the authority of the NCPC with regard to the security of the White House was limited and that perhaps there was a need for either better coordination or a greater federal role in protecting the White House.

Concerned that the federal interest in the District of Columbia "may not be adequately protected" under current processes governing building height limitations, Senator Frank Lautenberg (D-N.J.) requested the GAO to carry out an investigation of building height limitations in the District of Columbia. He requested an assessment of whether current laws and regulations satisfactorily protected the federal interest with respect to security and to the architectural and aesthetic character of the city as the nation's capital.[45]

The GAO reports, submitted to Senator Lautenberg in July and September 1986, indicated that the District Council was not prohibited by the provisions of the Home Rule Act from enacting the Schedule of Heights Amendment Act of 1979, which allowed the construction of Metropolitan Square to a height of 130 feet. The reports found that the administrative apparatus in place to enforce the Height of Buildings Act of 1910 and the Schedule of Heights lies with the District government. In this respect, "protection of the Federal interest is locally enforced."[46]

Although the NCPC is responsible for protecting the federal interests in the District of Columbia and the national capital region, it does not have approval authority over the heights of proposed private sector buildings and is not typically involved in the review of private sector building projects unless an alley closing (over ten feet wide), zoning change, or planned unit development is proposed. It does have approval authority over federal building projects throughout the District and over District government building projects within the central area.[47]

Citizen Litigation

After concluding that the national government was not going to move against the Metropolitan Square project, a lawsuit was brought by three longtime District residents with "interest in the architecture, history and planning of the District of Columbia."[48] The plaintiffs sought the removal of the top three stories of phase I of Metropolitan Square, alteration of the project plans for phase II, and a declaratory judgment that the Schedule of Heights Amendment Act of 1979 was unlawful "and is therefore void." The defendants in the case were the District of Columbia, Mayor Marion S. Barry, and the Oliver T. Carr Company.[49]

While the United States District Court did not deny the plaintiffs' standing to sue, it dismissed the case on the principle of *laches*—that the plaintiffs waited too long to bring action. Subsequently, a three-judge appeals court panel gave summary affirmance to the lower court ruling. Therefore, the substantive legal questions raised in the case were not considered by either court. After the case was dismissed by the appeals court, the plaintiffs filed a petition for rehearing *en banc*—asking the full court to hear the case. They also prepared a detailed report for Attorney General Edwin Meese III, requesting the United States government to intervene in the case on the side of the plaintiffs.

In the final analysis, the Department of Justice did not intervene in the case. The United States attorney for the District of Columbia, Joseph diGenova, preferred not to get involved, and the petition for re-hearing *en banc* by the appeals court was denied.[50] With the substantive issues in their lawsuit never examined by the lower courts, the plain-tiffs took their case to the United States Supreme Court. In January 1986, the long and often bitter struggle over Metropolitan Square came to a final conclusion when the Supreme Court denied *certiorari* in the case. Later in the year, phase II of the project was completed at a total height of 157 feet, and now two large flags—of the United States and Metropolitan Square, respectively—wave peacefully in the wind high on the rooftop of this controversial building, overlooking the White House and its grounds.[51]

The problems growing out of the construction of Metropolitan Square revealed that a critical gap existed over the lack of controls or guidelines for private development in the area which potentially im-pacts upon the White House precinct. None of the existing federal agencies with responsibilities or roles regarding the White House area and its environs appeared to have the authority to institute adequate controls over private development.

The primary agency charged with protecting the federal interest, the NCPC, has no authority over local planning and development un-less there is a negative impact on the federal interest. This gives the NCPC a fairly broad mandate to advise on a wide range of local plan-ning and zoning matters. In the Metropolitan Square case, the NCPC generally took a conservative view of its limited powers and role where private development was concerned. On the other hand, Mayor Barry and city officials made skillful use of all the powers available to them as "the central planning agency for the District Government."

It is generally agreed by officials at both levels that national au-thorities should protect the federal interest and the local government should settle local matters. The basic problem rests upon the defini-tions of federal and local interests in the nation's capital. Federal and local interests have become so intertwined over the years that clearly defining or separating them is a tough challenge to lawmakers. Border-line cases, such as Techworld, present the most serious problems. Both the federal and local governments endorsed economic development and historical architectural concerns but assigned these "vistas" signif-icantly different degrees of priority.

The local government prevailed in these land-use cases partly because the federal government did not perceive a very strong interest in them. The eventual congressional involvement in the Techworld case created a bifurcated national involvement. Congress entered the case on the side of local government and at the behest of a parochial rather than a genuine national interest. The federal executive branch involvement was driven by special interest groups. In Metropolitan Square, the federal interest and involvement were again divided, with executive branch agencies on both sides of the issue. Even the White House was in support of District action during the policy formulation stage of this issue. Matters were complicated further in this case by uncoordinated and delinquent procedures. Although these cases represented fragmented national interests that did not prevail in the final analysis, even the national involvement that took place was largely a response to pressure from interest groups and the promotion of parochial interests by members of the Virginia congressional delegation. Consequently, the cases offer very little support for the Rowat thesis of an inevitable conflict between federal and local interests.

N O T E S

1. The term land use, as employed here, refers to general development, including building location, design, and height.
2. Charles W. Harris and Neeka Harris, "Conflicting Vistas in the Nation's Capital," *Catholic University Law Review* 38 no. 3 (Spring 1989), 602.
3. Significantly, one of the preservationist groups that voiced concern over the planning authority in 1973, the Committee of 100 on the Federal City, later became embroiled in the Techworld controversy. Ibid., 604–05.
4. *Washington Post*, 29 June 1973, A-30.
5. Composition of the NCPC prior to home rule—twelve members: five eminent citizens appointed by the president and seven ex officio members from the federal and District governments. Under this arrangement, the District government had only one representative out of the twelve members.

Composition of the NCPC after effective date of home rule (1975)—twelve members: three members appointed by the president and two by the mayor. Effective 1 July 1974 the seven ex officio members became the secretaries of defense and the interior, the administrator of general services, the mayor and the council chairman of the District, and the chairmen of the Senate and House Committees on the District of Columbia. Under the new arrangement, the District government has four representatives out of the twelve members. Harris and Harris, 606–07 n. 44.

6. As of 1994, eight federal elements and eleven District elements had been adopted. The final District element was adopted on 16 March 1985 and, subsequently, respective ward plans have been completed. The eighth federal element was completed in 1984. Two federal elements have not yet been adopted: the monumental incorporation element and the transportation element. The latter's future, however, is in question. District of Columbia Office of Planning, *Comprehensive Plan for the National Capital Elements,* 1985. Jerry Gilreath, community planner, NCPC, telephone conversation with the author, 29 June 1993.

7. Harris and Harris, 608.

8. The main developer of the World Technology Trade Center was International Developers, Incorporated (IDI). Other developers included Techworld Realty, Inc., Techworld Development Corporation, Techworld Hotel Associates, and FF Realty Corporation. IDI was a Delaware corporation with its principal place of business in Virginia. It was a developer and managing partner of Techworld. In legal papers, the developers were referred to as IDI *et al.* In this study, the term *developer* generally refers to IDI and/or its president.

9. Giuseppe Cecchi was president of IDI, a development firm based in the suburbs (Rosslyn, Virginia) of Washington, D.C. As of mid-1994 there were no definite plans to develop the fourth quadrant of this property, which would likely involve another office building. Vice President Philip Ricciardello, Techworld Associates, telephone conversation with author, 4 June 1993 and 21 July 1994.

10. Without the Eighth Street closing, IDI could not join buildings on the two parcels with its proposed sky bridge.

11. The reviewing agencies sought to limit the impact of the closing on the public welfare by requiring the developer to: (1) grant the city a permanent easement for emergency vehicles; (2) grant a 45,000-square-foot easement for pedestrian circulation; (3) grant another easement to preserve the view along Eighth Street from the Carnegie Library to the Museum of American Arts/National Portrait Gallery; (4) commit to the basic components of the development; and (5) install a sprinkler system throughout the project. Harris and Harris, 614.

12. Although the substance was the same, both emergency and permanent legislation were approved authorizing the closing of a portion of Eighth Street, Northwest, and public alleys in square 403: District of Columbia Act 5-206 and District of Columbia Law 5-148. *Eighth Street Closing Acts,* 31, *District of Columbia Register* 1984, 5984–87.

13. See United States Complaint for Quiet Title Action, *United States vs. Techworld Hotel Associates,* 648 F. Supp. 106 (D.D.C. 1986) (C.A. No. 86-0837).

14. *Techworld Development Corporation vs. District of Columbia Preservation League,* 648 F. Supp. 106, 108 (D.D.C. 1986).

15. For a full discussion of the legal issues, see Harris and Harris, 624–634.

16. *Reorganization Plan Number 3 of 1967,* 81 *Statutes at Large* (section 402) 948, 961 (1967).

17. *Street and Alley Closing Acquisition Procedures Act of 1982,* D.C. Law 4-201, sec. 726, 30 *District of Columbia Register* 148 (1983); *Techworld,* 648 F. Supp.

114–15. For the additional arguments on the local authority to close federally owned streets under the Home Rule Act, see Harris and Harris, 626 ff.

18. *National Historic Preservation Act,* U.S. Code, sec. 470–470W-6 (1982 and Supp. IV 1986); *Techworld,* 648 F. Supp. 119.

19. Ibid.; see also Harris and Harris, 631.

20. Ibid., 123; see also Harris and Harris, 634.

21. D.C. Code Ann., sec. 5-405(a) (Replacement Volume 1988).

22. Robert A. Peck, president, District of Columbia Preservation League, interview with author, Washington, D.C., 18 September 1987.

23. One of the charges made before the Zoning Commission by the preservationists was that trademarts in other cities were not as successful as originally anticipated, and that if the project failed as a technology mart, it could become just another office building. This diagnosis has been proven fairly accurate with regard to Techworld. Although it was originally designed to consist of office and showroom space for companies dealing with computers, office automation, and telecommunications, this plan proved unfeasible when the building was placed in operation. Instead, Techworld has become largely a regular business office complex with auxiliary services that include retail, hotel, restaurants, a conference center, and parking. Techworld Trade Associates, *Techworld Plaza* (promotional brochure), Washington, D.C., 1992, 2–8, passim; Philip Ricciardello, Techworld Associates, interview with author, Washington, D.C., 20 August 1992 and 21 July 1994.

24. Located on square 224, it is within the White House precinct and is bounded by 15th, G, F, and 14th Streets, Northwest. With its buildings of historical and architectural distinction, this square is along the presidential inaugural procession route and is considered important to the overall downtown program. Letters from Oliver T. Carr, Jr., to James O. Gibson, dated 27 July and 21 August 1979, Washington, D.C.

25. Don't Tear It Down, Inc. (DTID), the leading organization representing preservation interests in the District, was founded in 1971. In September 1984 the organization changed its name to the District of Columbia Preservation League (DCPL). Nicholas Hill, "Preservation Group's Name Change Reflects a New Market Climate," *Business Review* 9, no. 37 (10–14 September 1984): 1.

26. Category I landmarks are considered to be of national importance, while category II landmarks are of local importance. This system was abandoned in 1979, with the implementation of District of Columbia Act 2-318— *Historic Landmark and Historic District Protection Act of 1978,* 25 *District of Columbia Register* 6939 (26 January 1979); District of Columbia Law 2-144—*Historic Landmark and Historic District Protection Act of 1978,* 25 *District of Columbia Register* 8683 (16 March 1979).

27. Letter from Oliver T. Carr, Jr., President, Carr Company to James O. Gibson, Assistant City Administrator, Washington, D.C., dated 21 August 1979.

28. To allow increased height for the project required legislation amending the Schedule of Heights of Buildings Adjacent to Public Buildings, established under the Height of Buildings Act of 1910. D.C. Code Ann., sec. 5-405(a) (Replacement Volume 1988); 36 *Statutes at Large* 452, 455.

The Schedule of Heights Amendment Act of 1979 was introduced in the District Council on 24 January 1979 as Bill No. 3-85. It was approved by the council on 9 October and signed by the mayor on 2 November 1979; after congressional review it became effective as D.C. Law No. 3-43. Letter from David A. Clarke, Chairman, District Council, to Charles McC. Mathias, Jr., Chairman, Subcommittee on Governmental Efficiency and the District of Columbia of the Senate Committee on Governmental Affairs, dated 19 July 1983, Washington, D.C.

29. District of Columbia Council, "Bill 3-85 Fact Sheet," related documents, 2 April 1979, Legislative Services Unit (LSU), microfilm collection, council period 3 (1979).

30. In April 1978 the District of Columbia state historic preservation officer invoked the first six-month delay, which expired on 4 October 1978. Then the Carr Company allowed six more months for the city and groups to continue their search for sources of funds and also to process an application for a $7.2 million grant from the Urban Development Action Grant Program (UDAG), U.S. Department of Housing and Urban Development. Ibid.

31. Letter from Oliver T. Carr, Jr., to James O. Gibson, dated 27 July 1979, Washington, D.C.

32. This commitment included any order (under the new Historic Landmark and Historic District Protection Act of 1978) or action that might prevent demolition of Rhodes Tavern. In late August 1979, Carr wrote to Gibson to emphasize that the city's support meant the elimination of Rhodes Tavern. *Citizens' Committee to Save Historic Rhodes Tavern* vs. *District of Columbia Department of Housing and Community Development,* D.C. Cir. 29 May 1981, no. 80-179, pleadings, 13; see also letter from Oliver T. Carr, Jr., to James O. Gibson, dated 21 August 1979, Washington, D.C.

33. Joseph N. Grano, Jr., "self-appointed guardian" of Rhodes Tavern, was cofounder and chairman of the Citizens' Committee to Save Historic Rhodes Tavern and waged a virtual one-man battle to keep the structure from falling victim to the wrecking ball. Grano quit his $20,000-a-year job as an attorney with the Veterans' Pension Board to devote his full time to efforts to save Rhodes Tavern. Built in 1799, Rhodes Tavern was the oldest commercial building in downtown Washington. It was an early city hall, site of "home rule" protests, the first Riggs National Bank Office, and the place where Admiral Robert E. Peary announced the discovery of the North Pole. Dirk Olin, "Preservations Required," *Regardie's* (September 1984), 58; *Los Angeles Times,* 7 July 1981, part I-A, 6.

34. D.C. Code Ann., sec. 5-405(a).

35. Letter from Elizabeth Rowe to Willie J. Hardy, Chairman, District of Columbia Council Committee on Housing and Economic Development, dated 6 April 1979, Washington, D.C.

36. Letter from James O. Gibson to Oliver T. Carr, Jr., 6 August 1979.

37. Griffith's letter was discussed within the office of the mayor and with staff members at the Department of Treasury, the White House, and the NCPC. The city officials decided that it was a matter that did not need to go beyond this point. *Washington Post,* 26 May 1983, C-1.

38. After a short time, the White House resumed the North Portico greetings but used a large portable white screen to block the view from the Metropolitan Square site. The Secret Service was still concerned; the threats to White House security outlined in its letter to the NCPC nearly four years ago were now a reality. *Washington Post,* 26 May 1983, C-1.

39. Letter from John R. Simpson, Assistant Director, United States Secret Service, to Reginald W. Griffith, Executive Director, NCPC, 10 October 1979; Washington, D.C.

40. *New York Times,* 12 May 1983; *Baltimore Sun,* 27 December 1984; *Times-Picayune,* 1 September 1985.

41. Clarke further pointed out that the height limits for the Metropolitan Square block or any other city block that was "adjacent to public buildings" are not "contained in" the Height of Buildings Act of 1910. Instead, some time since 1910, Congress, in the same act and section of the code, authorized that such height limitations be set by the Board of Commissioners. The legislative history of the Home Rule Act provision that restricted the authority of the council to raise the height limitation in the District of Council did not support an argument that the elected council was to obtain less power than its predecessor commissioners. Rather, it was not to receive new authority to amend any provision of the Height of Buildings Act of 1910. The Schedule of Heights Amendment Act of 1979 was within the above legal parameters. D.C. Code, Ann., sec. 5-405; letter from Clarke to Mathias, 19 July 1983; Public Law 93-198, *District of Columbia Self-Government and Government Reorganization Act,* sec. 602(a) (6).

42. Letter from Marion S. Barry, Jr., to Charles McC. Mathias, 20 July 1983, in Joint Collection, University of Missouri Western Historical Manuscript Collection and State Historical Society of Missouri Manuscripts, Columbia, Mo.

43. Letter from James O. Gibson to Oliver T. Carr, Jr., 6 August 1979, Washington, D.C.

44. Letter from Oliver T. Carr to Senator Thomas F. Eagleton, 19 July 1983, Washington, D.C.

45. Letter from Senator Frank R. Lautenberg to Charles A. Bowsher, Comptroller General of the United States, GAO, 22 January 1986, Washington, D.C.

46. Letter from Gene L. Dodaro, Associate Director, General Accounting Office to Senator Frank R. Lautenberg, dated 18 July 1986, in General Accounting Office, *Height Limitations—Limitations on Building Heights in the District of Columbia* (Washington, D.C., July 1986).

The request to GAO from Senator Lautenberg resulted in two reports; the second report was *Height Limitations—D.C. Government's Authority to Amend Building Height Limitations,* September 1986.

47. The area generally bounded by Pennsylvania Avenue, 15th Street, Florida Avenue, New York Avenue, New Jersey Avenue, North Capital Street, and Constitution Avenue, all in Northwest D.C. District government projects outside this central area are reviewed by the District of Columbia Department of Administrative Services.

Federal agencies such as the Secret Service, the Commission of Fine Arts, and the Pennsylvania Avenue Development Corporation provide advice to the District government on private sector building heights in some situations. General Accounting Office, *Height Limitations on Building Heights in the District of Columbia*, 2, 8.

48. Plaintiffs Carol Currie, Kathryn A. Eckles and Anne Sellin also affirmed that they were frequent visitors to the White House precinct and that their individual, aesthetic, environmental and recreational use of the area was injured by the presence of Metropolitan Square which overwhelmed the White House and other public buildings in the area. Carol Currie, Kathryn A. Eckles and Anne Sellin, "Why the U.S. Government Should Intervene in the *Currie v. District of Columbia* Lawsuit," Report to the Attorney General of the United States (Washington, D.C., 21 August 1985, Xeroxed), 1.

49. *Currie et al* vs. *District of Columbia et al*, Civil Action No. 84-3824 (D.C. Cir., No. 85-5649, 17 December 1984).

50. Craig Stoltz, "Up on the Roof," *City Paper* (Washington, D.C., 18–24 October 1985), 10.

51. Letter from Frank R. Lautenberg to Charles A. Bowsher.

8

The Challenge of Dual Democracy: National Representation and Statehood

While many Americans sympathize with a city that lacks full representation in the national legislature, this sympathy has not been translated into national support for converting the nation's capital into the fifty-first state. Even many proponents of statehood acknowledge that, outside the Washington area, the issue has sparse support and limited but passionate opposition. A 1987 national survey showed that the American public, by a nearly eight to one ratio (78 percent), believes that District residents should have the same rights as other citizens, but only 52 percent said they supported the bill to grant statehood to the District; approximately 24 percent disagreed and 24 percent had no opinion. Democrats were more supportive of statehood than were Republicans or independents, and women were more supportive than men. The survey showed that many Americans know little about the nation's capital. One in four believed that the District already was a state, while three out of four were unaware that the District's 630,000 residents were not represented in the Senate and had only a nonvoting delegate in the House.[1]

From the standpoint of democratic principles and practices, there are at least three issues that must be confronted when considering a restructuring of the District of Columbia government: representation in the national legislature, autonomy in policymaking, and protection of the federal interest. The most serious of these issues at this time is representation in the national legislature. Although most Americans would not deny this right to their fellow Americans in the District, they differ on the method for its implementation. There are many approaches to the issue of representation in the national legislature. Since most of them would include changes in the local governmental structure, I shall deal with this general question as well. The list of proposals includes the following:

Retrocession to Maryland
Semi-retrocession: participation in federal elections in Maryland
Full voting rights—version I
Full voting rights—version II
Full self-determination
Statehood: national representation and home rule

Proposals such as retrocession and statehood would automatically provide national representation and respective versions of full local autonomy. Full self-determination as discussed below deals only with local autonomy. Still other proposals, such as semi-retrocession and full voting rights, would only address the representation problem. Some of the proposals would make no change in the present organizational structure for protecting the federal interest, while others would require major adjustments.

Each of these approaches will be discussed, with more attention devoted to statehood, which is the issue before Congress in the 1990s. They will be evaluated based on the following criteria: providing representation, providing local autonomy, protecting legitimate federal interests, and political feasibility.

RETROCESSION TO MARYLAND

In accordance with the Exclusive Power (District) Clause of the Constitution, the states of Maryland (1788) and Virginia (1789) ceded their respective lands to the federal government for the purpose of creating the nation's capital. In a single act in 1790 Congress accepted these cessions of land to form the federal district that became the seat of government of the United States. The original federal district was 10 miles square, lying on both sides of the Potomac River at the head of navigation. In 1846 Congress approved legislation to return to Virginia that portion of the federal district lying in that state and, following a favorable vote by the local residents, President James K. Polk issued a proclamation declaring Alexandria County retroceded to Virginia.

If most Americans would like to see the nation make good on the principles of democracy for the citizens living in the nation's capital, the most conservative approach to this problem has been retrocession to Maryland. Some of the most outspoken opponents of statehood offer retrocession as the preferred resolution of the representation problem. Since the District would become a part of Maryland, local autonomy would be provided in accordance with the system in this state.

Representative Ralph Regula (R-Ohio) introduced a retrocession bill in the 101st Congress (1989–90) and Representative Dana Rohrabacher (R-Calif.), a member of the House District Committee, observed that adding the city of "Washington, Maryland" would "hardly be overwhelming to Maryland," as it would constitute only the fifth most populous jurisdiction (counting cities and counties) in Maryland.[2] In a possibly tongue-in-cheek comment in 1990, Maryland Governor William Donald Schaefer indicated that he would have no trouble with the District of Columbia becoming a part of Maryland. Retrocession, however, would require formal action by the state legislature and there is no evidence at this time that this body, or the citizenry in general, would favor such action.[3]

As when retrocession took place in Virginia, the desires and wishes of the District residents would have to be considered. In a high-stakes political issue of this kind, much would depend upon the options and alternatives at the time the question is formally put to the respective jurisdictions. Certainly, there is no indication that District residents would favor retrocession to Maryland. First and foremost, there would be concerns about the dilution of power in both the District and Maryland. This would be especially true for District residents who, within the constraints of the Home Rule Charter, are in full control of policy-making within the jurisdiction. Joining the District with its Maryland suburbs would dilute power in general and further diminish the political clout of Baltimore and other parts of the state.

Then there is the matter of customs and traditions. The affinity between the District and its suburban Maryland counties may be strong, but this relationship does not extend to other parts of the state. Both Maryland and the District are justifiably proud of their own historic political communities and boundaries and probably would not be willing to give them up. Consequently, this approach receives a low rating in terms of political feasibility.[4]

In spite of their different objectives, there is a type of de facto coalescence between statehood and retrocession advocates on cordoning off the National Capital Service Area (NCSA) and having it serve as the seat of the government. Under the present configuration of the NCSA, it does not appear that the federal interest would be well served under either option.

The NCSA would be a very small federal district—a total area of approximately 11.55 square miles.[5] Many federal operations, and almost all foreign chanceries, are outside of it. During the consideration of the Foreign Missions Act back in 1982, it was repeatedly stated by members of both the House and Senate that no other issue provides perhaps the clearest example of shared federal interest and local interest in the District of Columbia as does the issue of the location of chanceries within the nation's capital (see chapter 5, pp. 109–11). There is a legitimate federal interest and a legitimate local interest involved in this issue that must be reconciled.

SEMI-RETROCESSION: PARTICIPATION IN FEDERAL ELECTIONS IN MARYLAND

Another possibility for providing District of Columbia residents with voting representation in the national legislature is to enable them to vote for federal legislators in Maryland. In other words, they would be treated as Maryland residents for purposes of federal elections and apportionment. The governmental structure of the District would remain as it is, while its residents would be empowered to vote in the Maryland congressional elections. Under this approach, District residents would elect a full-voting House member, in place of a nonvoting delegate, and vote for Senate candidates in the neighboring state of Maryland. A sensitive political factor in this plan, especially for Republicans, is that it would allow District residents to have voting representation in the Senate without increasing the Democratic Party's strength in this body.

Although voting representation on this basis could be accomplished by an ordinary act, an amendment to the Constitution would be necessary to repeal the Twenty-third Amendment (concerning presidential electors for the District of Columbia). This idea was discussed, mainly among the conservative members of the House and Republican Representative Stan Parris of Virginia introduced a bill in the 101st Congress (1989–90) to implement this plan. The plan would maintain the existing home rule government and repeal both the nonvoting delegate law and the Twenty-third Amendment to the Constitution.[6] It made no provision for a federal enclave, a vital aspect of both retrocession and statehood, and, assuming no change in the District charter, it would avoid a commuter tax. The sponsor of this plan said that it was inspired by historical precedent. From the time the federal district was created in 1790 until 1800, District residents voted for president and for members of Congress in Maryland. (Parris said that the system was never outlawed but appeared to have faded away.[7])

For many years Parris had been an outspoken congressional foe of District autonomy. Consequently, District leaders had reason to suspect the motives behind any plan offered by their political nemesis from across the river. Many District officials and politicians summarily dismissed Parris's bill as an effort to block the statehood campaign that was beginning to gain some visibility in Congress. Mayor Marion Barry said that the plan "wouldn't make much sense" and the Reverend Jesse L. Jackson called it "another expression of colonialism"— an attempt to "annex us" without the consent of District residents.[8]

Before introducing a measure that involved Maryland so directly, one would have expected Parris to consult with the congressional delegation from that state. Apparently this was not the case: Maryland Republican Representative Constance A. Morella, whose district is adjacent to the nation's capital, responded that Parris "may be serious about the proposal, but it is not a serious proposal." Maryland Democratic Representative Steny Hoyer, whose congressional district, like Morella's, is adjacent to the District of Columbia, indicated that he did not support the plan, but he praised Parris for supporting some form of congressional representation for the District.[9] Maryland Governor William Donald Schaefer, in a news conference in the capital city of Annapolis, declined to discuss the proposal in detail but said that if the District residents and officials wished to join Maryland voluntarily, he would welcome them. However, he did not oppose statehood.

This proposal would maintain the present structure and procedures for the protection of legitimate federal interests but would not address the issue of providing local autonomy, nor would it remedy the ongoing interference by Congress in local affairs.

In spite of strong opposition to the semi-retrocession proposal by District officials and politicians, one legal scholar sympathetic to statehood for the District feels that the plan may offer the best intermediate tactical step to full statehood for the District.[10] He argues that under this plan District residents would have voting representation in Congress and thus "real leverage and leadership for their statehood drive," while preserving or possibly enhancing their limited home rule status. Since the persons campaigning for United States Senate seats could become partly dependent on votes of District residents, the District electorate might be able to trade its support for a pledge from prospective senators to work for statehood.

Although this plan may sound like a logical and sharp tactical move, the political risk of irreparable damage to the statehood cause would be too high for the District to buy into it. Coalitions in Congress develop around certain issues at a given time and then fall apart, a fact of life in the history of the District's quest for self-determination. It would be extremely difficult to develop successful coalitions for both participation in Maryland federal elections and for statehood, or a single coalition involving these two steps. Once District residents had voting representation in Congress, policymakers would see the problem as solved and not want to revisit the divisive statehood issue.

In spite of the lack of support for the retrocession plans, they may have contributed to some of the other options. Nearly everyone, supporters and opponents of increased political liberty for the District, agreed that, on balance, the retrocession proposals had the effect of focusing attention on, and enhancing the case for, full representation in Congress for the District. Moreover, the proposal for full retrocession carved out a federal enclave for legislative authority and control by Congress. In so doing it established a precedent for support of a reduction in the size of the federal district by those who were opposed to statehood.

FULL VOTING RIGHTS—VERSION I

An effort was made by the District and its nationwide supporters to achieve full voting rights or nominal statehood (as it is sometimes called) in the late 1970s and early 1980s. Under the proposed full voting rights amendment to the Constitution, the District would not have been a state but would have been treated as if it were a state for purposes of representation in Congress. It would have been entitled to representation by two senators and at least one member of the House of Representatives. In addition, the District would have participated in the ratification of amendments to the Constitution and would have elected representatives to the electoral college in proportion to its population.

With solid backing from the administration of President Jimmy Carter, optimism was extremely high among District officials and supporters when the required two-thirds majority of Congress proposed the Full Voting Rights Amendment in August of 1978. By its own terms, the amendment established a timetable of seven years (1978–85) within which ratification by the required thirty-eight states (three-fourths majority) had to be achieved. Although the Full Voting Rights Amendment did not address the problems of limited home rule, District officials and supporters were prepared to press forward to make it a reality. Many felt that with voting representation in Congress, it would be easier to remedy the deficiencies of home rule. This amendment would have no direct bearing on the existing protection of legitimate federal interests which, ostensibly, would not be affected under its implementation.

As the District began to travel the long and difficult road to ratification, its optimism and positive outlook began to wane. During the initial year of the ratification period, it was common practice for a star-studded delegation from the District to fly into a state that was considering the amendment and make a patriotic appeal—arguing that it was the American way for District residents to have representation in Congress. They soon learned that the justice of their cause alone would not win ratification of the Full Voting Rights Amendment. In time the strategy shifted to supplying information and resources and having the District residents with local ties play a supportive, behind-the-scenes role in the respective state.

The ratification drive was plagued by inadequate funds, and the launching of an effective nationwide educational campaign never materialized. District leaders said that money was needed to battle an array of weak or irrelevant arguments, among them that the Founding Fathers did not intend for the District's residents to have voting rights; that some states have counties bigger than the District, but those counties do not have two senators; and that representatives from the District are likely to favor urban issues, be Democrats, and be black. They maintained that all of these arguments could be countered as part of a positive program that explained to the people of the nation, and especially to the state legislators, the reasons why District of Columbia residents were entitled to full representation in the national legislature. Mounting a national campaign of this scope required substantial funding (several hundred thousand dollars) which was not available.[11] In the final analysis, however, the real problem with granting full voting rights to the District was partisan politics (an historical factor in statehood issues), compounded by race.

The leaders and supporters of the proposed amendment had to struggle, with only partial success, to achieve a unified, District-wide campaign on behalf of ratification. First, the main organization involved in the ratification campaign was the Coalition for Self-Determination for the District of Columbia, a national alliance of civic, religious, political, labor, business, and other groups.[12] Then a separate group was established under the sponsorship of the mayor, the council chairman, and the congressional delegate, known as the District of Columbia Voting Rights Service Corporation. Subsequently, to avoid duplication of effort, that corporation closed its offices, leaving the Coalition for Self-Determination as the only ratification drive in town (and the nation).

There were other shortcomings of the ratification campaign. The business community, a prime source of needed funds, had not been effectively enlisted as an equal partner in supporting full voting rights. Congressional leaders and members, who proposed the amendment, were in an ideal position to press for action in the states, but were hardly involved in the campaign. Equally important, the ratification effort needed to be truly bipartisan, which meant reenlisting the Republican Party in the campaign. It was significant that no Republican-controlled chamber of any state legislature voted to ratify the amendment. There were several key Republicans in support of ratification, for example, national party chairman Bill Brock, Senator Bob Dole of Kansas, and Representative Stewart McKinney of Connecticut. These Republicans were natural sources of assistance in recruiting additional party support.[13]

By the final stage of the seven-year ratification period for the amendment, the attention and efforts of local leaders had shifted to the statehood effort. The slow pace of ratification made it clear, long before the seven-year deadline, that the amendment would not be successful. By the end of 1983, only thirteen of the thirty-eight states had ratified it. The movement for statehood was to become the battleground of the 1990s.

In light of the fact that this approach to voting representation in the national legislature has been put before the nation and found wanting, it would appear that it has earned a place at the bottom of the list of alternatives. It makes sense for District officials and supporters to put all of their energy and resources behind a single approach, which at this time is statehood. But until District residents have full voting representation in the national body, the door cannot be completely closed on any alternative, even one that has been tried and failed. The art of forging compromises and the revisitation of issues and problems due to changed circumstances are primary ingredients of United States politics and public policy. As legislators come and go and coalitions form and dissolve around issues and problems, what is rejected or vetoed at one time may be approved at another.

FULL VOTING RIGHTS—VERSION II

A practical compromise in the full voting rights option would be for the District to settle for a single senator instead of two, with other aspects of the amendment remaining the same as in version I. This option would probably bring howls from District leaders, but no possibility can be ruled out completely as long as the status quo remains in effect. This plan would be called up for consideration only in case of the failure of other options of higher preference. Enactment of this compromise version of full voting rights would still require ratification by thirty-eight states. Members of the House represent people on a proportional basis; senators represent chunks of territory called states—in which varying numbers of people live.[14] As of 1992 the dwindling District population was still larger than the populations of the states of Alaska, Vermont, and Wyoming and was in the same general range as that of Delaware, North Dakota, and South Dakota.

A Senate vote is a Senate vote and it is hard to play down its importance. Trading and bargaining in the Senate is on an individual member basis rather than by state pairs, which at times may be split between the two major political parties. And because of how the Senate operates, a single senator is likely to have more power than the fraction 1/101 seems to imply.[15] This is especially true in votes to cut off a filibuster in the upper chamber.

The fact that the number of senators plus the vice president would be even with the addition of a single senator for the District is not considered a serious problem. The vice president can vote only to break a tie, not to make one. Since all senators rarely are present to vote and the Senate has occasional vacancies, the total vote on any given occasion is as likely to be odd as it is to be even. Moreover, this arrangement would reduce the number of important occasions in which it would be necessary to call upon the vice president to break a tie.[16]

Assuming that the District remains a Democratic stronghold with a commitment from the Democratic Party, now, at a time in which the party is in control of both Congress and the White House, there is a good chance that state legislators would listen seriously to a single-senator voting rights amendment that would effectively capitalize on the District's unique status. There is a serious danger, however, that if either of the full voting rights amendments is approved by the states, it would be the final resting place for the political aspirations of the District—certainly not a stepping stone to statehood, as some legal scholars have argued.[17]

FULL SELF-DETERMINATION

With the exception of full retrocession to Maryland, approval of any of the above approaches would achieve voting representation in the national legislature for District residents, as a distinct jurisdiction, but would not automatically provide them with the full self-governing rights exercised by the residents of the various states. Conversely, steps may be undertaken to increase local autonomy without providing District residents with voting representation in Congress. Under its present limited home rule system, the District's self-governing deficiencies include the following: a variety of constraints on legislative autonomy, inadequate budget authority, and lack of control over the judicial and criminal prosecution system. Moreover, the tenuous nature of the present system means that it can be taken away by Congress at any time.

Legislative Authority

Under the current District home rule system, legislation is enacted by the District Council, usually after well-attended and televised public hearings, extensive debate, and two readings. With the exception of emergency legislation of short duration (ninety days), however, this enacted legislation cannot become effective until at least thirty legislative days after it has been transmitted to Congress for review. This period is extended to sixty days for matters affecting the District's criminal laws. During the review period, Congress may repeal the statute by joint resolution, which requires presidential concurrence.[18]

This restraint on local policymaking could be removed with little or no harm to the legitimate federal interests which it was designed to protect. Congress would still have its constitutional power to repeal any District action and to legislate on the District's behalf at any time. Only three District acts have been formally vetoed during twenty years of home rule. The net gain from a removal of the review period would have to be weighed very carefully. Because of the set period for review, Congress customarily has put itself under pressure to either disapprove District action during the appointed time or leave it alone, avoiding a continuous "open season" approach. The review process not only undermines local autonomy but is also demeaning to the District and, considering its minimal contribution to the federal interest, should be removed.[19]

Probably the most important step toward increased legislative authority for the District would be the removal of the ban against the imposition of an income tax on nonresident commuters who work in the District. Lifting this ban would open up channels of revenue to the District that are used by the states and other major cities. Through the annual appropriations process for District revenues, Congress may force changes in District policies and practices by attaching a rider to an appropriations bill. As noted earlier, this provides an informal congressional veto. Congress has expressly denied the District certain other legislative powers, for example, the District cannot revise the congressionally imposed height limit on District buildings.

Budgetary Autonomy

For purposes of budget approval, Congress treats the District as though it were a federal agency rather than a local government. The District of Columbia section of the president's budget appears under the caption "Other Independent Agencies." A most important lever in this process is the power of Congress to appropriate the entire District budget, including the share—usually more than 80 percent of the total—financed by locally raised revenues. A first step toward greater local autonomy would be to allow the District Council to appropriate the local revenues as it deems fit.

The District's annual budget is recommended to the council by the mayor and revised and adopted by the council after extensive public hearings, debate, and compromise. The budget is then reviewed by the Office of Management and Budget and submitted by the president to Congress. In spite of the rigorous review of the District budget at the local level, the process starts all over again when it reaches Congress. Full rounds of public hearings are sponsored for input from local citizens and groups. Even the smallest and most routine expenditures by the District government are subject to annual congressional scrutiny. The annual appropriations bill gives Congress a ready-made vehicle to intervene in virtually any decision the District government makes.

This procedure is not necessary to protect legitimate federal interests and, in the interest of local autonomy, should be discontinued.

Judicial Nomination Authority

One important characteristic of true self-determination is the power of the local government to control the selection of judges. The citizens of the District do not elect their judges, nor does the mayor appoint them. The District state judges are appointed by the president of the United States and are confirmed by the United States Senate. Under the provisions of the Home Rule Charter, the president is required to select nominees from among three names proposed by a seven-member commission, of which only three are chosen by District government officials. Federal law, rather than local law, determines the judicial term of office.[20]

Shortly after President Bill Clinton took office, the District gained an important partisan power long enjoyed by the fifty states: a lead role in selecting its federal prosecutors, judges, and marshals. The Clinton administration agreed to seek the recommendations of the District congressional delegate in the same way it does of the Democratic senators from each state. This new system is not a legislated change but the result of an arrangement between President Clinton and Delegate Eleanor Holmes Norton (D-D.C.). District officials and supporters viewed this move as an opportunity for racial progress and more local involvement in law enforcement matters.[21]

Control Over Criminal Prosecution

The United States attorney, not an official chosen by District officials or voters, prosecutes all crimes other than violations of minor regulations. With the exception of the District, every state and most local jurisdictions select the officials who will prosecute local crimes. For many years, District officials have sought without success to have this authority transferred to the local government. Although President Clinton allows the District congressional delegate to play a role in the judicial selection process, local officials say the system deserves still more change: a city prosecutor to take over local functions from the United States attorney for the District. They argue that full control of the criminal justice system at the local level would contribute to its overall improvement.[22]

Formula for Federal Payment

For years the District has sought a federal payment authorized annually on a permanent basis pursuant to a statutory formula. In 1991 the Bush administration and Congress approved legislation authorizing a formula-based federal payment; authorizations for fiscal years 1993 through 1995 were to be based on a fixed rate of 24 percent of audited local revenue levels.[23] The formula was supposed to help stabilize the budget process by enabling the District to calculate the compensation for services rendered to the federal government rather than waiting for the announcement of an arbitrary figure. When the fiscal year 1993 budget was unveiled by the Bush administration, no mention was made of the formula, resulting in a freezing of the payment at the amount for the previous year ($630.5 million).[24] Full budget autonomy for the District would mean that congressional appropriation of the federal payment would represent the only annual involvement of Congress in the District budget process.

The Tenuous Nature of District Home Rule

Although the current home rule government has been in effect for twenty years, it rests on a rather tenuous base. At any time Congress can rescind the home rule powers that it has delegated to the District. This ever-present threat under which District officials must live has been labelled "anticipatory colonialism" by some members of the media. To see anticipatory colonialism at work, they say, "you only have to watch the city council and mayor tackling a really controversial issue like the sodomy law or pot legalization."[25] At times of mistrust of the local government, behind-the-scenes comments and questions are raised over whether home rule is going to work. Moreover, if Congress decides to violate the spirit or the letter of the Home Rule Charter, who will stand in its way? Congress's annual practice of passing legislation for the District in the guise of appropriations riders is a case in point, and so far the District has found no remedy to deal with these violations of the home rule compact.

STATEHOOD: NATIONAL REPRESENTATION AND HOME RULE

In the United States, federalism has facilitated growth through the admission of new states to the Union. The basic principle of American federalism is fixed in the Tenth Amendment to the Constitution, which provides that the national government is to have those powers dele-gated in the Constitution with all other powers reserved to the states. The American states exist by right, not just by the whim of the national government.

The primary advantage of statehood over other forms of repre-sentation at the national level is that it would provide to District resi-dents full legal and political rights equal to those of residents of the existing states. Under statehood, these rights would be automatic and permanent, rather than subject to reversal when there is a change in political coalitions and circumstances.

The basic arguments for and against statehood have not changed much over the years. The critical factor today, as it has been in the nearly two-hundred-year history of this issue, is the interest in and re-ceptivity to statehood for the District among other citizens throughout the United States and their elected representatives.[26] There is nothing radical about statehood as a procedure for gaining self-government. It has happened thirty-seven times since the first thirteen colonies banded together to form the Union. The Constitution makes the process comparatively simple. In fact, it has been far easier to create new states and permit their residents to vote than it was to establish the right to vote for blacks and women.[27]

The most serious disagreement between advocates and foes of statehood is not over whether the District should or should not be a new state. Opponents argue that statehood is illegal unless the Con-stitution is amended, whereas, supporters argue that the new state can be admitted through the same process followed in the admission of thirty-seven other states of the Union—a simple majority vote of Congress.

The national Democratic Party has endorsed statehood for the District in its last three platforms (1984, 1988, and 1992). President Clinton ran on a platform that stated:

And we need fair political representation for all sectors of our country—including the District of Columbia, which deserves and must get statehood status.[28]

The Republican Party took the opposite position, calling for closer congressional scrutiny and tighter fiscal restraints over expendi-tures. The 1992 Republican platform stated:

We oppose statehood as inconsistent with the original intent of the Framers of the Constitution and with the need for a federal city belonging to all the people. . . .[29]

When the Democrats won control of the White House and Congress in the 1992 elections, it appeared that the stage was set for the statehood issue to move forward during the 103d Congress (1993–94). But with President Clinton facing problems implementing his national agenda, the early stages of his administration seem to indicate an unwillingness to expend much political capital on the statehood issue.

There were developments in 1993, however, that were viewed as advancing the cause of self-determination for District residents. Additional power for the District delegate in the city's judicial process and in congressional voting, along with House floor debate of statehood (discussed later in this chapter) are cases in point.

At the beginning of the 103d Congress, the nonvoting representatives from the District of Columbia and the four territories (Puerto Rico, the Virgin Islands, Guam, and American Samoa) were given a vote on the House floor. The Constitution restricts House membership to representatives of the states and only a constitutional amendment can change this. Technically, the delegates won a right to vote in the Committee of the Whole (the whole House sitting as a committee), where most of the House business is conducted. Most of the floor sessions and roll-call votes in the House are in meetings of the Committee of the Whole and legislation is rarely altered during official House votes on final passage. Previously, the representatives of the District and territories could vote only in the smaller legislative committees.[30]

House Republicans and Democrats clashed angrily over rules expanding the voting privileges of the District of Columbia and territorial delegates. Republicans charged that the move was unconstitutional, "a raw grab for power" by the Democrats, and quickly took the matter to court. In early March 1993, a federal judge upheld the rule change but the Republicans proceeded with an appeal and promised to continue their demands for revoting legislation on which the delegates had cast a floor vote. In January 1994 the United States Court of Appeals upheld the right of the delegates to participate in votes on the floor of the House.[31]

In the media and in public discussions at local and national levels, a series of arguments for and against statehood have been presented and many of these arguments shall be summarized below. In some cases, the pro and con arguments on a common issue tend to rebut each other, while in other cases a counterargument is included in the discussion of the issue.

Some of the Arguments: Pro and Con

Many arguments have been advanced on both sides of the statehood issue. Hardly any point of the respective sides has been left unanswered in this ongoing political struggle. Considering the nature of the arguments and counterarguments, a clear separation between them was not always achieved under the pro and con captions.

Equity: A Matter of Fairness and Justice
PRO

Responsibilities of Citizenship. Statehood advocates point out that District residents bear all of the burdens of citizenship, but do not share the most cherished right of citizenship—full representation in Congress. All other Americans are represented in the national legislature; why are District residents different? Statehood advocates say, "It is time to right the wrongs" and they assert that the fairness issue overrides the worries of the adjacent states of Virginia and Maryland about a commuter tax. Speaking at the 1992 Democratic National Convention in New York City, Mayor Sharon Pratt Kelly and District Delegate Eleanor Holmes Norton emphasized their strong belief that the District has not received the fair treatment it deserves from the national government and that the only way to correct this is by granting statehood.[32] These arguments are supported by pointing to the strength of the District's record in carrying the responsibilities of citizenship such as taxation and wartime participation.

Equal Taxation. The District is subjected to "taxation without representation," a rallying cry that inspired the American Revolution. For the year of 1988, on a per capita basis, the District was third highest in the nation in the ranking of all states in the payment of federal individual income taxes. It ranks second among all states, next to Alaska, in the amount of taxes per capita raised from its own resources.[33] Some 60 percent of all income earned in the District is exempt from District taxes and approximately 50 percent of all real estate and 50 percent of all sales are exempt from taxation mainly because of the federal presence.[34]

There may be some misconception that the District is supported by the federal government. In actuality the federal contribution to the District's total operating budget has been less than 20 percent in recent years. For example, about 19 percent of the District's fiscal year 1992 budget was funded through the federal payment.[35] On the other hand, the amount of federally imposed tax exemptions for fiscal year 1992 was nearly triple the level of the federal payment.[35]

Wartime Participation. District residents have fought and died for their country in time of war. It is against the American tradition to require a young person to fight for his or her country on the battlefield without providing local representation in Congress to help decide if the war should be fought. In the Vietnam War, the casualty level for the District was higher than that of ten states.[36] In testimony on statehood for the District, House Majority Leader Thomas Foley (D-Wash.) stated that, proportionately, more District residents died in military service in Vietnam than was the case for forty-seven states.[37] While not rejecting some of the facts presented by the supporters, the opponents of statehood offer a number of counter-arguments to deal with the matter of equity.

CON

The District Belongs to the Entire Nation. The District of Columbia does not belong solely to the people who live there; like the Constitution and the federal government, it is the common property of all Americans. The District has a special status to be enjoyed by all, and all should have a voice in its operation.[38] This counterargument often includes constitutional and legal points which will be covered in a separate section later in this chapter.

"They Knew What They Were Doing." When confronted with the fairness issue, some statehood opponents have countered with the argument, "they knew what they were doing." In the 1991 congressional hearings on District of Columbia statehood, James C. Miller III, former director of the United States Office of Management and Budget in the Reagan administration, reminded members of the House District Committee (Subcommittee on Judiciary and Education) that residents of the District were well aware that they did not have the benefits of statehood and voting representation in Congress when they moved to the District.

If residents were born in the District, then they could always move out to Maryland, Virginia, or elsewhere in the country when they reached voting age. They were not forced to remain in the District.[39]

Population and Territory.
PRO

A Sufficient Population. Based on comparative data, the District population is sufficient for statehood. With a 1990 population of 607,000, the District exceeded the populations of Alaska (550,000), Vermont (563,000), and Wyoming (454,000). It is within the range of the populations of the states of Delaware (666,000), North Dakota (639,000), and South Dakota (696,000). The District's population is close to Hawaii's 663,000 and over two-and-a-half times Alaska's 226,000 in the 1960 census, one year after these states were admitted to the Union.

While an urban state would be unique in this country, there are examples in other countries with federal systems of government such as Bremen, Hamburg, and Berlin (future national capital) in Germany; Lagos (former national capital), Nigeria; and the capital city of Vienna, Austria.

An Indigenous Community. District officials and supporters of full autonomy argue that residents of the federal district comprise an organic community with indigenous rights and should not be viewed as an appendage or adjunct to the national government. The assurance of democratic rights and principles to the local people represents the basic premise.

CON

The District is a City, Not a State. The opponents of statehood are not without a rebuttal to the arguments concerning population and physical size. They emphasize the fact that the District is a city and to grant it statehood would be unfair to other cities of equal or greater population and size.

The District is only one-twenty-third the physical size of the state of Rhode Island. With its small and completely urban land area, the District meets qualifications of a city, not a state. Congress essentially functions as a state government for the District.[40] Opponents of statehood point to the small area of the District, 68.26 square miles, and the lack of land for expansion and population growth. The other small-population states have the space for growth and expansion.

If the District were to be granted statehood, it could be argued that many other large cities of the United States should have statehood. With a population fourteen times that of the District, New York City is cited as a prime example of a jurisdiction that could be represented as a distinct unit instead of a part of a state. Of course, New York City residents presently have about fourteen voting representatives in the House and they participate in the vote for two United States senators from their state—a status that is lacking in the District.[41] Although the power of New York City residents could be strengthened further if they had their own two senators to accompany their voting congressional representatives, the rights New York City already holds are, presumably, enough to offset the need for statehood status.

Readiness for Statehood.

Pro

Self-Government Experience. In spite of negative charges from the opponents of statehood, District officials (and statehood supporters) quickly defend their record of government experience and overall readiness for statehood. The current local experience with self-government has been in effect for two decades. Including the incumbent, there have been three mayoralty administrations during this period. The District has emerged from an era of worldwide attention and considerable congressional mistrust during the latter stages of the three-term administration of Mayor Marion Barry. Since that time, the District has demonstrated maturity in its local government by electing new and stable leadership, winning congressional confidence, and ridding itself of corruption.

Statehood supporters make the point that government corruption is not an uncommon occurrence in American politics, and it has not caused the residents of the respective jurisdictions to lose their democratic rights or their representation in Congress. The District's image may have been tarnished during the administration of Mayor Marion Barry, but most statehood supporters view the performance of District officials as a separate issue from basic democratic rights and voting representation. Senator Edward Kennedy (D-Mass.) said, "It would be unfortunate to hold the people of the District of Columbia hostage to that issue." He referred to statehood as "the right answer before the mayor's problems and it will be the right answer afterward."[42]

Con

Mismanagement and Corruption. Some of the opponents of statehood maintain that even if this status were granted, it should not be at this time. In their view, the District is not ready for statehood. They argue that an extended era free from excessive urban problems, mismanagement, and corruption is necessary before statehood for the District can be seriously considered. Their supporting examples include the high crime rate and the overall status of public safety, high rates of infant mortality and single parenthood, and the series of financial crises that have plagued the city in the 1990s.

Economic Viability.
Pro

A Viable Economy. Proponents of statehood argue that the District has a viable economy that would enable it to meet and sustain the costs of full self-government. In its favorable report on the District of Columbia statehood bill of 1987, the House District Committee stated that District earnings by industry are very diverse and rank higher than many states in several categories. The following rankings were cited in support of this assertion: "In finance, in insurance, in real estate activities the District of Columbia ranks higher than 14 states. . . . In business services, it ranks higher than 41 states."[43]

Seeking an answer to those who had suggested that the city could not sustain itself as a state, the District of Columbia Statehood and Statehood Compact Commissions contracted with economist Andrew F. Brimmer, former Member of Federal Reserve Board, to study the economic prospects of the District as a state. A 115-page report was released in September 1986, in which Brimmer concluded that the city's economic growth, while less robust than that of Maryland or Virginia, "will not be significantly altered by statehood." At the time of this study, it was projected that statehood might allow the District to collect more than $300 million a year in nonresident revenues (from persons who live in other jurisdictions but work in the District). Pointing out that the federal payment, set at $425 million for fiscal year 1987, is granted to cover the loss of taxes not collected from federal property, as reimbursement for services, and to offset the costs that arise from being the nation's capital, Brimmer said that the new state should lose neither its current federal payment nor its eligibility for federal grants and programs given to cities.[44]

In the 1991 congressional hearings on the House statehood bill, District officials were confronted with the charge that the economic base of the city is too small to make up for lost revenues if it were cut off from the federal payment. Mayor Kelly and Council Chairman John Wilson testified that if the District "had the autonomy of a state," it would be better off economically. "We could support ourselves," and would be willing to forego the annual multimillion dollar federal payment to the city. Although it was not emphasized at the hearing, "having the autonomy of a state" means having the power to levy a non-resident income tax on commuters who work in the city.[45]

CON

A Dependent Economy. The opponents of statehood emphasize the city's ties to the federal government. President George Bush and the Republicans expressed concerns about the economic viability of the proposed new state, saying that it would be radically dependent upon the federal government for support. They reject the District's response to the charge that its residential and commercial base is too small to make up for lost revenues if it were cut off from the federal payment. The deepening financial crisis of the District government in 1994 is cited by statehood opponents as further support of their position.[46]

Diversity.

PRO

Levels of Diversity. The District population is said to be "too liberal, too urban, too black, and too Democratic," and, therefore, not representative of America's population. Rather than an overt assertion by statehood opponents, the above argument is usually cited by statehood advocates in characterizing how they believe statehood opponents feel.

The proponents of statehood respond by explaining that diversity can be approached on different levels and scales. If diversity on a macro scale is a valid objective for the nation as a whole, then states such as Maine, New Hampshire and Vermont, with populations over 98 percent white; Hawaii, with a 61.8 percent Asian and Pacific Islander population; and the District, with a 65.8 percent black population, should not present a problem.[47] The District's completely urban and dense population, 13,900 per square mile of nonfederal land, would be balanced by the rural and sparse populations of Alaska and some other western states.

This balancing idea is ennobled by the faith that our nation can summon from its myriad diversity the deepest measure of unity. Therefore, micro diversity or diversity within a respective state may not be as important as optimal balance within the nation as a whole.

CON

Not Representative of America. The opponents of statehood charge that the District lacks diversity in several respects, especially in its employment base and overall economy. The argument is sometimes made that the District is a "company town," revolving around the federal government. Of the 687,900 jobs located in the District in 1990, only 220,400, or 32 percent, were federal government jobs.[48] It is estimated, however, that another 25 percent of the District jobs were in "service industries closely associated with the federal government." If this is a fair approximation of government spin-off employment, then over half of the jobs in the District are directly or indirectly dependent on the federal government.[49]

The 1980 census reports that of the 237,686 federal government jobs located in the District, 66,771, or 28.1 percent, were held by residents of the District, with residents of suburban Maryland and Virginia holding the vast majority of the remaining jobs.[50] Of the 323,000 District residents who were in the labor force in 1980, the 66,771 residents who worked for the federal government constituted 21 percent.[51] These statistics are not that convincing for either side of the statehood issue and their interpretation and use vary over a wide range.

Intervention and Micromanagement
PRO

The appropriations process has become a common device for arbitrary congressional intervention and micromanagement of District of Columbia affairs. Statehood would provide an opportunity for self-government to function properly and prevent Congress from "meddling" in local affairs under the thinly veiled guise of protecting the federal interest.

CON

The opponents of statehood see no real problem here. They have little or no objection to Congress's handling of oversight and feel that it may be necessary to adequately protect the national interest. They do not view it as an abuse of congressional power.

The Partisan Factor

Although it may not be a part of the official record, the statehood issue is heavily influenced by political factors. The electorate in the District of Columbia is 78 percent Democratic, followed by independents who comprise 12 percent. The percentage of Republican voters is only 8 percent.[52] The District's completely urban population is predominantly black. Under these circumstances, its representatives to Congress are almost certain to be Democratic and black. The Republican members of Congress would have little incentive to vote for statehood under these conditions and their forty-three members in the Senate of the 103d Congress (1993–94) are quite enough to present a real stumbling block through a filibuster.

Constitutional Issues

The Department of Justice, under Republican President Ronald Reagan, asserted in 1987 that statehood for the District of Columbia is neither a racial issue nor a civil rights issue: "It is a constitutional issue that goes to the very foundation of our federal union. A change in the status of the District of Columbia would signal a substantial change in our form of federalism."[53] Over the years, legal scholars on opposing sides of the statehood issue have argued the constitutional issues in great detail. The crux of these arguments centers on whether or not Congress may permanently surrender its exclusive authority over the District without a constitutional amendment. The Republicans argue that a constitutional amendment is required and that even if a District of Columbia statehood bill is enacted, it would be struck down on constitutional grounds. The high points of some of the constitutional issues are presented below.

Original Intent

There is concern by some (mainly opponents of District of Columbia statehood) that statehood for the District would conflict with the original intent of the Framers of the Constitution, who envisioned a national capital on neutral ground "outside the borders of any state." Consequently, a federal district was devised as a means by which the federal government would remain independent of the states and, in turn, the states would remain independent of the federal government. The argument in defense of this point is that statehood for the District would change the balance between the states and the federal government that the Framers so carefully struck in Philadelphia.

The Justice Department under President Bush argued that the Framers intended that the District, comprising the seat of government, would be permanent, and that they never intended this District to become a state. The main aspects of the argument on original intent can be dealt with in two parts, "fixed form" and "fixed function," both of which focus on the Exclusive Power (District) Clause of the Constitution, which states that the Congress shall have power

> [t]o exercise exclusive Legislation in all Cases whatsoever, over such District (not exceeding ten Miles square) as may, by Cession of particular States, and the Acceptance of Congress, become the Seat of the Government of the United States, . . . (U.S. Constitution, art. 1, sec. 8)

Fixed Form. Opponents of District of Columbia statehood have construed the District Clause to prohibit Congress from altering the present form of the District of Columbia. They argue that this clause gave Congress plenary legislative authority over not just any district that may become the seat of the government from time to time but over only the "district" that, by cession of lands from Maryland and Virginia, became the District of Columbia. By the acts of cession of lands from Maryland and Virginia, and their acceptance by Congress, the latter body exhausted its authority to determine the form of the federal district that became the seat of the government. Thus, the form of the original District of Columbia was finally fixed and is unchangeable by Congress without a constitutional amendment.[54]

The supporters of District of Columbia statehood present many arguments against this interpretation. First, they point out that the federal district would not be eliminated. It would simply be shrunk to the small enclave of federal buildings and installations that comprise the National Capital Service Area. The remainder would then be admitted as the state of New Columbia. Thus, the statehood concept is not inconsistent with the federal intent. Second, in their "plain language" interpretation of the District Clause, statehood supporters argue that the only restriction regarding boundary that is imposed by this clause is that Congress may not use its authority to create a district "exceeding ten miles square." They point out that the inclusion of this ceiling restriction suggests that the omission of any floor restriction in the District Clause is legally significant and deliberate. Thus, the end, according to their interpretation, is to attain what is desirable in relation to the seat of government within the ceiling.[55]

Historical precedents, with respect to boundary changes already executed in the federal district, are used to support the argument against a fixed form. The 1846 House Committee on the District of Columbia rejected the fixed form interpretation of the District Clause in deciding to give back to Virginia one-third (the areas of Alexandria and Arlington) of the original District. Congress then passed and the president signed the retrocession bill into law. The judgment of these two political branches that the change in the size of the District was constitutional is presented as weighty evidence that the District Clause permits such changes.[56] The constitutionality of this judgment was rounded out when the Supreme Court, thirty years later declined the opportunity to reject the judgment when it was asked to rule on the constitutionality of the retrocession.[57]

Another change in the boundary of the original District took place in 1791, less than one year after Congress had voted to accept the cession of land for the District. The First Congress amended the act of acceptance to change the southern boundary of the District. Thirteen of the original Framers, including James Madison, voted for the amendment. Apparently, they did not believe that a constitutional amendment was required to effect this change.[58] These precedents support the argument that Congress's authority to fix the form of the District was not exhausted by any single legislative act.

The supporters of statehood also point out that the District Clause is immediately followed in the Constitution by a grant of authority "to exercise like authority over all places purchased [within the states] for the erection of forts, magazines, arsenals, dockyards, and other needful buildings. . . ." (U.S. Constitution, art. 1, sec. 8,). It has long been construed that this authority allows Congress to convey, as well as to acquire, such places; it does not exhaust its authority by using it to acquire these places. If Congress can thus change the form of such federal places, then it has "like authority" to do the same to the District—as long as such changes do not fundamentally alter its function.

Fixed Function. In their case against District statehood, proponents of the fixed function argument assert that the Framers' original intent was to locate the seat of government in a federal town outside the jurisdiction of any state. Their rationale for establishing an autonomous federal enclave was to assure Congress of authority over its immediate surroundings, "to forever secure the independence of the federal government, avoiding the overweening influence of any one state, as well as to avoid interstate and sectional rivalries."[59]

The broader and longer-range concern of the Framers was securing the general independence of the operation of the federal government from any state. It is arguable from the historical materials that these functions presupposed creation of a federal district outside the boundaries of any state, not just a federal enclave within one. The fixed function argument is completed by the assertion that District of Columbia statehood would impinge on the intended functions of the federal district in that the truncated federal enclave would lie within the state of New Columbia and be completely dependent on it for essential services. District of Columbia statehood would eliminate the federal city, converting it into a small unit comparable to existing federal enclaves in the states. The members of the government could not reside in the reduced federal district.

Supporters of statehood admit that the fixed function argument presents a serious challenge to the constitutionality of District of Columbia statehood. But the case may be vulnerable due to an incorrect gauging of the impact of statehood on the federal government functions and the scope of such impact can be gauged more appropriately by Congress in its political discretion.[60]

Statehood supporters are not without a rebuttal to the fixed function argument. They begin by pointing out that it was not a lack of government authority that worried the Framers who wrote the District Clause. It was the lack of physical power and armed force, which the federal government has long since acquired. Today there is no question that the national government possesses the power to secure the seat of government, whether in its present or a reduced form. In spite of the Bush administration's concern about a small federal enclave, surrounded by the state of New Columbia, the statehood advocates argue that no state has the power to prevent the national government from performing its duties. The second part of their counterargument is that the National Capital Service Area, to which the District would be reduced, is arguably no more an enclave inside a state than is the existing District, surrounded on three sides by Maryland. The only difference would be that of size.[61]

What about the argument that the District is now a functioning city, not just a geographic construct within the state of New Columbia? Statehood supporters respond that national legislators, executive officers, and federal judges already live in the states of Maryland and Virginia. Changing the size of the District by creating a new state will not change the practical interdependence of all of the metropolitan District of Columbia areas.

Finally, congressional discretion would be expected to gauge the impact of the new state on the functions of the reduced federal district. Congress would always have the power to legislate against state encroachments on the independence of the federal government.[62]

The Twenty-third Amendment.

The opponents of District of Columbia statehood assert that the Constitution, by the Twenty-third Amendment, recognized the District as a permanent entity. This amendment provides for the District to have three electors in presidential and vice presidential elections. To reduce the District to a small federal enclave with virtually no one living there would effectively nullify the Twenty-third Amendment, which can only be done by another constitutional amendment.

The supporters of statehood maintain that the Twenty-third Amendment empowered Congress to "direct" the manner in which electors from the District are to be selected and, in the words of the amendment, "enforce this article by appropriate legislation." Implementing legislation would determine whether the new federal enclave would have the three electors authorized in this amendment. Congress, of course, could propose repealing the amendment if and when deemed appropriate.

Consent From Maryland.

The Justice Department under President Bush, in its argument against statehood for the District, testified that consent of Maryland might have to be secured before the District could be admitted to the Union. Since Maryland originally ceded the land that is now the District for purposes of establishing a seat of government, erecting a new state from this territory would, arguably, nullify the cession.[63]

After reviewing the wording of the cession, legal scholars in support of statehood stated that the Maryland grant of land was unconditional. Moreover, they maintain that even if the intent were implied that the land could only be used for purposes of creating the national capital, the fact that the land has been used for that purpose for over 190 years "may" have constituted "substantial compliance" with the original intent.[64]

THE POLITICS OF STATEHOOD

The road to statehood for the District is encumbered by many hurdles and potential barriers, ranging from partisan political factors on the national and state levels to internal conflicts on the local level. The latter has included differences over the substance of the statehood constitution, procedures for dealing with Congress, timing of protests and other activities designed to influence national government officials and the general public. Some of the major developments and conflicts to date are reviewed next.

The Constitution of New Columbia.

Drafted in a ninety-day period in 1982 by forty-five specially elected convention delegates, the District of Columbia statehood constitution received only lukewarm support from city leaders—many of whom immediately called for major revisions in the document. The constitution was approved by the voters in six of the city's eight wards and passed with a total vote of 60,333 in favor and 53,914 opposed.[65]

When it cleared the hurdle of voter approval on 2 November 1982, the proposed constitution still faced an uncertain future. Who would make the changes in the document—the District of Columbia Council, Congress, or the convention delegates, who had considerable time left in their three-year terms? Would the revised document be returned to the voters for referendum approval, and when would the mayor exercise his statutory authority to submit it to Congress in the petition for statehood? Many supporters felt that with the constitution in its present form, statehood would have little chance of approval by Congress because the document was viewed as "too radical." Some of the controversial provisions included the right of public employees to strike, a guaranteed job or minimum income for all citizens, a guaranteed right to abortion, and a prohibition against "fishing expeditions" by grand juries.[66]

The delegates to the District of Columbia Statehood Constitutional Convention finally completed the legislative history to the document in September 1983, thus clearing the way for the controversial constitution to be sent to Capitol Hill. Without further delay, Mayor Marion Barry forwarded to Congress the District's petition for statehood and Delegate Walter E. Fauntroy followed up by immediately introducing a bill on 12 September 1983 to grant District of Columbia statehood based on the proposed document.[67]

District officials readily conceded that many obstacles stood in statehood's way. After years of agonizing over its slim chances for approval, they finally proceeded to deal with the one hurdle that was clearly in their power—revising the substance of the document.

Early in 1987 a majority of the District Council, meeting privately with Delegate Fauntroy, agreed to a strategy for winning congressional approval of statehood legislation which, in effect, meant abandoning the constitution as approved by the voters in 1982. In essence the strategy was to combine parts of the current Home Rule Charter with a bill of rights, patterned after the first nine and the Fourteenth Amendment[s] to the United States Constitution, which would be substituted for the voter-approved document. Backed by Delegate Fauntroy and Mayor Barry, the council, in effect, passed its own version of a statehood constitution for the District.[68] As the leader in this strategy, Fauntroy convinced the members of the council that the objective was to have the District present to Congress a "bare bones" document that was simple, clear, and familiar, so as to focus debate and action on the issue of statehood and not on the contents of the proposed constitution.

As a result of its action the council found itself castigated by a stream of witnesses at a day-long public hearing on the revision of the constitution. It was charged with having usurped democracy by abandoning a constitution approved by the voters and for postponing the election of statehood lobbyists.[69] Although the council was urged to submit its changes to the voters before sending them to Congress, this was not done. Commenting on the council's action, the president of the defunct District of Columbia Statehood Constitutional Convention, Charles I. Cassell, said he believed that the will of the people had not been respected.[70]

With the trimmed down constitution accomplished in 1987, the final stage was set for action by Congress—a process that was still going on in 1994. Until his departure at the end of the 101st Congress (1990), Delegate Fauntroy was the chief engineer in directing the statehood legislation on Capitol Hill.[71] The high hopes for a debate and vote in the House in 1987 were to no avail. Although the House District Committee, under Chairman Ronald V. Dellums (D-Calif.), reported out a statehood bill in June 1987, the House was not asked to vote on the measure.

Delegate Eleanor Holmes Norton took her seat in the House at the beginning of the 102d Congress (1991–92) and assumed a leadership role in the strategy to win congressional approval of statehood for the District. On a straight party-line vote of seven to four, the House District Committee approved a District of Columbia statehood bill in April 1992, at which time Chairman Dellums vowed to bring the issue to the floor for a test vote as soon as possible. Supporters had expected the pressure of election-year politics to help the statehood cause. As the year wound down toward adjournment, it was clear that the opposite had taken place. Election-year politics had driven down the potential support for statehood, causing the leaders to drop their efforts to bring the issue to the floor in the 102d Congress.[72]

The Statehood Party and Related Commissions.

Formed by the late District Council member Julius Hobson, Sr., community activist Josephine Butler, and others, the Statehood Party is a homegrown political entity. Its main goal is expressed through its name. From its barely noticed beginnings in 1969, the party developed into a small but significant political force in the pre-home rule politics of the District of Columbia School Board.[73] Since the beginning of the party, its goal of making the District the fifty-first state has been in conflict to some extent with the concept of limited home rule that the District was granted in 1973. The Statehood Party platform, accepted at its 1972 convention, contained a number of extremely liberal planks. For example, its platform included tax-supported free health care for all people, replacement of penal institutions with rehabilitative programs of fixed maximum terms, a taxi system to be owned and controlled by taxi drivers and citizens, and the right to strike by all government employees and teachers.[74]

Although the Statehood Party remains small in membership, District residents began to gravitate to the statehood cause after it became clear that the Full Voting Rights Amendment would not be approved.[75] The Statehood Party can be given major credit for keeping the statehood issue alive and, after the death of the voting rights amendment in 1985, the movement was embraced by the local Democratic Party, leaving the Statehood Party with very little separate identity in the struggle for statehood. As of 1994, at-large council member Hilda Mason was the party's only elected official.

In accordance with the statehood initiative, two related commissions were established in the early 1980s to promote the statehood movement: the Statehood Commission and the Statehood Compact Commission.[76] The Statehood Commission is a twenty-four-member appointed body (with three members from each of the city's eight wards) that uses its annual funding for educational and promotional activities and materials to advance the proposition of statehood in the District of Columbia and elsewhere. The smaller Statehood Compact Commission (with members drawn from the Statehood Commission— one from each ward) is somewhat like a subcommittee of the former body. It is entrusted with the responsibility of developing the technical framework (the appropriate legislative and administrative actions) that would be needed to facilitate the transfer of authority and functions from the District to the state of New Columbia. For several years, each of these bodies received one-half of a $150,000 annual appropriation. Although both commissions are still in existence, their financial support has not been consistent. In the city's budget for fiscal year 1990, the funding for these bodies was redirected by Congress to the Metropolitan Police Department and was not restored until fiscal year 1994.[77]

The House Debates Statehood—1993.

Near the end of the first session of the 103d Congress (November 1993), the bill to admit the state of New Columbia into the Union was brought to the House floor for full debate and a vote, climaxing the efforts led by District Delegate Eleanor Holmes Norton and Representative Fortney "Pete" Stark (D-Calif.), with solid support from the Congressional Black Caucus. Ultimately, this debate became a conflict of two basic issues: the rights of District residents versus the District's unique place in history and in the Constitution. Although the statehood bill was defeated by a vote of 277 to 153, the sponsors and supporters of the measure portrayed the vote as a major political victory. It was the first time in fifteen years that Congress had considered any major change in the structure of the District government. Never in history had either the House or the Senate debated statehood for the District in plenary session, and the number of members voting in favor of the bill exceeded expectations by some twenty or thirty votes.[78]

Statehood opponents called the outcome of the vote a serious set-back for the cause and predicted that it would be many years before another vote would be taken. No committee hearings or other action on statehood took place in the Senate during the first session of the 103d Congress (1993).

Bringing the statehood issue to the House floor in 1993 was a strategic move that was sought by statehood leaders. They saw it as a milestone and felt that they were gaining momentum in what may be a very long struggle. They led twenty-one consecutive weeks of protests on Capitol Hill, which resulted in about 230 supporters being arrested in the name of statehood. In spite of the expected negative vote, the issue gained national visibility and only time will determine the true meaning of this historical development.

RACE AND POLITICS

Hardly anything can complicate an issue more than race and politics, and statehood is a case in point. Although President Bush and the Republicans were on record against District of Columbia statehood, President Bill Clinton said during the 1992 presidential campaign that he would sign legislation making the District the fifty-first state.[79] With the Democrats in control of the White House and Congress, the assumption by District officials and supporters was that a new urgency had been given to the statehood question.

The District of Columbia statehood issue has the makings of a hot political topic—with charges of racism and discrimination on one side, and violations of the Constitution on the other. After a statehood bill was introduced in 1987, Delegate Fauntroy said, "There are still a few racists who would deny the citizens of the District of Columbia voting representation because the majority [68 percent] of people here happen to be black." "That's totally ridiculous," replied Representative Stan Parris (R-Va.), a leading opponent of statehood. "It is an attempt to intimidate Members by shifting the focus of debate away from the constitutional issues." In a poll of members of Congress, many said their constituents did not seem to care about the issue.[80]

The racial question in the United States has been the subject of considerable research and study since the early years of our nation. Based upon this research, it is generally conceded that institutional racism, in various amounts, permeates the general society of the United States.[81] With its predominantly black population, the District is probably the target of more than its share of racist thinking. In grappling with the financial problems of the city, Mayor Sharon Pratt Kelly has made urgent calls for statehood, based on the charge that the national government does not play fair with the District. She has contended that Congress pays little heed to District officials, most of whom are black, and has said that race is very much a part of the equation in which the city finds itself.[82]

As indicated at the outset of this chapter, the most serious aspect of the territorial status of the residents of the District of Columbia is the lack of representation in the national legislature. Of the residents of federal capital cities in the countries of the Western world, only those in the District of Columbia are without this basic right. Statehood would be the quickest and most forthright way to establish the full political rights of the residents of the District. Would the District be economically viable without federal support? There is a standoff between the advocates and foes on this question. A commuter tax would generate the reciprocal factor and, since the majority of the federal workers in the city would probably work in the federal enclave and hence not be subject to the tax, further study may be needed on this question to ascertain a better estimate of the net income.

Although statehood receives a low political feasibility rating, it would provide representation and local autonomy for the District. Both statehood and retrocession call for the implementation of the NCSA. The main federal buildings are within the federal enclave, but important aspects of the federal establishment and most of the embassies are outside of it.

Approximately 95 percent of the foreign missions are located within the District of Columbia, in the northwest section of the city. Finding suitable and adequate locations for chancery facilities has been a continuous and growing problem. It has been stated repeatedly by members of both the House and Senate that the issue of the location of chanceries within the nation's capital provides perhaps the clearest example of shared federal and local interests in the District of Columbia. There are legitimate federal interests that are broader than the compact area that comprises the NCSA. The challenge of dual democracy demands a fair and equitable reconciliation of interests. In the case of statehood, it may mean a compromise on some attributes and prerogatives as has already been done in the proposed statehood bill to protect the skyline.

NOTES

1. The lead question asked respondents was whether citizens of the District should have the same rights as citizens of the fifty states. Seventy-eight percent said "yes"; nearly 11 percent said "no"; the remainder had no opinion. In the follow-up question, respondents were asked whether they agreed or disagreed with a bill to grant statehood to the District. Fifty-two percent said "yes"; nearly 24 percent said "no"; 24 percent had no opinion. The margin of error in the survey was plus or minus three percentage points. Released by the office of the District of Columbia Delegate, this nationwide survey of one thousand people, age eighteen and over, was conducted by Decision/Making/Information, a Washington, D.C. research firm, headed by then-President Ronald Reagan's pollster, Richard Wirthlin. Reported in the *Washington Post*, 16 May 1987, B-3.

2. Edward M. Meyers, "An Examination of Statehood and other Political Alternatives for the Residents of Washington, D. C." (Ph.D. diss., Georgetown University, Department of Government, 1992), 52.

3. Although the position of the governor, as chief of state, would be a key factor in any steps toward retrocession of the District to Maryland, formal action by the legislature would be required to execute this transaction. A survey of the Maryland House of Delegates and Senate in 1989 revealed views that were in opposition to those of Governor Schaefer. Of the 47 percent of the members of the House of Delegates and 51 percent of the senators that responded, 82 percent of the delegates and 92 percent of the senators replied that they would reject retrocession even if Congress continued to provide a financial subsidy to the District. Only one senator and six delegates out of the ninety-one legislators who responded were willing to take the District back. These unpublished survey results are summarized in Philip P. Scharg, "The Future of District of Columbia Home Rule," *Catholic University Law Review* 39, no. 2 (Winter 1990), 320 n. 53; *Washington Post*, 26 February 1990, A-6.

4. Meyers, 53.

5. Information on square mileage of the NCSA secured via telephone from the office of the National Capital Planning Commission, Washington, D.C., 27 May 1994

6. In tandem with the bill introduced in the House, Representative Parris introduced a joint resolution proposing an amendment to the Constitution to repeal the 23d Amendment. Garrine P. Laney, *D.C. Statehood: The Historical Context and Recent Congressional Actions*, Washington, D.C.: Congressional Research Service, Library of Congress (12 March 1992), 8.

7. Representative Parris introduced the National Capital Civil Rights Restoration Act of 1990 (H.R. 4193), Committee on the District of Columbia, 101st Cong., 2d sess., 1990; see also *Washington Post*, 2 March 1990, D-1.

8. *Washington Post*, 7 March 1990, D-1.

9. Parris recalled the early system from 1790 until 1800, when District residents voted for president and members of Congress in Maryland. Based on his legal research, Parris went so far as to say that "the system could be reinstated by Congress without approval of Maryland officials," which, of course, was not a likely possibility. Ibid.

10. Jamin B. Raskin, "Commentary: Domination, Democracy, and the District: The Statehood Position," *Catholic University Law Review* 39, no. 2 (Winter 1990), 54.

11. *Washington Post,* 22 August 1980, A-14.

12. Coalition for Self-Determination for the District of Columbia was a group of over sixty local and national organizations that worked for full home rule. It worked with state affiliates of the national member organizations and helped to organize and develop strategies for the ratification campaigns in the respective states. *Washington Informer,* 26 January–1 February 1984, 11.

13. *Washington Post,* 22 August 1980, A-15; 25 August 1985, B-8.

14. Based on the 1990 census, the average congressional district contains 572,466 people. *Washington Post,* 6 September 1992, C-8.

15. For a discussion of how a single senator may affect the agenda of the body as well as the policies of some executive departments by the skillful use of his/her power, see Schrag, 326 n. 79.

16. Ibid.

17. To guard against this eventuality, it has been suggested that a full voting rights amendment should provide that both it and the Twenty-third Amendment (which provides electoral votes for the District) would become void if the District is admitted to the Union as a state. Ibid.

18. Although it is expected that Congress would review and act on District of Columbia legislation during this review period, there is nothing to bar Congress from repealing District of Columbia legislation at any time.

19. Intermittent proposals to reduce Congress's power over the District government have been made without success by members of the House District Committee and, in 1991, by Mayor Kelly and Council Chairman John Wilson. These efforts have been met with solid opposition from the Republicans on the committee. *Washington Post,* 8 November 1991, D-1.

20. This seven-member commission comprises one member appointed by the president, two by the board of governors of the District of Columbia Bar, two by the mayor, one by the council, and one by the chief judge of the United States District Court. Schrag, 342 n. 157.

21. In July 1993 the first African American, former District of Columbia Superior Court Judge Eric H. Holder, was appointed by President Clinton to serve as United States attorney for the District. *Washington Post,* 30 July 1993, B-1.

22. Ibid., 25 March 1993, A-24.

23. Meyers, 48.

24. *Washington Post,* 16 February 1992, C-8; 9 October 1992.

25. Ibid., 12 October 1980, C-4.

26. Meyers, 2.

27. *Washington Post,* 12 October 1980, C-4.

28. Democratic National Committee, *1992 Democratic Platform,* (Washington, D.C. 14 July 1992), 11.

29. Republican National Committee, *The Republican Platform—1992,* (Washington, D.C., 17 August 1992), 49.

30. Delegate Eleanor Holmes Norton (D-D.C.), a former law professor and constitutional scholar, conducted research on the legal issue and drafted the legislation that led to the delegates' right to vote. She argued that since the delegates were allowed to vote in committees, they could legally vote in the Committee of the Whole. The House Democrats voted on this matter late in the 102d Congress (1992). All of the District and territorial representatives are Democrats. No Republicans supported the move, calling it unconstitutional and a Democratic "power grab." They finally took legal action in their efforts to block it. *Washington Post,* 6 January 1992, A-1; 9 March 1993, A-1.

31. Ibid., 9 March 1993, A-1; 27 January 1994, B-3.

32. Ibid., 15 July 1992, A-23.

33. Bureau of the Census, *Statistical Abstracts of the U.S.: 1991,* 111th ed., quoted in Meyers, 20–21.

34. *Washington Post,* 16 February 1992, C-8.

35. Meyers, 57.

36. Judith Best, *National Representation for the District of Columbia* (Frederick, Maryland: University Publications of America, 1984), 5.

37. Foley became speaker of the House on 6 June 1989. Congress. House Committee on the District of Columbia, Subcommittee on Fiscal Affairs and Health, *Hearings and Markups on H.R. 51—Admission of the State of New Columbia into the Union,* pt. 1, 100th Cong., 1st sess., 17 March 1987, 31.

38. Meyers, 32.

39. House Committee on the District of Columbia, Subcommittee on Judiciary and Education, *Hearing and Markup on H.R. 2482—Admission of the State of New Columbia into the Union,* vol. 1, 102d Cong., 2d sess., 24 March 1992, 37.

40. *Washington Post,* 23 June 1987, B-1.

41. New York City Federal Affairs Office, official information via telephone, Washington, D.C., 23 February 1993.

42. *Washington Post,* 18 May 1990, D-1.

43. House Committee on the District of Columbia, *New Columbia Admissions Act,* 100th Cong., 1st sess., 17 September 1987, H. Rept. 305, 12, quoted in Meyers, 38.

44. *Washington Post,* 30 September 1986, B-1.

45. *Washington Times,* 15 November 1991, B-2.

46. *Washington Post,* 4 May 1992, B-1; Rudolph A. Pyatt, Jr., "D.C.'s Deteriorating Economy is Fueling Its Fiscal Troubles," ibid., 23 May 1994, Washington Business Magazine, 3.

47. Exclusive of other non-black groups, the white population is 90 percent or above in 20 states; there are nine states with a black population of less than one percent. Bureau of the Census, *Statistical Abstracts of the United States, 1990 Census of Population* (Washington, D.C., 1993), 343–50.

48. District of Columbia Office of Policy and Program Evaluation, *Indices: A Statistical Index to District of Columbia Services* (Washington, D.C., 1991), 171.

49. Best, 74.

50. Bureau of the Census, *Census of the Population, 1980,* vol. 2, Subject Reports, (Washington, D.C., 1984) 126.

51. District of Columbia Office of Policy and Program Evaluation, *Indices,* 172.

52. Statistics provided by the District of Columbia Board of Elections and Ethics, Washington, D.C., February 1993.

53. Office of Legal Policy, *Report to the Attorney General on the Question of Statehood for the District of Columbia* (Washington, D.C., April 1987), 50.

54. Peter Raven-Hansen, "The Constitutionality of D.C. Statehood," paper presented at the 1990 annual meeting of the American Political Science Association, San Francisco, 31 August 1990, 5.

55. Ibid., 6.

56. Ibid., 7.

57. *Phillips v. Payne*, 92 U.S. 130 (1875), summarized in Raven-Hansen, 7.

58. This act of 3 March 1791 repealed the requirement of the first act, which had set the location of the district on the Potomac "at some place between the mouths of the Eastern Branch and Conococheague . . . ," and substituted a location "below said limit, and above the mouth of Hunting Creek, . . . so as to include . . ." portions of what are now Anacostia and Alexandria. See also House Committee, *Hearing and Markups on H.R. 2482—Admission of the State of New Columbia into the Union*, 184.

59. Raven-Hansen, 9.

60. Ibid.

61. Ibid., 11.

62. Ibid., 11–12.

63. House Committee, *Hearing and Markups on H.R. 2482—Admission of the State of New Columbia into the Union*, 85.

64. Raven-Hansen, 14.

65. The constitution was opposed by a margin of more than 4 to 1 in the predominantly white Ward 3, lying west of Rock Creek Park, while the residents of Ward 2, which includes Dupont Circle, sections of Georgetown, Southwest, and the central city, rejected it by a margin of some 600 votes out of approximately 12,000 cast. *Washington Post*, 4 November 1982, A-21.

66. Ibid., 16 May 1984, C-4.

67. Ibid.

68. The revised statehood constitution was cosponsored by twelve of the thirteen members of the council; at-large Republican member Carol Schwartz was the lone dissenter. *Washington Post*, 12 March 1987, A-18; 31 March 1987, B-3.

69. The council voted to put off for three years the elections of three "shadow representatives"—two senators and one representative to promote in Congress and in the nation the cause of District of Columbia statehood. Ibid., 31 March 1987, B-3.

70. *Hilltop*, Howard University, 13 March 1987, 5.

71. Delegate Fauntroy did not seek reelection to Congress in 1990 but chose instead to run for the position of mayor of the District of Columbia; he was defeated in the 1990 Democratic primary.

72. *Washington Post*, 6 October 1992, C-6.

73. Five Statehood Party members—Julius Hobson, Sr., his son Julius, Jr., Hilda Mason, Charles I. Cassell, and Bardyl Tirana—held seats on the school board at one time or another within the party's first five years of existence. The elder Hobson was elected as at-large member of the first home rule District Council in 1974 and served until his death in 1977. Mason was appointed to succeed Hobson on the council in 1977. Later that year she defeated nine other candidates in a special election to serve out Hobson's term. In 1978 she won a full term and remains as a member of the council in 1994 through successive reelections since that time. *Washington Post*, 1 March 1979, D.C.-3; 30 October 1982, B-1.

74. *Statehood Call: Voice of the District of Columbia Statehood Party*, 23 March 1981, 2-3.

75. In 1979 the Statehood Party had only about 1,500 members. During the current statehood era, membership of the party increased to 3,605 by November 1993. Statistics provided by the District of Columbia Board of Elections and Ethics, Washington, D.C., 4 January 1994.

76. *Washington Post*, 12 October 1980, C-1.

77. Telephone interview with Ms. Josephine Butler, former chairwoman of both the Statehood Party and the Statehood Commission, Washington, D.C., 11 March 1993; House, *District of Columbia Appropriations Bill, 1994*, 103d Cong., 1st sess., 1994, H. Rept. 152.

78. Only one Republican voted for statehood and 105 Democrats voted against it. *New York Times*, 22 November 1993, B-8.

79. *Washington Times*, 17 November 1992, A-1.

80. *Roll Call: The Newspaper of Capitol Hill*, 20 September 1987, 16.

81. For a definition of institutional racism and its relationship to racist policies, see Louis Knowles and Kenneth Prewitt, *Institutional Racism* (Englewood Cliffs, N.J.: Prentice Hall, Inc., 1969), 5–6.

82. *Washington Post*, 27 September 1992, B-1.

9

The Challenge of Dual Democracy: Foreign Models

Democratic federations face the challenge of trying to balance the demands of democracy between the nation as a whole and the capital city. Although varied in their political cultures and governmental organizations, these countries confront basic problems that are surprisingly similar in the development of their capital cities. For example, control of the police forces and the keeping of public order can be a ticklish issue in the relations between the central government and the national capital. Practically all of the capital areas are undergoing rapid population growth, which has further complicated their problems. Obviously, some of the federal countries have met the challenge of dual democracy more successfully than others.

In this chapter I shall review capital city governance in several foreign countries that have federal systems of governments to see how they have responded to their problems. My main concern will be with the existence and powers of the basic local governing institutions—legislature, executive, and judiciary—with comments in some instances on security, budget, and planning. My purpose is to see what can be learned from these systems—especially the institutional mechanisms—that would promote democratic principles and practices in the federal district of the United States. In making this determination within the domestic context, I shall seek to apply the same criteria that were applied in the last chapter to evaluate the proposals for meeting the challenge of dual democracy: representation in the national legislature, local autonomy, protecting legitimate federal interests, and political feasibility. In other words, what can we import from these models that might contribute to an optimal balance in democratic principles and practices in our national capital? Although there will be some comment on the experiences with these arrangements within the respective country, it is not my objective to carry out a political/cultural evaluation.

The number of countries that can be identified as federations depends upon the definition that is used. I have avoided the problem of trying to determine which countries are genuine federations by including countries that claim to have federal constitutions. There were eighteen countries with federal constitutions, most of which will be identified below. Since the USSR and Yugoslavia have fallen apart, the working number is now at sixteen. A complete list of these countries, along with a discussion of their capital cities, was prepared by Donald C. Rowat in 1973 and updated in 1991.[1]

Federal capital cities fall into three categories, with some similarities and variations in the problems encountered by each group. These categories are: (1) capitals within a state, (2) capitals as city-states, and (3) capitals as federal districts or territories. Each of these arrangements has its own problems and none of the countries seems to be entirely satisfied with the system of government for the capital. I shall discuss each of these categories, with the most attention devoted to capitals in federal districts, the same arrangement that was adopted in the United States.

CAPITALS WITHIN STATES

Examples of capitals located within the jurisdiction of a state or province include Ottawa (Canada), Bonn (Germany),[2] and Bern (Switzerland).[3] As will be shown below, the main problem with this arrangement is that the federal government does not have direct control over its own capital. Although the national government should have a definite role in developing the capital in the interest of the nation as a whole, the constitutional power to do this may not exist. The powers in the federal constitutions are usually divided in such a way that the central government cannot preempt state or local jurisdiction in certain policy areas, such as municipal governmental structure, transportation design and construction, registry activities, security, planning, and zoning. There is often too much emphasis on provincial and local views, to the neglect of national interests. The laws, influence, and culture of the governing state tend to dominate the capital city, rendering it less representative of the nation as a whole.

These complaints have often been made by national officials in Canada, where the national seat of government in Ottawa falls under the laws of the province of Ontario. A similar situation holds true in Switzerland, where the capital city of Bern is also the capital of the canton of Bern, within which it is situated. The central government complains about having inadequate control over its own capital. It does not control planning in the capital city and, in fact, cannot even control the location and construction of its own buildings. When building projects are planned, the central government must secure the necessary permits from the city planning department. Speaking of his own country, Donald C. Rowat categorizes Ottawa as one of the most difficult federal capitals to govern, pointing to Canada's very decentralized system and the predominant control of the province of Ontario over the capital city. Moreover, the National Capital Region lies on both sides of the Ottawa River, partly in the province of Quebec and partly in the province of Ontario. The region's municipalities on the north side of the river fall under the laws of Quebec, while Ottawa and the other municipalities on the south side of the river come under the laws of Ontario. Rowat states: "So the federal government has no control over its own capital."[4]

In Bonn, the central government is represented on the regional planning bodies of North Rhine Westphalia, the state in which the capital city is located. The regional planning bodies establish the land use plans to which the local governments, including Bonn, must adhere.[5]

The situations in the capital cities of both Ottawa and Bern are complicated further by language and cultural problems. The French-speaking people of the province of Quebec feel that Ottawa, as an English-speaking city governed by an English-speaking province, is not sufficiently representative of the nation as a whole and that the country would be better served by a federal capital territory surrounding Ottawa (because it would include a part of Quebec north of the capital). They argue that this arrangement for the capital would symbolize bilingualism and biculturalism. The situation in Bern with respect to language and culture is similar to that in Ottawa except that German, rather than English, is the predominant language. Bern is a German-speaking city governed by a German-speaking canton, and the French-speaking Swiss federal civil servants have an adjustment problem in the capital city.

One complaint of local government officials in state-controlled capital cities is that they do not receive adequate financial help from the central government to meet the cost of their function as the national capital. Because the national government does not carry its own weight in the relationship, a financial hardship is created for the city. Thus, state-governed capitals have a high degree of self-government but they suffer from the problems of divided jurisdiction and financial insufficiency.

The perspective in dealing with governance issues is affected by the degree of centralization that exists within the respective federal system. Although Islamabad (Pakistan) and Kuala Lumpur (Malaysia) are now examples of federal district capital cities, when Rowat prepared his original list in 1973 they were within states but were governed almost exclusively by federal law. Because these countries are highly centralized federal systems, there was slim chance of serious disagreement between the state and central government. Capitals such as Ottawa and Bern are in decentralized systems and the reverse situation is encountered. As demonstrated above, the central government is often lacking in sufficient powers to control adequately the planning and development of its own capital area.[6]

CAPITALS AS CITY-STATES

The best example of a city-state capital is Vienna (Austria). Berlin (Germany) will also represent a city-state capital when the transfer of the German capital from Bonn to Berlin is completed. While a city-state arrangement assures that the residents of the capital will enjoy democratic rights and privileges on a par with other citizens of the country, it may give the central government even less control than when the capital city is within a state or province.

If the city-state is not made large enough at the time of its creation, the urban population may eventually spread far beyond its boundaries into other states, thus causing a serious problem of metropolitan government. City-states are usually small in physical area compared to other states of the federation. Their dense populations often expand across their boundaries into adjacent states, creating interjurisdictional difficulties in dealing with the problems of the larger capital city area.

In the greater Vienna metropolitan region, the jurisdictional boundary lines between the city-state and the outlying areas are strongly reinforced by partisan political affiliations. With a population of over 1.54 million, Vienna is the largest city, as well as the largest of the nine states, of Austria. It has been and continues to be a stronghold of the Social Democratic Party. The surrounding state of Lower Austria is a strong Christian Democratic area. While there is satisfactory cooperation between the two states, neither one would support any change in the present boundaries due mainly to political reasons. The national government would have little or no leverage to influence this situation.[7] Due mainly to the lack of control over the city's development,

Rowat, in his comparative studies of federal capitals, advised against this arrangement.

CAPITALS IN FEDERAL DISTRICTS

In light of the unique position held by federal capitals, many countries have treated them in a special way by placing them in a separate federal district or territory. This arrangement has been defended as a principle of federalism, the argument being that the national seat of government should not come under the jurisdiction or domination of any of the federated states, but should be equally accessible to all states.

The United States is the oldest example of this governmental arrangement and its capital city has served as a model for the other countries of the world that have adopted it. Traditionally, this category has included the following seven capitals: Buenos Aires (Argentina), Caracas (Venezuela), Brasilia (Brazil), Mexico City (Mexico), Canberra (Australia), and Delhi (India). In addition to the previously mentioned transitions to this category—Kuala Lumpur and Islamabad—the capital of Nigeria has been moved from the city-state of Lagos to a newly created federal district in Abuja.[8] Our discussion here will focus on the capital cities that have had long years of experience as federal districts.

The main motivation behind establishing the seat of government in federal territory is the desire of the country to develop and have adequate control of its capital. And although this goal may be achieved, experience with federal districts has shown that other basic problems of governing the capital are left unsolved. The central government may dominate the public affairs of the city at the expense of the democratic principles upon which the nation is founded. Later in this chapter, Mexico City will be discussed as a prime example of this problem. Moreover, the federal district capitals experience the problem of fragmented decision-making at the national level. Many departments, agencies, and commissions become involved in administering the capital city, and the difficulty of coordinating their activities is a serious one.[9]

In some cases the local residents are denied the basic political rights that are enjoyed by the citizens of the nation as a whole; capital inhabitants can be subject to taxation without representation in the national legislature. Because the residents of the federal district have very little political power, they cannot effectively engage in the process of defining federal and local interests, nor can they defend or protect their interests.

In countries where a new planned capital city is created, the problem of political representation tends to grow with the population. The issue is hardly raised when only a handful of residents, all of whom work for the government, are involved. Washington, New Delhi, Canberra, and Brasilia are examples of such cities. Only Washington made provisions for some self-government at the very outset. However, Washington did not maintain this momentum and now finds itself lagging behind the other federal district capitals on the issue of national representation.

In spite of the problems and issues, the federal district arrangement seems to be the growing trend among federal systems. The number of countries in this category has grown from seven in the early 1970s to approximately ten in 1993. When the capital is located in a federal district, however, the basic dangers remain: domination from the center, lack of self-government for the local residents, and the neglect of local interests.

FEDERAL DISTRICT CAPITALS: VARYING DEGREES OF SELF-GOVERNMENT

In democratic federations, the essential challenge in governing the capital city is to strike a balance between national and local interests. But this is easier said than done. Although the United States model is the oldest of the federal capital cities and has served as a prototype for countries all over the world, the United States has not been able to lead the way in striking such a balance in democracy. Consequently, its task, along with that of many other democratic federations, is unfinished.

With respect to their local governments, some of the federal capital cities with federal districts—Canberra, Brasilia, Caracas, and Delhi—have a significant degree of self-government with good results. The federal districts in Mexico and Argentina represent examples of capital cities with limited self-governing powers.

Considerable strides toward full self-government have been made in the federal district of Venezuela in recent years.[10] Before 1986, the federal district comprised two centrally governed departments: the Libertador Department, which included the city of Caracas, and the Vargas Department. The new Organic Law of the Federal District, promulgated in 1986, introduced two major changes in the governance of the federal territory. First, the two former departments of Libertador and Vargas became, respectively, Libertador Municipality, with its capital at Caracas, and Vargas Municipality, with its capital at La Guaira; each municipality has its own elected council. This new arrangement with respect to municipalities placed the federal district on a par with the rest of the country. Second, the organic law divided the governance of the federal territory into district and municipal functions.

In 1988 further reforms in the Organic Law of Municipal Regime introduced the office of mayor, which assumed the administrative functions in each of the municipalities. There is still a governor, appointed by the president of the Republic, who represents the federal government and has jurisdiction over the whole federal district, but the election of mayors in the municipalities was an important self-governing step. Legislation required for the federal district above the municipal level is passed by the national congress.

In Buenos Aires there is a city council of limited powers. The national congress enacts basic laws that are applicable to the federal district, covering such matters as municipal governmental structure, the court system, and the registry office. With twenty-five deputies in the Chamber of Deputies, the federal capital has the second largest representation in this body.[11] Each province, as well as the federal capital, has two members in the senate. In the current administration of President Carlos Saul Menem, leader of the Justicialist Party (1989–95), there is ongoing discussion and debate on the question of amending the national constitution to allow for the election of the mayor of Buenos Aires.[12]

A key aspect of the democracy exercised by the residents in federal territories is the right of representation in the national legislature. While the residents of the federal district of the United States have only a nonvoting delegate in the lower house of Congress and no representation in the Senate, the other countries have voting members in their national legislatures. On this important aspect of democracy, the United States has fallen behind other democratic countries.

In several countries, such as Australia, Brazil, and India, as well as the United States, the capitals in federal districts began as planned new cities. There were only a small number of residents in these districts at the outset and the lack of provisions for self-government was not a big problem. The seriousness of this issue tends to grow along with the population and soon demands increasing attention from the central government until it is dealt with.

Our examination of federal district capitals reveals that none of these countries allows the full gamut of self-government that is usually available to the citizens of the other federated states within the country. Our assessment was conducted on an institutional basis, with full cognizance of the drawbacks of this approach. Differences in the political cultures in the respective countries affect the meaning and interpretation that should be attached to the presence or absence of certain aspects of self-government. For example, the emphasis on local self-government in the United States has been very strong throughout its history. This is not the case in Australia. The movement for self-government in Canberra was not a local initiative; in fact, there was resistance to it at the local level. The reason for and the extent of the resistance are explained below in the section on the Australian federal district.[13] As late as 1993 President Carlos Salinas of Mexico argued that increased democracy for the residents in the federal district of his country was not a top priority with them.

Although none of the federal district countries allows the full gamut of self-governing powers to the local residents of their capital cities, the limitations may vary from one country to the next. For example, in Mexico City, the elected Representative Assembly has very limited powers and cannot legislate in the true sense. It is more like an advisory body. In some of the more advanced self-governing systems, such as those in Brasilia and Canberra, the powers of the federal district are roughly on a par with those of the states. Even in these cities, however, the national government has retained some key levers of control, for example, the power to disapprove local legislation and, in Canberra, control of the planning powers.

The governing system in the federal territory of India is rather complex, with three jurisdictions—New Delhi, Delhi, and the Union Territory—having some claim on being the seat of the national government. The capital was shifted from old Delhi to New Delhi in 1931 and Delhi became a union territory in 1956. While it is New Delhi that is most frequently cited as the capital in official documents, the situation is not free of anomaly and ambiguity. Although there are statutory limits of the New Delhi Municipality as well as the jurisdiction of the New Delhi Municipal Committee, the name itself is a loose and ill-defined geographical expression which refers to an area far more widespread than the official boundaries.[14]

New Delhi was built adjacent to the existing city of Delhi, which has since surrounded it. The National Capital Region of Delhi, with a population of over nine million, comprises three adjacent cities—Delhi, New Delhi, the Delhi military cantonment (controlled by the central government)—plus a rural area of 214 villages. Through a constitutional amendment in 1991, the region was provided with a legislative assembly comprising seventy seats along with a seven-member council of ministers headed by a chief minister.[15]

The major organs of the federal government and the diplomatic enclave are located in New Delhi. It is governed by a federally appointed committee, while Delhi has its own elected governing council. Executive power in Delhi is held by a commissioner who is appointed by the central government. The Union Territory has an elected metropolitan council of limited powers (sixty-one members, five appointed), and it is represented in both houses of the national parliament. Executive power in the Union Territory is held by the lieutenant governor (part mayor, part city manager, part governor), assisted by a chief minister and council of three ministers, all of whom are appointed by and serve at the pleasure of the central government. The relationship between the ministers and lieutenant governor is considered sacred, with matters of utmost secrecy and of great public importance being discussed between them.[16]

Once a graceful colonial capital of tree-lined avenues and pleasant gardens, New Delhi has degenerated into a chaotic Third World megalopolis. Rapid population growth, corruption, excessive pollution and a consumer-driven economy have all combined to impair the functioning of the capital city. More than half of the city's residents live in substandard housing, many without access to running water or proper sanitation facilities. Maintenance of city services is virtually nonexistent, with efforts dwarfed by the immensity of the task of caring for the city. When New Delhi's first elected mayor took over in 1993, he discovered that 40 percent of the city's street lights did not work and that hundreds of schools did not have running water, electricity or bathrooms.[17]

In 1990 the central government (Janata Dal Party) announced plans to convert the Union Territory into the twenty-sixth constituent state of India. Considerable opposition to this idea soon developed, on the grounds that it would be harmful to the interests of both Delhi and the nation. Although statehood would mean a higher political status for the capital territory, the great fear was that the new state would face grave financial losses and its present all-around development would come to a halt. The charge of inadequate protection of national interests focused on security and a number of factors connected with the central government becoming a tenant of the proposed state government.[18]

I have selected three of the federal district capitals—Canberra, Brasilia, and Mexico City—for further analysis of their overall development to their present status. The two Latin American countries are presidential systems and are chosen because they seem to be at opposite ends of the self-governing spectrum. The federal district of Mexico was created around an existing old city and, to date, its residents have very little self-government. The federal district of Brazil is a planned new city whose residents enjoy comparatively strong self-governing powers. Canberra, also a planned new capital city, represents a parliamentary system in which its residents enjoy significant self-governing powers.

Each of these federal districts will be discussed further in an effort to identify any aspects that can be drawn from them to support and improve democracy for the residents of the federal district of the United States. Are the residents of these foreign capitals represented in their national legislatures? Would their governmental mechanisms improve local autonomy in the capital of the United States? Would they protect legitimate federal interests, and are they politically feasible?

CANBERRA

Canberra was planned and built as a completely new city, in a specially created federal district, to serve as the capital of Australia. The principle was established early in the move toward independence (at the constitutional conventions of the 1890s) that a federal district of at least one hundred miles square would be created to serve as the seat of the national government. While the United States Constitution did not name a particular state or geographical region for the location of its federal district, the Australian constitution declared that the seat of government would be in the state of New South Wales and not less than one hundred miles from Sydney.[19] After a number of alternative sites were considered, an area of 2,359 square kilometers (1,474 square miles), lying approximately 320 kilometers (200 miles) southwest of Sydney, was transferred to the Commonwealth.[20] The site that was chosen for the capital is about halfway between the country's two largest cities—Sydney and Melbourne—and is on land that was virtually unoccupied when it became the property of the federal government.

The necessary enabling acts to establish the Australian Capital Territory (ACT) were passed by the Commonwealth and New South Wales governments in 1908 and 1909, respectively. The territory that was established is 910 square miles, which is over thirteen times the size of the District of Columbia (68.26 square miles). Although construction of the capital began around 1913, it was interrupted by World War I and overall progress was slow. There were very few people living in the area and local self-government was not an issue.

In 1927 the parliament house was opened and the federal legislature began meeting in Canberra instead of Melbourne. The principal growth of the city as a major government center and as a city in its own right began around 1958. Although the city had no elected city government, by 1930 a local advisory council had been established, consisting of four federal officials and eight elected members. In 1969, however, the elected members resigned in protest against alleged failure on the part of the central government to consider their advice or keep them informed on developments.[21]

From 1948 to 1967 residents of the ACT were allowed to elect a member to the federal House of Representatives, but the member could only vote on matters relating to Canberra. In February 1967 their representative was granted full voting rights. In 1972 this member was appointed minister for the ACT.

Under the provisions of two important acts, approved by the Commonwealth Parliament in 1973, the Australian Capital Territory was given effective representation in that body. The ACT Representation Act of 1973 provided the territory with a second seat in the federal House of Representatives and, following the enactment of this measure, it was divided into two electoral divisions. The Senate (Representation of Territories) Act provided for two senators to be elected from the ACT. Senators serve a six-year term and members of the House of Representatives are elected for the duration of the Parliament, which is limited to three years but may be dissolved sooner by the governor-general.[22]

As the population of the territory grew, proposals were made for a partly or fully elected governing council. With the administration of Canberra mainly in the hands of executive branch departments of the national government, there was concern among professionals about the fragmentation of authority among the departments and agencies administering the territory. Many of the local residents, however, were satisfied with the existing arrangement and were opposed to any change in the system.[23]

In 1974 the local advisory council was replaced by a fully elected Legislative Assembly of eighteen members, chosen by proportional representation. Limited mainly to giving advice and making recommendations, the assembly was not a legislative body in the true sense. For several specific reasons, there was growing opposition to the idea of self-government among the local residents. The ACT had been reasonably well governed and financed under federal control and there was fear of a decrease in the level of services and/or an increase in taxes. Moreover, many civil servants working for federal agencies feared being transferred to an ACT government. When a referendum on local self-government was held in 1978, a majority vote (63.5 percent) was cast in favor of no change in the existing system.

The proponents of local self-determination continued their activities for home rule. The ACT government unit was established in March 1988 to assist in the development of the proposal for an ACT government. Its responsibilities included policy development, drafting of establishment and consequential legislation, and project coordination for the implementation of a new government. The unit planned and executed an effective program of public consultation and information. In April 1988 a discussion paper was released which formed the basis for dialogue with the community and community groups. An information booklet was distributed to all Canberra households and a telephone hotline was instituted so that the public could raise any concerns or questions they had about the proposed system of government.[24]

Finally, with the approval of the Australian Capital Territory Act of 1988 and related legislation, the federal district was established as a body politic with self-governing powers and responsibilities similar to the states. The self-government package was passed with bipartisan support and established a Legislative Assembly of seventeen members to make laws for the peace, order, and good government of the territory. The executive consisted of a chief minister and three other ministers to exercise the executive power; thus, four of the seventeen members are full-time ministers. In addition to supporting democratic principles, self-government transferred to the local residents some of the costs of the territory.

Opposition to the establishment of local self-government in the federal territory was sufficiently strong to generate formally organized political parties: the No Self-Government Party and the Abolish Self-Government Coalition. When elections were held for the first local assembly in March 1989, the No Self-Government Party won three seats and the Abolish Self-Government Coalition won one seat. The formal transfer of power from the Commonwealth to the ACT followed in May 1989.[25]

Under the above legislation, the Commonwealth transferred most of its powers and responsibilities concerning the administration of the federal territory to the new ACT government. As in the United States, some important powers of control were retained. The functions which were not transferred included the ACT courts, policing functions, and the power for the ACT to determine its own electoral system and the size of the executive branch. The federal government may also disallow actions of the ACT legislature, and it can be dissolved by the governor general.

The transfer of judicial power was to be on a gradual basis, with the ACT being responsible for the magistrates' and coroners' courts and the criminal law by 1990, and the supreme court by 1992.[26] By 1 July 1992 all state-type court functions in the ACT had been transferred to the local government. The federal courts in the ACT remain under federal control. As of 1994, the Australian Federal Police (AFP) operate in the capital territory on an agency basis, that is, the ACT pays the federal government over $50 million in quarterly payments for the AFP to undertake community policing within its borders. To a large degree, the assets of the AFP—the police stations and equipment—have been transferred to the ACT. Police cars remain federal property and the salaries of the police officers are paid from the $50 million. The agency arrangement, which is currently under review (1994), operates under a policing agreement between the two governments.[27]

Similar to the situation in the United States, comprehensive planning for the ACT must conform with the plans produced by the National Capital Planning Authority. Contrary to the situation in the United States, however, the Australian planning body has no representatives from the local government.[28]

The governmental arrangement in the ACT is a dual system of democracy, with final say on the integrity and character of the national capital remaining in the hands of the Commonwealth Parliament, as well as the power to protect and preserve the Commonwealth's interests.

The development of local self-government in Australia and the United States, respectively, reflects a point of difference in the political culture of the two countries. The influence of Thomas Jefferson and other advocates of local self-government during the seedtime of the American Republic meant a strong heritage throughout the nation in this aspect of democracy. The same is not true for Australia. Local government developed in the ACT more as an imposed duty than an asserted right, as a device used by higher government to encourage and then to require local citizens to accept some responsibility for financing and administering their respective areas. Unlike the situation in the United States, the residents of the ACT were not faced with a situation where self-government seemed the likeliest way to have their needs met.

The ACT has its own treasury and general control of its finances. The objective was to place its finances on a basis consistent with those applying in the states. It receives a payment from the national government. The Commonwealth Grants Commission decides on the amount in the same way as it does for the states (and the Northern Territory), taking into account the additional costs that arise from the federal district serving as the seat of the national government.[29]

As with the District of Columbia, the governmental powers conferred on the ACT made it a cross between state and local government.[30] Its size and population pattern with respect to the growth and development of surrounding cities, widely separated from Canberra proper, have raised questions about a further devolution of power within the territory. Two of its satellite cities have populations larger than central Canberra and a third has a population almost as large. A logical arrangement would be to grant these cities local governing councils, similar to other Commonwealth cities, and allow the ACT government to exercise state powers and functions. For all practical purposes, however, Canberra is considered coterminous with the territory.[31]

Although the ACT has self-governing powers and responsibilities similar to the states, there are important differences. The 1988 legislation was very strong on transferring most of the state-level legislative and administrative powers from the Commonwealth to the ACT government. But the local electoral system was not transferred, nor were the judicial system and policing functions at the outset. The federal government is specifically authorized to disallow acts of the local legislature, and the local government has no representation on the planning body for the territory. The legitimate federal interests seem to be well protected.

BRASILIA

With a territory of some 3,285,619 square miles, Brazil is the fifth largest country in the world. The official estimate of its population as of mid-1991 was 153.3 million. Its population is growing at an approximate rate of three million per year. The country comprises twenty-six states, the federal district, and the territories. With a mid-1991 population of 1.8 million, Brasilia is the fifth largest city in Brazil, behind Sao Paulo, Rio de Janeiro, Belo Horizonte, and Salvador.[32]

Several places have served as the seat of the national government in Brazil, but the idea of creating a capital in the central plateau was present even in colonial times. In 1763, while Brazil was still under Portuguese rule, the capital was transferred from Salvador, Bahia, in the northeast part of the country, to Rio de Janeiro. The emergence of gold and diamond mining in the state of Minas Gerais, in the central part of the country, dictated this move by the Portuguese crown for economic and administrative reasons. Rio de Janeiro had become the principal port in the country and it gained new status as the seat of the royal court. The royal family's move to Brazil in 1808, when Portugal was invaded by Napoleon's armies, increased the importance of Rio de Janeiro as the imperial capital city while Napoleon occupied Iberia.[33] After the overthrow of Portuguese control and the establishment of the Brazilian monarchy in 1822, Rio de Janeiro remained as the capital.[34]

Following independence, Brazil was divided into provinces. The city of Rio de Janeiro was detached from the province bearing the same name and, indicative of its status as the national capital, was transformed into what was called the Neutral Municipality. Influenced by the model in the United States, with the proclamation of the Republic in 1889 and the establishment of a federation, the Neutral Municipality was designated as the federal district. The city was governed by a popularly elected council and a mayor appointed by the president of the Republic with the approval of the senate. Because of the strong powers that are granted to chief executives in Brazil, the prevailing idea was that national interests in the capital were incompatible with popular election of the mayor.

Apparently, the idea of moving the nation's capital to the interior first arose in 1789 with the ill-fated rebellion known as the Inconfidencia Mineira, the first attempt by the colony of Brazil to free itself of Portuguese control. Even the colonial administrators pointed out the disadvantages of having the capital on the coast in a major port city, which mitigated against focusing on the many problems of the huge country, whose boundaries were barely known at the time. The idea of a capital city located in the interior was reiterated in 1822, when Brazil gained its independence from Portugal, and it was embodied in the constitution of 1891.

Although the exact site for the Brazilian capital—on the central plateau at the meeting of the country's major watersheds—was chosen as far back as the beginning of the nineteenth century, the first practical step toward its creation was taken by the new republican government in 1892 when it sent a commission to the central region to mark off the area of the future federal district. In 1956 legislation was approved by the national congress to create a public contracting company for the purpose of building the national capital. The new capital was inaugurated at Brasilia in April 1960, only four years after this legislation was passed, an accomplishment for which President Juscelino Kubitscheck is given credit. The actual construction time took forty-two months.[35]

In 1987 Brasilia was added to UNESCO's list of sites that form part of the cultural patrimony of mankind. Selection of this modernistic capital marked the first time that a monument less than one hundred years old was so recognized by UNESCO. There is controversy within the country, however, over whether Brasilia has so far proved a success both as an architectural and urban experiment and as an instrument for opening up Brazil's hinterlands.[36]

The original plan for Brasilia provided only a model for a full-grown city, not for the process by which it would grow. Designed for a population of some 500,000, Brasilia by 1988 had over three times that number of people. The original plans for the city have been radically altered by the patterns of migration and the project's own necessities. The creation of satellite cities surrounding Brasilia was envisioned, yet there has been a natural development of suburbs as a consequence of the city's own growth process. Today, apart from Brasilia, the federal district contains nine satellite and suburban towns. While Brasilia itself has begun to show a decline in its population, the federal district is one of the most dynamic centers of population assimilation in the country.

In accordance with the federal constitution of 1969, the chief executive of the city was appointed by the president of the Republic with the approval of the senate. His official title was changed from mayor to governor and he could be removed by the president acting alone. A special committee of the senate served as the legislative branch for the federal district; it had no legislative body.

A new national constitution was approved in 1988, which provided for major changes and greater democratization in the government of the federal district. The governor and vice governor were now elected by popular vote for a term of four years, following the same procedures used in the election of the state governors and in the election of the president of the Republic.[37]

The constitution provided for the federal district to have the same legislative powers as the states and municipalities, but it is prohibited from being divided into municipalities. There is a legislative assembly for the federal district, whose size varies in accordance with the number of deputies in its delegation to the national Chamber of Deputies.[38] The federal district is to be governed by organic law enacted in accordance with the principles of the constitution and approved by a two-thirds majority of the local legislature. The local deputies are elected by a proportional representation system and serve a term of four years.

The federal district has representation in both chambers of the national legislature. Comparable with the states, the federal district has three senators who serve eight-year staggered terms. Representation in the Chamber of Deputies is based on population, with the necessary adjustments being made during the year prior to elections. No unit of the Republic is to have fewer than eight, nor more than seventy, deputies in the chamber.

There is a national judicial system in Brazil that includes regional courts and judges, and courts of the states, of the federal district, and of the territories. The federal district is on a par with the states in the distribution of the national courts, which include several special tribunals, such as labor courts, electoral courts, and military courts. For example, each state as well as the federal district is linked to one regional court at the appellate level. The constitution of Brazil authorizes the states to organize their own local judicial systems; this authorization includes the federal district.[39]

The Brazilian constitution provides the federal district with the same taxation and revenue powers (and limitations) as the states, and the federal district is generally in charge of its own appropriations and budget. Contrary to the situation with the capital of the United States, the Brazilian national congress does not have to approve the budget of the federal district. There is some sharing of national revenues with the states and the federal district in Brazil, and certain special payments are made to the federal district as the seat of the national government. Although there are nationally imposed restrictions and limitations on the comprehensive planning function, it is under the control of the local government.[40]

With the national constitution providing for the federal district to be treated as a state, it is strong in both local autonomy and representation in the Brazilian national congress. Although the expanded powers of the federal district have not been in effect very long, it appears that the federal interest is being protected. But a longer period will be required before a full evaluation can be made.

MEXICO CITY

The country of Mexico comprises thirty-one states and the federal district, which serves as the seat of federal powers. The Mexican national government has a long history of centralization and presidential domination. The country has a hegemonic party system and, since its founding in 1929, the Institutional Revolutionary Party (PRI) has held the presidency without interruption. Fraud has been a common practice in Mexican elections and demands for governmental reforms have intensified since the mid-1970s. These features of national politics have had direct influence on the governance of the capital city. With over 20 million inhabitants in its metropolitan area, the capital of Mexico is the second most populous urban center (next to Tokyo) in the world; the population of the federal district is 8.2 million.[41]

The constitution of 1824 authorized Mexico City as the seat of the national government and designated it as the federal district. The city was chosen as the capital city mainly because of its political preeminence, rather than for geographical considerations. In 1898 the boundaries of Mexico City and the federal district were established between Morelos and Mexico State. The constitution of 1917, signed after the Mexican Revolution and still the governing law, made no change in the boundaries of the federal district.

The aim in 1898 was that Mexico City would lie within the federal district, although today the terms "Mexico City" and "federal district" are synonymous or equivalent. The federal district is actually composed of sixteen sections. Some of these sections are densely populated and others are not. Generally, the urbanized parts of the federal district, along with a few southern sections of Mexico State, comprise what is referred to as "metropolitan Mexico City."[42]

A constitutional reform in 1928 canceled the autonomous municipal status of the federal district and transferred the district executive power to the president of the Republic. The chancellor (regente) of Mexico City, however, legally exercises the executive power for the president. The chancellor of the federal district, perhaps the second most powerful official in the country, is appointed and removed by the president. He is assisted by an appointed council in the discharge of his executive functions.

The federal district has a Representative Assembly composed of sixty-six members, elected by popular vote for a term of three years. They handle some municipal matters on an advisory basis, for example, rules of good government and security, but cannot legislate.[43] By comparison, the states of Mexico have their own representative governments and are sovereign in local matters. Both the state governors and the members of the state legislatures are elected by popular vote. The states are divided into municipalities which are governed by locally elected councils. The federal district is divided into delegations (sections) which are comparable to the municipalities or counties, except that the delegates, the local equivalent of borough presidents, are appointed by the governor. Neither the delegates nor their appointed subordinates have a fixed term.[44]

In the strict sense, the federal district is governed by the national government through a primary official called the chief of the department of the federal district, who is a member of the president's cabinet. This means that, essentially, one of the largest cities in the world is run like a government department. The chief follows to the letter the dictates of the national government and, increasingly, the people of the city are blaming their problems on the authoritarian way in which they are governed. Contrary to the claims of the national officials, an increasing percentage of the residents of Mexico City seem unwilling to accept the explanation that the absence of democracy can be justified by the role of the federal district as host to the federal government.[45] Self-government advocates say that the compass of the country points north, citing the United States as the source of many of their political ideas and aspirations. The recurring question is: Why can't we have elected authorities like the residents of Washington?

The administration of justice in the federal district is not common to the rest of the country. Judicial authority is exercised by district judges and magistrates. The magistrates are appointed for a term of six years by the president of the Republic with the approval of the Chamber of Deputies. The judges are designated by the members of the Supreme Court of Justice of the Republic.

The budget of the federal district is presented by the president of the Republic to the national legislature (Congress of the Union) for approval, whereas the budgets of the states are presented to their local legislatures. The chief of the federal district is required to give an annual report to the national legislature on the implementation of the local budget. The governors of the states make their annual budget reports to their local legislatures.[46]

The delivery of public services is a major concern in the capital city metropolis. The sheer size of the population of Mexico City presents governance problems and the call is for service to prevail over authority. The most serious problems include rapidly increasing pollution, a corrupt police system, and traffic jams which have reached the ridiculous level. In the words of one Mexican writer, there is a critical need in the public services for "efficiency, attention, courtesy, consideration, economy, respect of people's dignity, fast service, etc."[47]

The struggle over how Mexico City and the federal district that it encompasses should be governed is a test of both the administration's willingness to cede authoritarian control and of the ability of the opposition to generate pressure for more democracy. In early 1993 a non-binding plebiscite was organized by six members of the Representative Assembly and a disparate group of democratic activists from all of the main political parties and civic organizations. Supported by the city's liberal intelligentsia, the plebiscite was seen as a test of the country's desire for democratic political change. Although the turnout was small percentage-wise (about 10 percent of the registered voters), approximately 331,000 city residents participated. The organizers attributed the low turnout to the near complete media blackout through which the referendum had to suffer. Most Mexico City residents did not know about the referendum.[48]

The results showed 85 percent in favor of electing the city chancellor; 84 percent supported the establishment of a local legislature with increased powers; and 66 percent approved turning Mexico City into the country's thirty-second state. Mayor Manuel Camacho Solis and the governing political party (PRI) opposed a new state and immediate elections for mayor. The opposition supported both.

In spite of the argument by many in the Mexican government that there is limited public interest in democratic reform, the organizers hoped that the plebiscite would generate enough public pressure to force the government of President Carlos Salinas de Gortari to move toward elective rule in the city before his term ended in December 1994.[49] His position is that while Mexicans are eager to have cleaner elections, there is only limited public interest in democratic reform. He maintains that the society is far more likely to mobilize around such issues as ecology, services, and land use.

With the exception of providing voting representation in the national legislature, there is nothing else to be drawn from the Mexico City model that would help respond to the challenge of dual democracy in the District of Columbia. With the Mexican national government in control of practically all aspects of the local government, the federal interest is predominant and local autonomy is almost nonexistent.

We now return to the question raised at the beginning of this chapter: What can the United States learn from the foreign models? The criteria to be applied in responding to this question include the following: providing for representation and local autonomy, protecting legitimate federal interests, and political feasibility.

All of the models provide voting representation in their national assemblies, which is absent in the United States. This gives all of the foreign models invaluable political clout at the national level. With a delegation of twenty-five deputies, the federal capital of Venezuela has the second largest representation in the national legislature. This delegation has important political clout in determining policies for the capital city. Buenos Aires, the Union Territory, and Mexico City are further examples of this.

The six foreign models do not fare as well on self-government when it comes to executive power. Only in Canberra and Brasilia is the chief executive elected by the local residents. There is something of a compromise situation in Venezuela, with an appointed governor as the top executive authority of the entire federal district, but locally elected mayors of the two comprising municipalities: Libertador and Vargas. There is some limitation on the powers of the legislatures in all of the foreign models. In Australia's parliamentary system, the national governor general can dissolve the local legislature.

Of the three foreign models examined in depth, only Mexico City does not have both an elected legislature and chief executive. Beyond these basic institutional mechanisms of local autonomy, there are trade-offs. Canberra has general control of its budget but is not represented on the local planning body and it did not have control of the policing function when self-government became effective. Although the comprehensive planning function in Brasilia is under local control, there are nationally imposed restrictions and limitations on it.

There has been no indication of inadequate protection of the federal interests in the foreign models. Obviously, the Mexican system offers the greatest protection to the federal interest and for national development of the capital city, but at the denial of basic democratic principles and practices. It should be noted that the reformed federal district systems in Australia and Brazil are very recent; longer experience with them may be necessary before evaluating their overall success.

Finally, it should be pointed out that the cultural context in each of the countries is different and any attempt to draw general conclusions about the efficacy of the respective arrangements would not be fruitful. For example, the residents of the national capital of Australia were opposed to self-government, while the residents of the District of Columbia consistently sought self-government and are now pressing for increased local autonomy. And President Carlos Salinas of Mexico argues that the residents of Mexico City are not that concerned about self-government.

NOTES

1. The list prepared by Rowat included the following countries: Argentina, Australia, Austria, Belgium, Brazil, Canada, Germany, India, Malaysia, Mexico, Nigeria, Pakistan, Spain, Switzerland, the United States, Venezuela, the USSR and Yugoslavia. Donald C. Rowat, *The Government of Federal Capitals* (Toronto: University of Toronto Press, 1973), xiii–xiv passim; "Canberra in International perspective," in W.K. Oakes and L.J. Reeder, eds., *Governing the Two Canberras*, Papers and Proceedings of the ACT Self-Government First Anniversary Seminar, 11 May 1990 (Canberra: Universary of Canberra, 1991), 28–45.

2. Approximately 90 percent of the national government headquarters and staff are still in Bonn as of 1994; however, the capital of reunited Germany is to be in Berlin. When the physical move to the latter city is completed, the German capital will fall in the category of a city-state.

3. Spain and Belgium have adopted federal systems of government in recent years—Spain in 1978 and Belgium making a gradual transition, with constitutional revisions in 1970, 1980, and 1988. Similar to capitals within states, their capital cities of Madrid and Brussels, respectively, are located within autonomous regions: Madrid Autonomous Community and Brussels-Capital Region. Spain, *Spain 1992* (Madrid: Ministerio del Portavoz del Gobierno, 1992), 115. Andre Alen, ed., *Treatise on Belgian Constitutional Law* (Deventer, Belgium: Kluwer Law and Taxation Publishers, 1992), 18.

4. Donald C. Rowat, "Canberra in International Perspective," in W. K. Oakes and L.J. Reeder, eds., *Governing the Two Canberras*, 32.

5. Donald Rowat, excerpted in Douglas H. Fullerton, *The Fullerton Report*, vol. 1 (Ottawa, Canada, 1974), 20.

6. Ibid.

7. Ulf Pacher, Press Counselor, Austrian Embassy, interview with author, Washington, D.C., 4 February 1994.

8. The physical move of the national government from the previous city-state capital of Lagos to Abuja, a planned new city, has been in process for several years, with only a few of the ministries yet to be transferred. Interview with Mohammed Bashir Sani, Attache, Nigerian Embassy, Washington, D.C., 27 April 1993.

9. Donald C. Rowat, "How Federal Capitals are Governed," *Indian Administrative and Management Review*, 2, no. 3 (July–September 1970), 44.

10. Rowat, "Canberra in International Perspective," 39; Señor Gustavo Leon, J.D., interview with author, Washington, D.C., 31 March 1993.

11. The province of Buenos Aires is represented by 70 deputies in a body of 257.

12. Alberto Föhrig, "the Governance of Buenos Aires as a Federal Capital City," unpublished research paper, Georgetown University, 1993; Señor Alberto Föhrig, J.D., interview with author, Washington, D.C., 3 March 1993.

13. Bruce Juddery, "Self-Government of the Australian Capital Territory," *Australian Journal of Public Administration* 48, no. 4 (December 1989), 411.

14. Donald C. Rowat, *Federal Capitals*, 136; K.M. Mathew, ed., *Manorama Yearbook 1994* (Kottagam, Kerala, India: Malayala Manorama Press, 1994), 705.

15. Mathew, 705.

16. Jag Parvesh Chandra, *Delhi Assembly: Background and Analysis* (New Delhi, India: Central News Agency (P), 1992), 56.

17. *Washington Post*, 31 August 1984, A-27.

18. Ibid., 57–60.

19. Commonwealth of Australia, *Constitution Act*, chapter 7, art. 125.

20. Australian Bureau of Statistics, *Yearbook Australia 1990*, no. 73, (Canberra, 1990), 799.

21. Ruth Atkins, "Canberra," in Rowat, *Federal Capitals*, 43.

22. *Yearbook Australia 1990*, 28–29; Constitution of the Commonwealth of Australia, pts. 2 and 3.

23. The National Capital Development Commission was responsible for planning and development in the territory. Rowat, "Governing Federal Capitals," 11.

24. ACT Government Service, *Annual Report, 1988–1989*, vol. 2, (Canberra, 1989), 45.

25. *Canberra Times*, 4 May 1989, 1.

26. Beginning in 1990 the appointment of Supreme Court judges was to be made upon the recommendation of the ACT government. Also, it was anticipated that an arrangement for the provision of community policing services would be entered into between the Commonwealth and the ACT governments. Ibid., 46, 60.

27. Australian Department of Foreign Affairs and Trade, facsimile from Brett Bayly, Public Affairs Officer, to Amanda Buckley, Counsellor, Australian Embassy, Washington, D.C., 8 February 1994.

28. The National Capital Planning Authority was created by the Australian Capital Territory (Planning and Land Management) Act of 1988. This comprehensive planning body is responsible for preserving Canberra's national capital character, involving a national capital plan and a territorial planning authority. Juddery, 420; see also W.K. Oakes and L.J. Reeder, eds., *Governing The Two Canberras*, 44.

29. Gary Punch, Minister for Arts and Territories, Government of Australia, media release, Canberra, 13 April 1988.

30. *Canberra Times,* 4 May 1989, 1.

31. Canberra's satellite cities include Belconnen, Woden, Weston Creek, and Tuggeranong. Rowat, "Governing Federal Capitals," 12; Juddery, 411.

32. Brasil Trade and Industry, *Brasilia: A World Heritage Site,* special supplement, (Brasilia, 1988), 8.

33. The presence of the royal administration in the colony for a period of fourteen years accelerated the process of independence. In 1815 Brazil ceased to be a colony and became part of a united kingdom with Portugal. *Brazil in Brief,* 10.

34. Diogo Lordello de Mello, "Brasilia," in Rowat, ed., *Federal Capitals,* 6–7.

35. *Brasilia: A World Heritage Site,* 6.

36. *New York Times,* 3 January 1988, 31.

37. Constitution of the Federative Republic of Brazil, (1988) chap. 5, sec. 1, art. 32.

38. The size of the legislative assembly corresponds to three times the number of delegates in its delegation to the Chamber of Deputies. When this number reaches thirty-six, it shall be increased by as many representatives as the number of federal deputies exceeds twelve. Constitution of Brazil, chap. 3, art. 27.

39. Constitution of Brazil, chap. 3, sec. 8, art. 125.

40. Professor Paul Singer, University of Sao Paulo, Brazil, interview by author, Washington, D.C., 16 July 1993.

41. Institute for Statistics Geography and Information, *Access Mexico* (INEGI 1990), 25; *New York Times,* 15 July 1987, A-4.

42. Mexican Cultural Institute, Washington, D.C., letter to author, 7 July 1993.

43. *New York Times,* 22 March 1993, A-2.

44. Manuel Moreno Sanchez, "La reforma de la Ciudad de Mexico," *nexos* 179 (November 1992), 27 ff.

45. This assertion is based primarily on the results of a 1993 plebiscite conducted in Mexico City. See p. 258; also *Excelsior* (El periodico de la vida nacional—Mexico, D.F.), martes 2 de marzo de 1993, 1.

46. "Reforma Politica Del Distrito Federal," mimeograph, la Ciudad de Mexico (January 1992).

47. Sanchez, 27 ff.

48. In the weeks leading up to the referendum, the television monopoly Televisa pretended that the event did not exist, while most newspapers either attacked the referendum or inflated expectations so much that the event would be judged a failure. *El Financiero International,* 5 April 1993, 12; *New York Times,* 23 March 1993, A-6.

49. *New York Times,* 24 June 1993, A-10.

10

Conclusions

This book has detailed federal and local interests in the nation's capital. The experience of the United States supports the assertion by Donald C. Rowat that every federal country faces a difficult problem, inherent in the very nature of federalism, in deciding how its national capital should be governed. The general conflict between local interests and desires for more autonomy on the one hand, and federal goals for the nation's capital on the other, is the basic source of the problem. The residents of most capital cities wish to exercise full self-government on a par with the citizens of other jurisdictions of the country, while the goal of the national government is to develop the city in the interests of the nation as a whole.

That there is a conflict between national governments and the governments of capital cities seems obvious. Whenever two governments share jurisdiction over a particular piece of territory, disagreement is almost inevitable. However, this study has demonstrated the need for refinement of the Rowat thesis, which leaves three important sets of questions unanswered. First, is conflict likely to be limited to a few issues or felt across a broad range of issues? On what issues is disagreement likely to be greatest? Second, is the conflict really between the federal interest and the interest of city residents, including their desire for self-government, or are there other forces at work? Federal interventions in local affairs do not necessarily represent assertions of legitimate national interests. Finally, when there is conflict between a national government and the government of a capital city, which side is likely to prevail and why?

When we include formal vetoes, challenges, and congressional action through the appropriations process, the conflicts in the United States between the national and District governments have covered a wide range of policy issues. Included are issues of public safety, land use, revenue, education, civil liberties, human services, public works/ transportation, general government and personnel. Precipitated by the city's desire for downtown revitalization and economic development in general, some of the most intense clashes between the District and national governments have been over land use policies. Serious conflicts have also erupted in the area of public safety.

The government of the United States clearly has important national interests in the capital city and they need to be protected. Public safety is an obvious concern, both for the protection of the nation's leaders and the members of the foreign diplomatic corps who reside in the District. Land use is another valid area of concern—the nation's capital serves as a symbol to both local and national citizenry. The general belief is that the national capital should be a place of beauty as well as safety. Beyond these clear national interests are a number of other areas where the federal government might be said to have some involvement, such as the provision of public services that impact on the operation of the national government.

Other Forces At Work

There are a number of grounds on which conflicts have arisen between the federal and District governments other than simply the assertion of legitimate national interests. In fact, there seem to be at least four distinct reasons behind federal interventions, although more than one may be evident in any specific case. Descriptions of these reasons follow in roughly declining order of importance.

Parochial Interests.

A major source of such conflict is the assertion of parochial interests under the guise of national interests. Three distinct parochial interests were revealed in this study of District affairs. First, certain interests within the city, notably historic preservationists, police and fire fighters unions, well-connected local citizens and groups, and residents of specific neighborhoods, successfully use Congress and/or federal agencies as a kind of appeals board after they have lost a political battle with the District government. For example, the fire fighters union had amazing success by going to Congress to prolong the life of Engine Company Number 3 and to get special equipment.

Second, the interests of the bordering states of Maryland, Virginia, and sometimes Pennsylvania impinge on such matters as prohibition of a commuter tax or fees on suburbanites, residency requirements for city workers, and the transporting of municipal waste. Legislators from nearby Maryland and Virginia districts do not always have the same interest in or share the same views on District matters, but when they are united on an issue, as they were in opposing a District commuter tax, they are a formidable force in congressional policy making. The members from the bordering states are often able to prevail because most legislators do not care that much about District of Columbia matters. As full voting members of Congress, the legislators from the suburban jurisdictions have often pressed policies that benefitted those areas vis-à-vis the District. Other legislators, who do not have a direct stake in these matters, may defer to their Virginia and Maryland colleagues or use such matters as a vote-trading opportunity to secure the support of Maryland and Virginia legislators on matters of concern to their own areas. Since the District must depend on congressional restraint and goodwill without full voting representation in Congress, it has no effective way of countering these "neighborly" activities.

Representing a third type of parochial interest are matters of concern to Congress and its members and employees. A variety of issues, such as taxation of persons residing in the suburbs but working in the city, as well as parking and other transportation matters, for example, the issue of taxicab meters, fall into this category. In some instances a personal interest or relationship may prompt congressional intervention in District of Columbia affairs. Examples include the death penalty referendum, initially sponsored by Senator Richard C. Shelby (D-Ala.), and the abortive effort by Senator Daniel Inouye (D-Hawaii) to include financial support in the District budget for the George Washington University Medical Center, a private institution in the city.

Moral Issues that Divide the Nation.

Comprising a second overall source of conflict between the District and federal governments are the moral issues that divide the nation as a whole, such as abortion and gay and lesbian rights. If the District were a perfect microcosm of the country as a whole, then Congress would not be tempted to intervene on these issues because the city would likely make the same decisions as Congress. But in the important categories of racial composition and political party affiliation, the District is far from a perfect microcosm. In addition, the District has a large and politically active gay community and carries a heavy social welfare burden. So the pressures that determine the votes of a majority of city residents are different from those that determine the votes of members of Congress. On questions of social or moral values, legislators have repeatedly challenged District policies that differed from their own views—although not necessarily from the views and policies of state and local jurisdictions that are beyond the reach of constant congressional control. With the constituents of their own home state or district in mind, members of Congress often use the District as a proving ground for their social or moral values. It is an opportunity to act on one's values and, possibly, reap political gain with few risks.

Mistrust.

A third source of conflict between the federal and District governments is what might be called the general mistrust on the part of federal officials that the District government will act in the best interests of its own citizens. Some mistrust can be attributed to the fact that officials of two different levels of government are involved. Also, trust across racial lines is a problem in American society as a whole and, considering the District's predominantly black population, the stage is set for a generous amount of racially based mistrust between the two levels of government.

Mistrust was perhaps most obvious in the creation of the National Capital Service Area and in denying control of the District of Columbia National Guard to the mayor of the city. As a motivator of congressional intervention, the degree of mistrust has varied with the different local administrations, reaching its peak during the administration of Mayor Marion Barry, amid frequent press reports of alleged abuses or administrative problems in the District government, the criminal convictions of a number of the mayor's top aides, and, finally, the conviction of the mayor himself on a cocaine possession charge.

Standard Operating Procedures.

Finally, some conflicts between the District and national governments have resulted from what might be called the standard operating procedures of federal officials, especially those in Congress. Because the members of Congress, through the appropriations committees in particular, have power over the District government, they tend to treat it like any other part of the federal government, rather than as a separate entity. In other words, the District government is a victim of routinized oversight behavior. Legislators are accustomed to dealing with federal agencies in specific ways and exercising particular kinds of power over them. Thus, the appropriations committees impose tight personnel ceilings, limit travel allowances, and restrict access to fringe benefits, such as use of chauffeured automobiles, because that is what appropriators do. And no exception is made for the District of Columbia.

There are some elements and attitudes which may not be major sources of conflict in their own right, but play a contributing role in tandem with other factors. Many legislators have low esteem for the District of Columbia government. Whether it is true or not, they believe that the city is mismanaged. Because of this opinion, which is probably enhanced by racial overtones, members of Congress do not fully respect the policy decisions and judgments of District officials, particularly when these differ from their own. This lack of respect, which is different from mere disagreement, contributes to the decisions of members of Congress to challenge District government actions. In addition, a certain amount of arrogance, growing out of their self-perceived superior status as *national* lawmakers, probably influences some members. When these factors are considered, along with the tremendous power of individual members to affect District policies and affairs, it is not surprising that there is often micromanagement of District affairs.

Winners and Losers

A final important question is why the District prevails in some conflicts and loses in others. The cases examined in this book do not suggest many hard-and-fast rules about whether District or national interests (which may or may not be genuine) will prevail on particular issues. Indeed, the District has sometimes won on an issue temporarily, for example, the abortion issue from 1980 to 1987 and the residency requirement from 1981 to 1987, only to lose later. Although they do not indicate clear conditions that make victory inevitable, these cases for the most part do suggest some factors that increase the prospects of one or the other government winning.

The closest to a sure-fire determinant of victory or loss involves federal interests in public safety and land use. In the Techworld land use case, parts of the federal government were on both sides of the issue, which more or less neutralized the outcome. The presence of a clear, legitimate federal interest is not a necessary condition for victory by federal institutions, but it comes close to being a sufficient condition. The federal government clearly seems to have adequate levers to ensure that the District's ability to serve as the nation's seat of government is not compromised by local government policies in such areas as the location of chanceries, the adequacy of the District police force, and the enforcement of building height limitations.

Having allies in the executive branch is especially helpful: when a federal agency declares that a District government decision clearly violates a federal interest within the agency's jurisdiction, as the State Department did in the case of restrictions on foreign embassy locations, the federal agency is almost certain to prevail. But this has happened very rarely. Much more typical is the treatment of White House security in the case of Metropolitan Square. In that instance, the relevant federal agency (the Secret Service) was not very persistent in making its views known when they might have had some effect. When a federal agency is lukewarm in its protests (as with the Secret Service in the latter case), stands on the sidelines, or supports the District, then District government interests are likely to win.

Federal actors have also won most of the time when federal interests were not so clear, however. As outlined above, federal intervention may be motivated by anything from moral conflicts to the parochial interests of local interest groups. Three general conditions determine or are important in determining who wins these conflicts: the degree of procedural protection afforded District interests in Congress, the strategic position of opponents of District interests, and the level of caution exercised by District officials.

Because District issues are of low importance to most national legislators, it is difficult for critics of District government policies to get their views on the agenda unless they either (1) hold a leadership position on specialist committees or (2) can mold the issue in such a way as to allow them to mobilize opposition to specialists. The protection afforded to District interests has varied both across issue areas and over time. The existence of a one-house legislative veto for criminal code changes made it relatively easy to overturn revision of the District's Sexual Assault Reform Law in 1981. The institution of a more involved veto procedure makes such actions harder to accomplish. Moreover, the use of omnibus appropriations to fund the District from 1983 through 1988 made it much harder to inflict the views of floor majorities on the District unless they could win over legislators on the specialist committees. With a separate District appropriations bill in 1988, a presidential veto became a credible threat.

A final observation on winners and losers, relating to District caution, is in order here: the administrative problems of the Barry administration exacted a high price in terms of congressional goodwill. The heightened level of distrust perhaps eroded any tendency legislators might have had to give the District the benefit of the doubt where the federal interest was questionable. District credibility improved during the administration of Mayor Sharon Pratt Kelly. With Barry having defeated incumbent Mayor Kelly in the Democratic mayoral primary in September 1994, it was expected that he would again be at the helm of the District government in 1995, giving him and Congress another try with their relationship.

The most disturbing aspect of our analysis is the finding that the federal government intervenes most often for reasons other than to protect a legitimate national interest. Parochial interests motivate many of these intrusions. If the federal government does decide to intervene, it should do so only when the legitimate federal interest in preserving the city's ability to function as a national capital clearly outweighs local residents' right to self-governance and when federal intervention is likely to produce a major improvement.

So far the record of federal interventions during home rule suggests that neither of these conditions is met very often. Federal interventions in District affairs have frequently gone beyond the areas in which the federal interest is clearest: public safety and land use. And even within these two areas, the federal interest at stake has sometimes been questionable. The congressional requirement that a particular District firehouse remain open is a case in point. In other instances, as in the case of prison overcrowding, the federal government has given the city conflicting signals: handing down orders to reduce overcrowding, while closing channels that would enable this to be done. Increased federal intervention is thus unlikely to solve many of the city's problems. Indeed, the record suggests that in most policy areas for the District, home rule should be strengthened, not weakened.

The federal government has prevailed forthrightly in disputes where legitimate federal interests are involved; therefore, no increase in its leverage is necessary. Because the federal government has ultimate constitutional and financial power, its avowed interests will predominate even if they do not represent true national interests, thus causing unnecessary interference in purely local matters.

Some conflicts between governments with shared jurisdiction are inevitable, but many can be avoided. Some conflicts may be beneficial, but others are counterproductive. Many of the conflicts between the federal government and the District of Columbia are neither inevitable nor beneficial. Whatever its own failings, the District of Columbia government has little to learn from Congress about how to run a city. Some structural reforms may be needed to ensure that legitimate federal interests are protected under normal operating procedures, while intrusions into primarily local matters are reduced.

Although the House District Committee has sought to establish standards for challenging District government action, these criteria have not been adopted by Congress. Moreover, the application of one of the committee's three standards—violation of the federal interest—can be a highly subjective matter, on which reasonable persons might differ. Because Congress has not established a definitive or generally accepted test of what does and what does not constitute a legitimate federal interest in the District, the local government depends almost entirely on federal restraint to prevent interventions that contravene the spirit and sometimes the letter of the Home Rule Charter. That restraint has been exercised too little.

Even the challenges and interventions that are relatively harmless instances of micromanagement send a powerful and dangerous message: namely, that virtually no District government policy is off limits. Moreover, the current system of federal control has perverse effects on the District's political system. It encourages interests that disagree with policies of the District government to run to Congress for redress rather than to work for change within the District's political system. It frees the District government from having to take responsibility for many of its own actions, for example, repeal of AIDS insurance (1986) and budget cuts (1994), because Congress will step in. And it encourages the District to seek additional congressional funding rather than solve its own fiscal problems. In short, it encourages just the sort of political immaturity that congressional critics of District affairs are always decrying.

Separating Federal and Local Interests

At the very outset, it should be clear that federal and local interests within a federal district cannot be separated completely. The very nature of the national union and its goals would defy this, even for the most autonomous states or regions. Second, there are no universal laws to be discovered that would allow federal countries to automatically separate federal and local interests. Since there are no universally accepted definitions of federal and local interests among the federal systems of the world, it must be the job of the national legislature of each country to reasonably spell out the federal interests that must be protected at the seat of the national government. In the United States this task could be approached on both procedural and substantive bases. From a procedural standpoint, the District could be treated as a state except where this arrangement would clearly interfere with its mission and function as the national capital. There is precedent for treating the District as though it were a state, and more will be said about it later.

As with substantive democracy, there are some basic powers which should not be taken away from the respective levels of government. The federal interest can be protected through appropriate sharing of power in the following policy areas: land use, public safety, public works, and delivery of services. Residual powers would be exercised by the local government. In any arrangement between the two governments, there would be an appropriate payment in lieu of taxes (PILOT) on federal properties at the local level.

Alternatives

Congressional meddling in District affairs can be limited in several ways. First, the Constitution could be amended to allow Congress to intervene only to protect statutorily defined federal interests in the District. Currently, the federal interest consists of whatever a majority of legislators are willing to say it is. A constitutional amendment would allow District officials recourse to the courts if they felt that Congress had overstepped the legitimate boundaries of the federal interest. If the Techworld case is any indication, the District would fare better under a judicial resolution of its conflicts with the national government. The District's continuing dependence on congressional goodwill suggests that the city would turn to the courts sparingly. But the fact that an appeal could be made might deter the most egregious congressional usurpations of District authority, and where a legitimate conflict arises, the courts could balance local and national interests in a way that Congress too rarely does today.

This constitutional approach faces severe political hurdles in that it is highly unlikely that Congress would agree to curtail its own authority over the seat of national government, or that three-quarters of the states would approve if Congress did agree. [Such a course of action may not be advisable in any case. Limiting federal intervention to specifically enumerated and narrowly defined situations might prevent interventions where a clear federal interest arises on a previously unanticipated issue.]

Under the present governmental system for the nation's capital, the most promising way to minimize federal intervention is to limit uses of the mechanisms that have been most prone to federal abuse. This is the reform that shows the greatest promise. The appropriations committees have been by far the greatest transgressors in local matters. These committees have used their power over the District government not just occasionally but almost constantly. Many of these interventions have been buried in fine print seldom debated outside of the committees, which means that most legislators do not explicitly consider the array of interventions deployed against the District. Few members feel a direct stake in challenging these interventions, and fewer still are likely to wish to challenge the powerful appropriations committees to defend the principle of District autonomy.

These repeated interventions through appropriations have been used, for the most part, not to assert legitimate national interests, but to assert parochial interests, the moral views of particular groups of legislators, or legislators' penchant for exercising power through micromanagement. The District appropriations bill has also been used as a vehicle for further interventions through floor amendments. When asked to defend invasions of local jurisdiction, appropriators can always reply that they are merely protecting the taxpayers' money, as represented by the federal payment to the city.

To remedy these problems, the appropriations committees should be stripped of their authority to tell the city how to spend its funds. Congress's authority over District funds should be limited to setting the size of the federal payment. A permanent formula should be established to determine the amount of the payment itself, based on the expenses and revenue losses the District incurs by serving as the seat of national government. An arbitrary percentage of the District's operating budget is unacceptable and will not meet the challenge of dual democracy. Even if the payment is not made a legal entitlement, it should be considered a revenue-sharing grant, rather than a vehicle to which innumerable strings are attached.

In addition, the House and Senate appropriations subcommittees on the District of Columbia should be abolished, and the responsibilities for setting the federal payment transferred to other subcommittees. Political institutions exist to exercise power and it is perhaps unrealistic to expect them to refrain from doing so. Instead of reforming procedures, a much more direct approach to the problem of institutions that abuse power is simply to abolish them. In this case, abolishing the subcommittees would result in little damage to the interests of either the District or the nation. These proposals would strengthen self-government in the nation's capital and are suited to immediate implementation by Congress.

A second approach to reducing inappropriate congressional interference is embodied in the proposal to create the state of New Columbia. This new state would include all of the current District except the National Capital Service Area. Statehood is the one solution that would take care of the District's political problems in a single stroke, conferring full local autonomy and representation in the national legislature. There are some questions about the economic potential of the proposed state. In light of the federal property that would likely be included in the new state and the reduced revenue from a probable nonresident tax (most of the federal establishment would be in the federal enclave), a federal payment or appropriate reimbursement for tax-exempt national properties would be in order.

In spite of the fact that the statehood option has been endorsed in the Democratic platform and by President Bill Clinton, it faces severe political difficulties. Many federal operations, and almost all foreign chanceries, would be outside the federal enclave. There would be a need for some mechanism to pursue federal interests in this broader area. Until satisfactory adjustments are made, national lawmakers are unlikely to approve a narrowing of the District's boundaries to the federal enclave. The boundaries of the new state, however, do not have to follow to the letter those that were established for the National Capital Service Area, and this offers an opportunity to resolve some of the problems that are being projected at this time.

In any event, the statehood issue is being considered by Congress with backing from the Democratic Party, now in control of both the White House and Congress. It should be supported as the quickest way for the District of Columbia to win full political rights. The city-state arrangement (without a federal enclave) is in effect in Austria with apparent success and it is to be in effect in Germany in the future. If one truly supports democracy, it is hard to be against any option, acceptable to the District and the nation, that would end the colonial status of the nation's capital. The movement to statehood must be allowed to run its course, hopefully with success in bringing full freedom and rights to District residents.

There is usually more than one way to achieve any goal, but it may also be prudent to mount only one campaign at a time so as not to have a diffused effort. If statehood is not successful, however, the District's political leadership should shift gears and press for the nation's capital to remain a district but be treated as a state (de facto statehood), as set forth in legal terms. This approach is similar to the Full Voting Rights Amendment that was before the nation a few years ago (1978--85), but it is not the same. This comprehensive approach would cover both local autonomy and national representation, minus the economic risks of statehood.

Under this arrangement, the District's residents would not only win voting representation in Congress, but would gain most of the other attributes of statehood. Implementation of this model means beginning with the full power and rights of statehood, and deducting only those powers that would clearly and absolutely interfere with the purpose and function of the national capital. Because a constitutional amendment would be required to implement this option, it should have a true "national origin" and endorsement. The amendment should not originate with Congress, like the Full Voting Rights Amendment of 1978, and become largely a project led or pushed by the District of Columbia. In that the whole nation will be needed to ratify this amendment (three-fourths of the states), it is important for the amendment to have a national base to help pave the way for its approval. Because the idea of the national capital remaining a district, but being treated like a state, draws elements from the positions of both the Democratic and Republican Parties on the governance of the nation's capital, it should receive a certain amount of bipartisan support.

To design this proposal, it is recommended that Congress authorize the establishment of a national panel, to be comprised of representatives from the District, states, cities, Congress, and White House. This panel would be prepared to design an acceptable model to meet the challenge of dual democracy. Representatives from some of the nation's large cities, who share common problems with the District, should provide critical input. The state representatives should be prepared to identify and assess state-level issues, while the congressional and White House panelists would ensure protection of the federal interest. All representatives, however, would be expected to embrace the common goal of protecting both local and federal interests, which is the essence of dual democracy.

The proposed panel should be provided with appropriate resources and be requested to complete its job within a relatively short period of time (not to exceed one year). The de facto statehood design recommended by the panel should be treated as a "privileged" proposal. It should be voted up or down by Congress, without changes or revision, as a proposed amendment to the Constitution.

The panel should remain intact to guide this amendment through the proposal stage in Congress and the ratification stage by the states. This would indeed be a national rather than a District project, designed to meet the challenge of dual democracy and to bring true democracy to the seat of the national government.

Being treated as a state does not have to be an alternative to the ultimate goal of statehood. Some legal scholars sympathetic to statehood feel that any plan offering voting representation in both houses of Congress could be an intermediate tactical step to full statehood. With voting representation in the House and Senate, District residents would have real leverage and leadership for their statehood drive, while possibly enhancing their limited home rule status at the same time.

The proposal to treat the federal district as a state has been implemented and seems to be working satisfactorily in other federal countries—especially Brazil and Australia, and also Venezuela and India. It appears that the residents of Brasilia and Canberra have most of the rights of the citizens of the other states within those countries. The states in the respective countries provided a pre-existing model for the powers granted to the federal districts.

Of all the democratic systems of the world with federal district capital cities, the United States is the only one where local residents do not have voting representation in the national legislature. Although they are devoid of most other democratic rights, even the residents of Mexico's federal district have voting representation in their national legislature. Taking care of this problem in the United States is serious business that cannot be put off any longer.

Regardless of the approach that is taken to democracy for the nation's capital—be it statehood, de facto statehood, or some other arrangement—the challenge to our country is to accept the fact that the residents of the federal district have "unalienable rights" that cannot be taken from them. Their existence as a community and body politic under American principles gives them these rights and powers, which have grown and expanded over the years as their numbers have increased. The size of the local community means that we are dealing with a local governmental problem that is very different and much more serious than the one faced in 1800 when the District of Columbia was established. The fact that a significant percentage of the residents are employed by the federal government is a point to be considered, but it does not alter their status as part of an indigenous community endowed with basic rights.

There is an American principle which undergirds the Constitution and the Declaration of Independence: the spirit of democracy. Democracy, above everything else, is a spirit that prevails in a society in which citizens believe that the rights and responsibilities of government can and must be shared by all the people. But the spirit by itself is not enough; without institutional mechanisms it would evaporate. The spirit of democracy is always and forever the same, but the system must remain flexible and adjustable. New situations may demand new systems in order that the spirit may flow freely and act creatively. The challenge to our country, with regard to its national capital, lies not so much in researching legal history as in having the political resolve to unite the spirit and the system.

The challenge of dual democracy requires the nation to take a double-minded approach to the local governance of the federal district:

The District of Columbia as a national capital

and

The District of Columbia as a place to live.

In the spirit of the advice of Thomas Jefferson, who was confident of the wisdom of each generation to resolve its own issues, this is our time to respond to the problem of democracy in the nation's capital.

Selected Bibliography

BOOKS AND MONOGRAPHS

Alen, Andre, ed. *Treatise on Belgian Constitutional Law.* Deventer, Belgium: Kluwer Law and Taxation Publishers, 1992.

Best, Judith. *National Representation for the District of Columbia.* Frederick, Maryland: University Publications of America, 1984.

Blaustein, Albert. *Constitutions of the Countries of the World.* New York: Oceana Publications, Inc., 1990.

Bowman, Ann O'M., and Richard C. Kearney. *The Resurgence of the States.* Englewood Cliffs, N.J.: Prentice Hall, 1986.

Brazil. Embassy. *Brazil in Brief.* Washington, D.C., n.d.

Brown, Letitia W. *Free Negroes in the District of Columbia, 1790–1846.* New York: Oxford University Press, 1972.

Canada. Royal Commission on Bilingualism and Biculturalism. *Report.* Vol. 5, 5; *The Federal Capital.* Ottawa: Queen's Printer, 1970.

Catholic University Law Review. District of Columbia Law Issue 27, no. 3, Spring 1978.

————. District of Columbia Law Issue 39, no. 2, Winter 1990.

Chandra, Jag Parves. *Delhi: A Political Study.* Delhi: Metropolitan Book, 1969.

————. *Delhi Assembly: Background and Analysis.* New Delhi, India: By the author; distributed by Central News Agency (P), 1992.

Collier, Barney. *Hope and Fear in Washington: The Story of the Washington Press Corps.* New York: Dial Press, 1975.

Commonwealth Grants Commission. *Third Report on Financing the Australian Capital Territory, Part Two—Analysis of Findings.* Canberra: Australian Government Publishing Service, 1988.

Democratic National Committee. *Democratic Platform.* Washington, D.C., July 1992.

Derthick, Martha. *City Politics in Washington, D.C.* Cambridge, Massachusetts: Joint Center for Urban Studies, 1962.

District of Columbia. *The Budget of the District of Columbia.* Fiscal Year 1981. Washington, D.C., 1980.

————. *The Federal Payment, Fiscal Year 1981.* Washington, D.C., 1979.

————. *Opinions of the Corporation Counsel.* Volumes 1 and 2, Washington, D.C., 1977, 1978.

————. *Proceedings of a Colloquium on the Report of the Mayor's Panel on Human*

Resources Organization and Management in the District of Columbia. Washington, D.C., 1977.

———. Office of Policy and Program Evaluation. *Indices: A Statistical Index to District of Columbia Services.* Washington, D.C., 1991.

———. Office of Planning. *Comprehensive Plan for the National Capital Elements,* Washington, D.C., 1985.

District of Columbia League of Women Voters. *Know the District of Columbia.* Washington, D.C.: District of Columbia League of Women Voters Education Fund, 1986.

Eggleston, Wilfrid. *The Queen's Choice: A Story of Canada's Capital.* Ottawa: Queen's Printer, 1961.

Eldredge, H. Wentworth. *World Capitals: Toward Guided Urbanization.* Garden City, New York: Anchor Press Doubleday, 1975.

Epstein, David. *Brasilia, Plan and Reality.* Berkeley: University of California Press, 1973.

Fauntroy, Walter E. *If You Favor Freedom.* Washington, D.C.: Office of the D.C. Nonvoting Delegate to Congress, 1986.

Gary, Lawrence, et al. *Attitudes and Perceptions of Black Police Officers of the District of Columbia Metropolitan Police Department.* Washington, D.C.: Howard University, Institute of Urban Affairs and Research, 1976.

Green, Constance M. *The Secret City: A History of Race Relations in the Nation's Capital.* Princeton University Press, 1967.

Harris, Charles W., and Alvin Thornton. *Perspectives of Political Power in the District of Columbia.* Washington, D.C.: National Institute of Public Management, 1981.

Knowles, Louis, and Kenneth Prewitt. *Institutional Racism.* Englewood Cliffs, N.J.: Prentice Hall, 1969.

Laney, Garrine P. *Shadow Representatives in Congress: History and Current Developments.* Washington, D.C.: Congressional Research Service, Library of Congress, 1991.

McMurtry, Virginia A. *Legislative History of the 23d Amendment.* Washington, D.C.: Congressional Research Service, Library of Congress, 1977.

McRae, Kenneth D., ed. *The Federal Capital.* Studies of the Royal Commission on Bilingualism and Biculturalism, no. 1. Ottawa: Queen's Printer, 1969.

Meyers, Edward M. "An Examination of Statehood and Other Political Alternatives for the Residents of Washington, D.C." Ph.D. diss., Georgetown University, 1992.

Noyes, Theodore. *Our National Capital and Its UnAmericanized Americans.* Edited by Benjamin M. McKelway. Washington, D.C.: Citizens' Joint Committee on National Representation for the District of Columbia, 1951.

Oakes, W.K. and L.J. Reeder, eds. *Governing the Two Canberras.* Papers and Proceedings of the ACT Self-Government First Anniversary Seminar, 11 may 1990, Canberra: University of Canberra, 1991.

Oldenburg, Philip. *Big City Government in India: Councillor, Administrator, and Citizen in Delhi.* Tucson: University of Arizona Press, 1976.

Parr-Moore, Rae, ed. *A Decade of Home Rule: The Challenge Continues.* Washington, D.C.: District of Columbia Government, 1985.

Republican National Committee. *The Republican Platform 1992.* Washington, D.C., August 1992.

Robson, William A., and E.E. Regan, eds. *Great Cities of the World—Their Government, Politics and Planning.* London: George Allen and Unwin, Ltd., 1972.

Rowat, Donald C. *The Canadian Municipal System.* Toronto: McClelland and Stewart, 1969.

———— ed. *The Government of Federal Capitals.* Toronto: University of Toronto Press, 1973.

Schmeckebier, Laurence F. *The District of Columbia—Its Government and Administration.* Baltimore: Johns Hopkins University Press, 1928.

Smith, Sam. *Captive Capital.* Bloomington: Indiana University Press, 1974.

Smith, Steven S., and Christopher J. Deering *Committees in Congress.* Washington, D.C.: Congressional Quarterly Press, 1984.

Spain. *Spain 1992.* Madrid: Ministerio del Portavoz del Gobierno, 1992.

Taylor, Duane R. *Home Rule in the District of Columbia: The First 500 Days.* Washington, D.C.: University Press of America, 1977.

ARTICLES, REPORTS, AND STUDIES

Australian Bureau of Statistics. *Yearbook Australia 1990,* no. 73. Canberra, 1990, 28–29, 799–809.

Australian Capital Territory Government Service. *Annual Report.* Volume II, pt. 1, 1988–89.

Brazil. Constitution of the Federative Republic of Brazil, 988. Brasilia, 1990.

Congressional Quarterly Almanac. 29 (1973), 734–41, 118H–119H, 425–35.

Congressional Quarterly Almanac. 35 (1979), 550, 118H.

Fullerton, Douglas H. *The Capital of Canada: How Should It Be Governed?* Volume 1, Ottawa: Information Canada, 1974. 64 pp.

Gelman, Norman I. "Self-Government for City of Washington." *Editorial Research Reports* Vol. 2, published by Congressional Quarterly, Inc., (10 July 1959): 513–532.

Harris, Charles W. "Congress and Home Rule in the Nation's Capital: District of Columbia Appropriations." Paper presented at the 1990 annual meeting of the American Political Science Association, San Francisco, 30 August–2 September 1990. 33 pp.

————. "Federal and Local Interests in the Nation's Capital: Congress and the District of Columbia Appropriations." *Public Budgeting and Finance* 9, no. 4 (Winter 1989): 66–82.

Harris, Charles W., and Neeka Harris. "Conflicting Vistas in the Nation's Capital." *Catholic University Law Review.* 38, no. 3 (Spring 1989): 599–639.

"Home Rule for District of Columbia is Approved by House." *In Common* (19 October 1973): 1–4.

Juddery, Bruce. "Self-Government of the Australian Capital Territory." *Australian Journal of Public Administration.* 48, no. 4 (December 1989): 411–12.

Leet, Rebecca. "D.C. Representation." Focus 6, no.9, published by Joint Center for Economic and Political Studies (9 October 1978), 4.

Lordello de Mello, Diogo. "Overview of the Different Political and Legislative Structures of Capitals and the Issues and Problems Relating to Them." Paper presented at Capitals of the World Conference, Ottawa, Canada, October 1987. 7 pp.

Olin, Dirk. "Preservations Required." *Regardies's* (September 1984): 53–64.

Raven-Hansen, Peter. "The Constitutionality of D.C. Statehood." Paper presented at the 1990 annual meeting of the American Political Science Association, San Francisco, 31 August 1990: 31 pp.

Rowat, Donald C. "Canberra in International Perspective." *Governing the Two Canberras*, edited by W. K. Oakes and L.J. Reeder. Papers and Proceedings of the ACT Self-Government First Anniversary Seminar, 11 May 1990. Canberra: University of Canberra, 28–45.

———. "Governing Federal Capitals: Washington, Canberra, Ottawa and Delhi." *Nagarlok* 24, no. 2 (April–June 1992): 3–28.

———. "How Federal Capitals are Governed" *Indian Administrative and Management Review* 2, no. 3 (July–September 1970): 39–47.

———. "The Role of a New Capital in National Development." In *Dynamics of Development—An International Perspective,* edited by S.K. Sharma. Delhi, India: Concept Publishing Company (1977): 672–77.

———. "Ways of Governing Federal Capitals." Paper presented at the Colloquium on Capital Cities, Canada's Capital Tri-University Study Group, Ottawa, Canada, 6–8 December 1990. 33 pp.

Sanchez, Manuel M. "La Reforma de la Ciudad de Mexico." *nexos* 179 (November 1979): 27–33.

Schrag, Philip P. "The Future of District of Columbia Home Rule." *Catholic University Law Review* 39, no. 2 (Winter 1990): 311–71.

Thomas, William V. "Washington, D.C. Voting preservation." *Editorial Research Reports.* Vol. 1, published by Congressional Quarterly, Inc. (5 January 1979): 3–20.

Vose, Clement E. "When District of Columbia Representation Collides with the Constitutional Amendment Institution." *Publius* (Winter 1979): 105–25.

Weaver, Kent R., and Charles W. Harris. "Who's in Charge Here? Congress and the Nation's Capital." *The Brookings Review* 7, no. 3 (Summer 1989): 28–45.

GOVERNMENT DOCUMENTS—District of Columbia

District of Columbia. *Fiscal Year 1993 Budget and revised Fiscal Year 1992 Request.* Washington, D.C., [1992].

———. *Fiscal Year 1994 Executive Budget (Including Revised Fiscal Year 1993 Request).* Washington, D.C., 1993.

———. Office of Mayor. *Report on Civil Disturbances in Washington, D.C.—April 1968.* Washington, D.C., 1968.

———. Office of Planning and Management. *People of the District of Columbia; A Demographic, Social and Physical Profile of the District of Columbia.* Washington, D.C., 1973.

————. Zoning Commission. *Application to Amend the D.C. Zoning Map from R-1-A to D/R-1-A for Lots 2, 9, and 821 in Square 2145 at West Side of 25 Block of 30th Street, Northwest—Imperial Embassy of Iran, Applicant.* Case no. 78-29, Order no. 294. Washington, D.C., 1979.

————. Zoning Commission. *Text and Mapping Amendments to Zoning Regulations for Chanceries and International Agencies.* Case no. 77-45. Washington, D.C., 1978.

————. Zoning Commission. *Zoning Text Amendment for Chanceries and International Agencies.* Case no. 77-45. washington, D.C., 1978.

GOVERNMENT DOCUMENTS–United States

Biographical Directory of the United States Congress, 1774–1989. Washington, D.C.: Government Printing Office, 1989.

Committee Prints

Congress. House. Committee on the District of Columbia. *The District of Columbia Self-Government and Governmental reorganization Act of 1973, as Amended.* 96th cong., 1st sess., 1979.

————. Committee on the District of Columbia. *Governance of the Nation's Capital: A Summary History of the Forms and Powers of Local Government for the District of Columbia, 1790 to 1973,* 101st Cong., 2d sess., 1990.

————. Committee on the District of Columbia. *Home Rule for the District of Columbia 1973–1974.* 93d Cong., 2d sess., 1974.

————. Committee on the District of Columbia. *Impediments to the Economic, Functional, and Aesthetic Development of the District of Columbia, the Nation's Capital* (committee staff report). 94th Cong., 2d sess., 1976.

Hearings and Markups

Congress. House. Committee on the District of Columbia, Subcommittee on Fiscal Affairs and Health. *H.R. 3861—Admission of the State of New Columbia into the Union.* 98th Cong., 2d sess., 15 May 1984.

————. Subcommittee on Judiciary and Education. *H.R. 2482—Admission of the state of New Columbia into the Union.* 102d Cong., 1st sess., 14 November 1991.

————. *H.R. 2482—Admission of the State of New Columbia into the Union.* 102d Cong., 2d sess., 24 March 1992.

House. Committee on the District of Columbia. *H.R. 51—District of Columbia Statehood,* 100th Cong., 1st sess., 17 March 1987.

————. Subcommittee on Government Operations. *H.R. 4394 and H.R. 5642—National Capital Service Area.* 94th Cong., 1st. sess., 10 June 1975.

————. *H. Con. Res. 75—Statehood Initiative.* 97th Cong., 1st sess., 4 March 1981.
————. Senate. Committee on Governmental Affairs. *H.Res. 208—District of Columbia Sexual Assault Laws.* 97th Cong., 1st sess., 30 September 1981.

Reports

Congress. House. *Commission on the Organization of the Government of the District of Columbia.* 92d Cong., 2d sess., 1972. H. Rept. 317.
————. Committee on the District of Columbia. *Activities and Summary Report.* 98th Cong., 2d sess., 1984., H. Rept. 1183.
————. 101st Cong., 2d sess., 1990. H. Rept. 1023.
————. ————. *New Columbia Admission Act.* 100th Cong., 1st sess., 1987. H. Rept. 305.
————. 102d Cong., 2d sess., 1992. H. Rept. 909.

D.C. Appropriations: Acts, Bills, Reports

FY 1988—P.L. 100–202, sec. 101(c). *District of Columbia Appropriations Act, 1988.* 101 *Statutes at Large* 1329—90 through 104. 100th Cong., 1st sess. committee print (containing act and reference report), 22 December 1987.
House. Committee on Appropriations. *District of Columbia Appropriation Bill, 1988.* 100th Cong., 1st. sess., 1987. H. Rept. 172.
Senate Committee on Appropriations. *District of Columbia Appropriation Bill, 1988.* 100th Cong., 1st sess., 1987. S. Rept. 162
FY 1989—P.L. 100–462—*District of Columbia Appropriations Act, 1989.* 102 *Statutes at Large* 2269. 100th Cong., 2nd sess., 1 October 1988.
House. Committee on Appropriations. *District of Columbia Appropriations Bill, 1989.* 100th Cong., 2d sess., 1988. H. Rept. 680.
Senate. Committee on Appropriations. *District of Columbia appropriations Bill, 1989.* 100th Cong., 2d sess., 1988. S. Rept. 398.
House. Committee of Conference. *Making Appropriations for the Government of the District of Columbia and Other Activities.* 100th Cong., 2d sess, 1988. H. Rept. 1013.
FY 1990—P.L. 101–168. *District of Columbia Appropriations Act, 1990.* 103 *Statutes at Large* 1267. 101st Cong., 1st sess., 21 November 1989.
House. Committee on Appropriations. *District of Columbia Appropriations Bill, 1990.* 101st Cong., 1st sess., 1989. H. Rept. 355.
Senate. Committee on Appropriations. *District of Columbia Appropriations Bill, 1990.* 101st Cong., 1st sess., 1989. S. Rept. 124.
House. Committee on Conference. *Making appropriations for the Government of the District of Columbia.* 101st Cong., 1st sess., 1989. H. Rept. 270.
House. *Veto of H.R. 3610—Message from the President of the United States.* 101st Cong., 1st sess., 1989. H. Doc. 114
FY 1991—P.L. 101–518. *District of Columbia Appropriation Act, 1991.* 104 *Statutes at Large* 2225. 101st Cong., 2d sess., 5 November 1990.

House. Committee on Appropriations. *District of Columbia Appropriations Bill, 1991.* 101st Cong., 2d sess., 1990. H. Rept. 607.

Senate. Committee on Appropriations. *District of Columbia Appropriations Bill, 1991.* 101st Cong., 2d sess., 1990. S. Rept. 397.

House. Committee of Conference. *Making Appropriations for the Government of the District of Columbia and Other Activities.* 101st Cong., 2d sess., 1990. H. Rept. 958.

FY 1992—P.L. 102–111 *District of Columbia Appropriation Act, 1992.* 105 *Statutes at Large* 559. 102st Cong., 1st sess., 1 October 1991.

House. Committee on Appropriations. *District of Columbia Appropriations Bill, 1992.* 102d Cong., 1st sess., 1991. H. Rept. 120.

Senate. Committee on Appropriations. *District of Columbia Appropriations Bill, 1992.* 102d Cong., 1st sess., 1991. S. Rept. 105.

House. Committee of Conference. *Making Appropriations for the Government of the District of Columbia and Other Activities.* 102d Cong., 1st sess., 1991. H. Rept. 181.

FY 1993—P.L. 102–382. *District of Columbia 1992 Supplemental Appropriations and Rescissions and 1993 Appropriations.* 106 *Statutes at Large* 1425. 102d Cong., 2d sess., 5 October 1992.

House. Committee on Appropriations. *District of Columbia Appropriations Bill, 1993.* 102d Cong., 2d sess., 1992. H. Rept. 638.

Senate. Committee on Appropriations. *District of Columbia Appropriations Bill, 1993.* 102d Cong., 2d sess., 1992. S. Rept. 333.

House. Committee of Conference. *Making Appropriations for the Government of the District of Columbia and Other Activities.* 102d Cong., 2d sess., 1992. H. Rept. 906.

FY 1994 House. Committee on Appropriations. *District of Columbia Appropriations Bill, 1994.* 103d Cong., 1st sess., 1993. H. Rept. 152.

COLLECTIONS

District of Columbia. Home Rule Papers. Washingtoniana Room. Martin Luther King, Jr., Memorial Library. Washington, D.C.

District of Columbia. Legislative Services Unit. Collection on District of Columbia Council bills, acts, and deliberations. Washington, D.C. Microfilm

Index